Radical Social Work

Edited by Roy Bailey and
Mike Brake

With an Introductory Chapter
by Richard A. Cloward
and Frances Fox Piven

PANTHEON BOOKS, New York

HV
37
R33
1975b

First American Edition

Library of Congress Cataloging in Publication Data
Main entry under title:

Radical Social Work.

   Bibliography: pp. 148–57
   Includes index.
   1. Social service—Addresses, essays, lectures. 2. Social service—Great Britain—
Addresses, essays, lectures. 3. Social services—United States—Addresses, essays,
lectures. I. Bailey, Roy Victor. II. Brake, Mike.
HV37.R33   1975b   361'.001   76–12937
ISBN 0–394–40919–1
ISBN 0–394–73265–0 pbk.

Manufactured in the United States of America

Contents

Acknowledgements

We should like to thank all the contributors to this volume not only for the work and time they spent on their contributions but perhaps more significantly for their patience and tolerance with us as editors. Our thanks are also due to our friends, our colleagues, our enemies and our critics whose interest in these and related issues has proved a major stimulus.

Our thanks must also be expressed to Mary Carver for her patient typing of the manuscript.

Spring 1975

ROY BAILEY
MIKE BRAKE

Notes Toward a Radical Social Work

Richard A. Cloward and Frances Fox Piven

Columbia University   Boston University

We are pleased that *Radical Social Work*, first published in England, is now being made available to audiences in the United States. When the publisher invited us to prepare an introduction to the American edition, we quickly agreed. Very little has been written in the United States which brings critical perspectives to bear on social work and on the agencies of the welfare state that employ social workers.

As for our own contribution to this volume, what began as an assignment to prepare a brief "introduction" soon evolved into a chapter. In effect, we emulated the contributors to this volume by setting forth our own views on the question of what constitutes radical social work. The reader will find that there are respects in which we agree with other contributors and respects in which we do not.

In particular, we attempted to be mindful of students in schools of social work. Professional education is, in our view, a major obstacle to the development of a radical social work, and we have tried to say why. Some case materials based on reports from students at various schools of social work are also included. As the reader will see, there are more than a few students who perceive the oppressive and conservative character of what is called professional social work education, and who are groping for a radical alternative.[1] We hope that our essay, together with the other essays in this volume, will help them in that search.

The agencies of the welfare state

There is no doubt that social welfare doctrines have become unsettled in

[1] The case materials used throughout this paper were taken, with permission, from term papers. Some students wished to be acknowledged, and so their names have been cited; others preferred to remain anonymous. Names, places, and agencies have been disguised, when appropriate.

the last decade or so. One only has to remember how liberals generally, and the professionals in the social services in particular, once confidently defined the social services as the progressive and humanitarian sector of American society. Services in health, education, welfare, housing, child care, and corrections were taken as the institutional proof that the American state had reached the stage where it was ready and able to intervene in the so-called free enterprise economy, and ready and able to protect people against some of its worst abuses. In other words, the United States, mainly through its public programs, and to a lesser extent through the voluntary sector, no longer tolerated the vagaries in human welfare produced by a capitalist economy, and no longer left the victims of the economy to fend for themselves. One had only to look at our splendid array of legislation, and the multitude of agencies spawned by that legislation, to know that this was so.

To be sure, liberals acknowledged that there were problems in the social service sector. Great progress had been made, but there was still a distance to go. The problems were largely attributed to the underfunding of social service programs. The agencies were inhibited by lack of money from doing what they knew how to do and urgently wanted to do to help people. Underfunding, in turn, resulted from the still backward attitudes of the American people who, the argument went, retained an old-fashioned skepticism about "big government," along with a lot of unenlightened hostility toward the poor and other unfortunates. But liberals always have unbounded faith in the educative force of their own beliefs, and there was not much doubt in the minds of those who defended the welfare state, and who pressed for its expansion, that Americans would in time come to appreciate the value of the social services and would provide political support for budgetary allocations on the required scale. Slowly but surely, then, progress would occur in the United States; the forces of capitalism would be curbed, their effects buffered by the gradual expansion of the social welfare sector.

The 1960s forced many of us to rethink this faith. We learned a great deal about how the social service agencies on which we rested our hopes for fundamental progress really worked, and about their effects on the lives of people. We did not learn this willingly. We did not re-educate ourselves. We were forced to learn by the turmoil that shook the United States, a turmoil generated by the black movements in the South and in the North, and by the student movement on the nation's campuses. Those movements forced issues of racism, poverty, and imperialism to the top of the American political agenda, and by doing so, made us open our eyes to, among other things, the widespread hardship and suffering that still prevailed in this country. And if there was still much hardship, then we had to wonder about the social service programs which we had so confidently believed were working to ameliorate the condition of the poorest and most exploited people in the United States.

We became at least skeptical. Skepticism opened the way for some of us to develop a different and more realistic way of understanding the agencies of the welfare state. We began to see that social welfare had not curbed capitalist institutions; it had supported and even enhanced them. And we began to understand some of the specific ways in which the social services had played this role. Let us quickly recapitulate some of our criticisms to show how fundamentally they broke with the conventional liberal faith.

We learned, for example, that the government health programs we had fought for, and had believed would make possible decent health care for all Americans, were not providing decent health care at all. More important, we realized that merely allocating more funds to health care, as liberals had advocated, did not improve the programs; it may even have worsened them. We had been fundamentally mistaken in our belief that health care institutions, and the professionals attached to them, knew how to help people and urgently wanted to do so. We began to understand that these institutions were shaped by quite different impulses, by the impulses for expansion and profit. We slowly deciphered the outlines of a health care industry composed of apparently neutral "not-for-profit" hospitals and medical schools, which in turn were linked to profiteering drug and equipment producers, and to profiteering private entrepreneurs called doctors (the highest earning occupational group in the United States).

In other words, we began to understand—we could not help but understand because the evidence was so overwhelming—that public expenditures for health had in fact been absorbed by the industry in ways which subsidized bureaucratic expansion and vastly enlarged profits, but did not much improve medical services. Health care institutions did not buffer capitalist institutions; they *were* capitalist institutions; they differed mainly in the extent to which they depended for their profits on the public sector. The arguments we had made, the campaigns we had waged for decent health care, had turned out in the actual world to be advertisements that smoothed the way for the expansion of a profit-based industry.

Similarly, we learned that the government housing programs initiated in the 1930s and expanded in 1949 under the legislative banner of "decent and standard" housing for all Americans were dominated and directed not by the housing needs of Americans, but by the construction and real estate industries and the downtown businesses. The vast government subsidies that we had promoted in the name of those who needed housing had gone to profiteers and speculators in urban land and to construction firms. Instead of modifying free enterprise by redirecting its activities toward the poor, public programs in housing have been a major source of profits for an important sector of free enterprise. Meanwhile, the subsidy programs, such as urban renewal, actually worsened the housing conditions of poor and working-class people, especially black people, by making it profitable to destroy their homes and neighborhoods so that their land could be turned over to private developers at costs underwritten by the public.

In other programs we came to see a less direct but not therefore less essential relation between the social services and what Marxists call "processes of accumulation." The public schools have been defined in liberal doctrine as vehicles for the opening up of the class structure, for equalizing opportunities among different strata. But we recognized that schools did nothing of the sort. Those who were poor or working-class were also at the bottom of the ladder of school achievement. More funds, more special programs, and more specialists of different kinds were needed, it was said. But these had simply not changed the failure and dropout rates among children at the bottom of society. Dimly, a new explanation began to emerge. Perhaps the schools were not institutions for equalizing opportunity. Perhaps they were institutions which mainly served to legitimate the low status to which many children were consigned by proving to them and to all around that it was they who had failed, not the society. Perhaps for many children the schools simply engrain and legitimate failure, meanwhile instructing them not in the skills and manners that would allow them to rise in the class structure, but in deadening rules of bureaucracy and in docility before bureaucratic authority—the proper education for the lower classes.

Similarly, we learned that public welfare programs inaugurated during the New Deal, that golden age of social welfare, were quite different in practice from what we had believed them to be. The introduction of a national system of public welfare had been regarded as a major step forward by social service professionals. American society had presumably advanced to the point where it was ready to ensure at least a minimal level of subsistence for its citizens, or so the legislation said. Thus consoled and deluded by the existence of legislation and of agencies who had the formal mandate to implement it, we did not pay much attention to what our public welfare agencies actually did. But in the 1960s, we were forced to learn that the public welfare system in fact reached very few of the poor, and that it exacted penalties of intimidation and degradation from those few it did reach. With these facts laid bare, a new explanation began to emerge, of public welfare not as a mechanism of state philanthropy, but as a mechanism by which the state enforced work and the search for work on those at the bottom, either by denying aid outright or by making the receipt of aid so degrading as to intimidate most of the poor into surviving as best they could given the vagaries and hardships of the low-wage labor market.

We also learned something about the apparatus of institutions the state had created for the criminal and mentally ill. We had been inclined to think of these institutions as places where a deviant was treated and thus rehabilitated, or at least that treatment and rehabilitation were slowly becoming the predominant focus of prisons and asylums. How we could have entertained such notions in view of the actual conditions in these institutions is puzzling, but at any rate, in the 1960s we began to understand that what had been created was an apparatus for stigmatizing and exiling those who could not cope with the stresses of lower-class life—those who protest their circumstances in bizarre ways full of flight, or in fearsome ways full of rage. As a "cure," these people were consigned to institutions of medieval awfulness, where the culture of the stigmatized enveloped and destroyed them. More recently, a new and perhaps more dangerous addition has been made to the arsenal of mechanisms for dealing with the casualties of capitalism: the promiscuous administration of drugs by the health, education, and social service bureaucracies. The drugging of the American under class has taken on the dimensions of a social movement, with the twin goals of social control and billion-dollar profits, and it is being led by the pharmaceutical industry and the psychiatric profession, with the unwitting acquiescence of other service professions.

Overall, the lesson we learned was shattering. We had now to somehow deal with the simple fact that during the forty years in which the social service sector in the United States had expanded, during forty years of progress, the incidence of crime, of mental illness, of school dropouts, all had risen, while the income of the lowest twenty percent of the population had hardly changed. In the United States, then, welfare capitalism had turned out to mean new areas of profit underwritten by the public sector and an enlarged state responsibility for disciplining the labor force. For the victims, welfare capitalism was capitalism, not welfare.

The quandary of radical practice

These new perspectives on the welfare state did not tell us, however, what we as professionals should do. The quandary was a difficult one, not only because the perspectives were too general to yield practical solutions, but because the criticism was focused on the agencies to which we as a profession were committed, if only because our livelihoods depended on them. Various solutions emerged among the more critical and radical groups in social work, most of them designed to evade rather than deal with the quandary.

One way in which the dilemma was popularized in the late 1960s was to state it as a stark dichotomy. Radicals in the social service professions (not just in social work), and particularly students entering these professions, became fond of boldly proclaiming that if we were politically committed, we would forsake our professions and become revolutionaries dedicated to a basic overhaul of American institutions. And if we were not prepared to do that, then we ought to resign ourselves to working within these professions and within the agencies, easing a little by our therapeutic efforts the hardships produced by the modern capitalist state. While this dichotomy reflected the depth of our disenchantment, it was foolish nevertheless. It was foolish because it posed an unreal alternative. Very few of those who took satisfaction in posing the stark choice had much idea about how to make a revolution in the United States or, more important, what specifically one would do if one chose to become a revolutionary.

It was foolish for another and more important reason. It encouraged us to ignore the actual political struggle for the rights of the poor, for the rights of those who were down-and-out, for the rights of the victims of American capitalism who were also frequently victims of the social service agencies. It encouraged us to ignore the unspectacular day-by-day strivings of particular people with particular problems, strivings in which we as employees of the social service agencies play a very large role. Our daily activities, our time, and our energies are all expended in the social agencies. The false choice—of whether we should become revolutionaries or merely be social workers—allowed us to avoid a series of much more important choices; more important because they were choices about actual and possible avenues of action, and about areas of activity in which we as social workers might make a difference. The issue was whether we were going to take sides with the agencies and further our careers, or with the victims of an aggressively cruel capitalist society. Were we in our daily work going to defend the practices and policies of the hospitals, courts, prisons, foster care agencies, welfare departments, and mental institutions for which we worked, or were we going to use our jobs to defend and protect the poor, the sick, the criminal, and the deviant against these agencies? That is the real and difficult challenge. It is not easy to be a professional, to lay claim to professional authority and esteem, and side with ordinary folks, especially poor folks. It is not easy to be a bureaucrat, intent on rising within the bureaucracy, and side with the clients and victims of that bureaucracy.

There were other false solutions, false because they helped us to avoid paying attention to the kinds of action which we might most effectively take, and helped us to avoid taking the professional risks of such action. One solution developed in the aftermath of disappointed revolutionism, as it often has before: the study group. Some among us urged that we should acquire a thorough grounding in Marxist theory and elaborate it in ways which would comprehend and explain the institutions of welfare capitalism.

Presumably this effort to develop and clarify an analysis was a precursor to developing guidelines for action, but the guidelines were not forthcoming. Instead, some among us became preoccupied with mastering the abstract and convoluted theoretical schemes produced by academic Marxism (paying obeisance to our special commitment as social workers by reiterating such general notions as the need for a "reserve army of labor" to explain the public welfare system), and satisfied themselves that by identifying with an intellectual tradition that had links with revolution, they were somehow becoming revolutionaries. But the more abstract the studies, the more elaborate the explanations, the more intense the preoccupation with differences of doctrine among Marxist scholars, the less we had to concern ourselves with the question of what social workers should do. We were doing something, after all; we were educating ourselves, so that some day we would know what to do. But that day did not and has not come, and in the meanwhile one cannot help but suspect that the preoccupation with an academic Marxism so abstract as to have no implications for action has led some of us not closer to struggle but, by a circuitous route, back to an inoffensive professionalism.

Other solutions to the quandary were adopted by those more firmly grounded in the profession. They tried to find new doctrinal footings with a minimum of professional upheaval, such as the turn toward community development or social planning. Presumably the failures of the welfare state could be accounted for by the limited role of professionals. Instead of working with individuals and families, we should work with entire communities; instead of working as the operatives of the social agencies, we should work as planners and administrators.

Both of these developments ought to be understood as efforts to take advantage of the assault on social welfare by expanding the jurisdiction of social workers, a not uncommon response by professions to crises in their institutions. In fact, whether we work with individuals or with community groups is not the issue; the issue is what we *do* when we work with them. When social workers in welfare departments shift from doing casework to doing community relations work, they do not necessarily change the relationship of domination and subordination between the agency and its clients. In fact, they may well enhance domination—for example, by allowing themselves to be assigned the function of smoothing out relations with groups of clients who might otherwise become insurgent.

The problems for practice posed by a radical critique of the agencies of the welfare state are surely not solved by what is called social planning, either. In fact, the premises of this false solution are totally at variance with the critique. Social planning is based on two key doctrines, both wrong. The first asserts that the planner is politically neutral, not taking sides in group and class conflicts; she or he works for something which is sometimes called "the community as a whole." The second belief concerns what planners do to advance the goals of the community as a whole. Social planners are presumably the rational decision-makers in the social services. It is their special role to assess the needs and goals of the community over time, to survey relevant action alternatives in the areas of program development or agency organization, and to assess the future impact of these alternative strategies on the community's needs and goals. Quite aside from the dubious assertion of a unitary public interest, it is surely not revealed in social planning activities. Rather, planners are committed to the bureaucracies and, more important, they are committed to the functions the bureaucracies perform in a capitalist society for a capitalist class. Nor is it true that social planners play a large role in these bureaucracies. The key decisions are made elsewhere. Meanwhile, the studies and proposals produced by the planners constitute a kind of techocratic public relations for the ongoing activities of the agencies. Social planning is extremely seductive as a remedy for our dissatisfactions with the social services, and it is everywhere expanding as a professional specialty, not because it comes to grips with those dissatisfactions, but because it promises to raise the status of social workers in the bureaucracies.

A third effort to establish new doctrinal footings has emerged in the training of those who provide direct services to individuals and groups. It is called "systems theory," and is now being taught in many classrooms. The chief virtue of this approach is that it modifies somewhat the emphasis on psychoanalytic theory which has long dominated the field of social work. But systems theory is not an analysis of bureaucratic power, or of the relation of social welfare agencies to capitalist ideology or institutions.

The systems theory approach invites social workers to view clients as "interacting" with a variety of "systems" in which we should ostensibly "intervene." The very blandness of the language denies any recognition of the realities of power. We learn that inmates "interact" with prisons; that mental patients "interact" with state mental hospitals; that recipients "interact" with welfare departments; that children "interact" with foster care agencies; that slum and ghetto dwellers "interact" with urban renewal authorities. But most clients do not interact with these systems, they are oppressed by them; and social workers ought not to intervene in these systems, they ought to resist them. In other words, this perspective—like earlier perspectives which dominate the field of social work—serves to conceal the true character of the agencies of the welfare state.

In these different ways, then, we have avoided the actual and important political choices that arise every day of our professional lives. And we have also avoided the risks to our careers which these choices pose for us.

Education for bureaucratic acquiescence

The kind of training we receive in the schools of social work does not make it easier to recognize these choices, or to understand concretely how to act on them in agency settings. There are few respects in which we can look to the schools for guidance, for they cannot afford to endorse perspectives that run counter to the needs of the bureaucracies of the welfare state. No school wants a reputation for training obstreperous students. It wants instead to ensure access for its students to field work placements, and access for its graduates to the best jobs. Consequently, professional training is itself a large part of the problem we face. The schools shape our ways of thinking and acting to ensure that we will fit into the agency scheme of things, and will accept the general dictum that what the agencies do is, finally, "in the best interests" of the client.

One striking feature of professional socialization is the frequent presumption that students know virtually nothing. No matter what their undergraduate preparation, no matter what their life experience (social work students are often older than students in other graduate departments) or work experience (which often exceeds or is at least more current than that of their instructors, many of whom have not practiced for many years), students quickly sense that they are often credited with very little. Although they may be mature, resourceful, and committed adults, they are frequently not assumed to bring much to the learning process, except perhaps personality traits that are "barriers" to learning. The dominant tendency is to infantilize students. One student described the reaction when she complained about the way in which she and other students were being treated in a unit:

I made an appointment with my faculty field adviser to complain. I was the first student in the unit (of six) to do so. I was met with what I unfondly call caseworking. My faculty adviser told me I was overly anxious and that I wasn't professional when I entered the school, but I would be when I left. She told me I have a lot to learn and asked me if I thought I knew everything. I tried to tell her what was going on at the agency but it was turned against me. I walked out of that office feeling verbally beaten up.

The infantilization of students is a fundamental mechanism by which the agents of oppression in the welfare state are created. Graduates of schools of social work, having been deprived by their training of much dignity or self-worth, often come to cope with this gnawing self-doubt by according the same treatment to others as was accorded to them.

Infantilization serves another purpose as well. Students educated to mistrust their own judgment, life experience, and feelings are then ready to be trained to acquiesce to the authority of others. Professional education is, in no small part, training in submission to bureaucratic authority, and to the supervisors who represent bureaucratic authority. In other words, we are educated to submit to the policies of our employers. The prominence of this theme is illustrated in the report of a student who had been placed in a residential treatment setting. One of her clients, a ten-year-old boy—whom she considered normal despite an institutional definition of him as schizophrenic—periodically ran away, especially in reaction to the threatening behavior of a sadistic child care worker. The student worked assiduously to help the boy control his panic. Still, he sometimes ran, and one day the student learned that, in her absence and without her knowledge, the boy had been placed on Thorazine:

When I returned to the center on Thursday I was told that Billy had been placed on Thorazine. The reason given by my supervisor was his "overwhelming anxiety." I questioned the reason for the medication, saying that he had been making progress in dealing with his anxiety as demonstrated by the less frequent attempts he had made to leave in the past few weeks. My supervisor took offense at my concern and replied that it had been Dr. R.'s decision (the agency psychiatrist). I asked to speak to him and she said I couldn't until a week from Friday, which was our student seminar day. In the meantime she said I was to inform Billy's parents about the medication. I said I needed to speak to Dr. R. first because as it stood I could not answer any of Billy's parents' questions since I did not see the need for medication. She immediately personalized the situation, commenting that "students" often had trouble seeing the need for medication. I replied that I didn't think this was my problem since I had trained at a psychotherapeutic nursery associated with a well-known hospital and had done my master's thesis in psychology on a brain-damaged hyperactive child who couldn't function adequately without medication. I said that Billy and I had been working on ways to deal with his anxiety and the fact that we were making good progress was a sign that he was learning to handle his feelings. She said angrily, "Well, talk to Dr. R. next Friday!"

When I saw Dr. R. the following week I raised the issue. My feeling was that my supervisor had already discussed my concerns with him, for he said sharply that Billy had been given medication because of the nightmares he experienced. This was not the same reason provided by my supervisor, but I did not comment, feeling that the supervisor had already undermined my argument regarding Billy's progress. Instead I raised the issue of Billy's sleepiness and described how differently he behaved and looked. I said he was pale, drowsy, and even his blue eyes looked lighter to me. Dr. R. said the initial sleepiness would diminish as time went by. To a degree it did, but not enough to bring back the enthusiastic little boy I had first known. Throughout the year I asked if we could take Billy off the medication, but Dr. R. said he would only consider it after Billy had been on it for a year.

I raised the matter again with my supervisor. She said, "You really are very stubborn. You just don't like medication and you won't admit it to yourself. You need to do some thinking." I agreed that I didn't like medication unless it was necessary and my "thinking" was that there wasn't a legitimate reason for using it with Billy. She countered by saying that my attitude was going to become a professional problem.

I raised this issue with my faculty adviser. Again I made him uncomfortable. He offered no support, no advice, but rather conveyed by his attitude that I was into something I shouldn't be. I found myself defensive, saying things like, "You know, I'm not totally against the use of medication, but in this case I don't think it is being used appropriately or to good purpose."

At another time I raised my concerns and when my supervisor once again commented on my student status, I replied that I had thought it was a "student's role" to question. She shook her head in exasperation but made no further comment.

In these situations, my concern was not that I be proven right, but that my clients be treated appropriately. . . . I may have been wrong, but no one provided me with an adequate reason to think so, and I feel that is an essential part of an adequate training program. In any case, by raising questions, I had incurred the anger of my supervisor, the agency psychiatrist, and my faculty field adviser.[2]

[2] Quoted with the permission of Patricia MacDonnell.

As this report reveals, another component of our socialization for acqui-escence to bureaucratic authority consists of socialization for acquiescence to psychiatric authority. Some fifty years ago, the mental hygiene tidal wave swept over the field of social work, and we have been drowning in it ever since. Because of the power of the medical profession in American society, psychiatrists have come to be the dominant figures in many of the agencies. Immersed in the doctrines of pathology, and subject to the power of psychiatrists in the agencies, many social workers have been led to deify psychiatric thought and psychiatrists. The truth is that psychiatrists know even less about social functioning than we do. They address themselves only to the client's inner life; they generally rely on a single (and unproven) theory about that inner existence; and in many settings (such as state hospitals) they apply that theory to the making of "instant diagnoses" in an almost assembly-line fashion. Many children, for example, end up in institutions because of the physical illness of their parents, or for other reasons that have nothing to do with them. How odd, then, that so many of the children in these institutions come to have such diagnoses as "schizo-phrenic reaction of childhood." Still, students are taught to accept all this as gospel, and to act as if they know nothing until the psychiatrist has rendered an "expert" opinion. Consequently, students find themselves paying tuition to be placed for field training in settings like this one:

The patients were so drugged, so subdued, so controlled that they were often unable to function. This created a "no-win" situation for them. On the one hand, they were instructed to go to their scheduled therapies (recreational, occupational, individual treatment) or to mop the floors and clean the toilets. Yet, on the other hand, they were forced to take medication which induced extraordinarily lethargic states. The patients were receiving two messages from the staff, and were therefore quite uncertain what was expected of them. If they did not take their medication, they were defined as "acting out"; therefore, they received no tokens. If they did take their medication, they were usually unable to participate in their scheduled therapies; therefore they also received no tokens.[3]

The more aware and humane students recoil from these practices. They grope for a way to understand and cope with the frustrations of their professional training. One student expressed her feelings in these words:

In my three different casework classes to date, we have not been permitted to discuss the field work agencies. It seems to be an unwritten rule that raising ques-

---

[3] Quoted with the permission of Janet Shupack Lichty.

tions about what is happening in field work is not appropriate, unless it is about our presumed failings as students. I see many things about the agency I have been in for a year that I think ought to be changed, and I would like a chance to talk about them. But it seems clear that I am not going to get that chance at this school.

Some students try to cope by continually reminding themselves that much of what they are being taught is wrong: "I got through the first year feeling that if this is what social work is about, then perhaps I'm in the wrong field, and if these are the people teaching me how to work with people, then I hope I don't learn anything." These students try to approach clients with openness, mutuality, and humility:

Mr. R. is a forty-four-year-old Puerto Rican male who was disabled in the Marine Corps during the Korean War. He has been using our hospital facility for twenty-five years. Although he has been entitled to a full disability, he was not totally incapacitated until a car accident, a year ago, which greatly aggravated his war-related back injury. His medical chart is filled with evidence that his pain is real and physical, although he has been charged with "faking it."

Mr. R. was referred to me by one of our psychiatrists who said he was depressed, suffering from a disease called "homosexuality," that his pain was probably all "bullshit anyway because Puerto Ricans are notoriously dramatic about everything," and he was "hostile, aggressive, and a know-it-all."

When I met with Mr. R., he was clearly depressed, and he still is. He is gay, but neither regrets it, desires to change, or sees it as a real problem. Rather than being a "know-it-all," he is a self-educated high-school dropout who is intelligent, introspective, and happens to know much more about his medical situation, the drugs he is taking, the effects of his injury, and so on than I do. Far from being dramatic about his pain, he makes great efforts to conceal his spasms and is embarrassed when his body contorts and he gasps involuntarily. He is very angry about the doctors who refuse to inform him about medical matters and who patronize him by answering his questions with answers like, "Don't worry about it, Professor."

Aside from this, I did request a new physical examination, and it turned out that Mr. R. is suffering from a deteriorated spine in the lumbar region, deterioration of the hip, and that his arthritis is spreading. I have been useless in the sense that Mr. R. knows as much about depression and psychological dynamics as I do, and because his depression is caused by the very depressing fact that his back is deteriorating, the condition is inoperable, he lives with daily pain, and he is facing the fact that one day he may not be able to walk.

Anyway, after a few interviews, I rejected the advice to "help Mr. R. explore his feelings." It was useless and patronizing advice. I also told Mr. R. very honestly that he knew as much as I did, and that I did not feel that he needed a social worker or a psychiatrist. Still, he said that having someone to talk to was helpful, so we agreed to meet weekly. We conversed as equals, sharing a bit of our lives with one another. The experience changed both of us for the better.

But most students succumb. They surrender their dignity, their capacity for critical reflection, and become the pliable materials out of which the "professional" is molded. Some surrender consciously, although usually gradually. In time, their adaptation comes to be justified by the belief that if they did not submit, they could not earn a degree and ensure their future job prospects. These students say what they think they are supposed to say, and leave unasked the questions that genuinely trouble them. When some of them write process records of their interaction with clients, they omit exchanges which they think will violate the perspectives of their supervisors; they invent exchanges that did not occur, and record them instead. From time to time, one student or another independently comes across the same line from R. D. Laing and quotes it to express his or her sense of the educational process: "They are playing a game. They are playing at not playing a game. If I show them I see they are, I shall break the rules and they will punish me. I must play their game, of not seeing I see the game." For these students the educational atmosphere is permeated with mistrust. Instead of being permitted to reach out to those from whom they can presumably learn, they shrink back, fearful and cautious, and expose as little of themselves as possible.

Evasiveness and accommodation are not simply individual responses; they come to be shared and to be incorporated in a student culture. New students are inducted into these modes of adaptation by other students, just as inmates are inducted by other inmates into the institutions of the welfare state. Sometimes the induction process takes place at the beginning of the year, when second-year students "orient" incoming students during a series of meetings.

When I received my notice of admission, I felt that this was the answer to my dreams. I had been accepted by a school with an excellent reputation in social work education. I believed it would provide me with the experience and knowledge to deal with the immediate and urgent needs of the poor, in particular blacks and Puerto Ricans.

But first of all, right from the start of my education, second-year students began educating me about how to behave in order to get through.

1. Do not confide in your professors, school administrators, field instructors, or agency supervisors.

2. Beware of what you write in your process recordings.

3. Beware of field work evaluations.

4. Do not challenge professors in class; just say what they want to hear.

5. Do not give field instructors and advisers the impression that you may be experiencing severe anxiety and tension.

6. Always maintain the impression that you completely agree with traditional social work values and professional ethics.

Much of what second-year students warned me about happened. During the beginning of the second academic year, I was a student leader in an orientation session and so I carried on the tradition:

1. FIRST-YEAR STUDENT: Should I confide in my field supervisor?
   MYSELF: Never, don't ever confide anything personal. They should not be trusted.

2. FIRST-YEAR STUDENT: What do the faculty look for in the students?
   MYSELF: In almost all cases, a reiteration of their own ideas. If you want to get good grades, do not challenge a professor's ideas.

3. FIRST-YEAR STUDENT: If I am under a great deal of personal pressure and anxiety, whom should I turn to?
   MYSELF: Just turn to other students for support.

One of the most dismal aspects of the process being described is that students knuckle under in order to obtain a degree. Once employed in the field, they continue to knuckle under, for there are promotions to be won, titles to be earned. The patterns of submission learned in the schools of social work are thus reproduced in the field. And of course, these patterns serve the bureaucracies of the welfare state well; they ensure that employees will not challenge and question, confront and disrupt. Even worse, the arrogance and inhumanity inflicted upon many students come to be incorporated as an essential part of their professional adaptation. The stresses generated by diminished self-esteem are solved by the model of professionalism. By emulating this model in their dealings with clients, students strive to recoup some of the pride that has been stripped away. Thus some students come to revel in their newly acquired facility to diagnose; they flaunt their ability to stigmatize others. How good it feels to sound so "expert," so superior, especially for students who have been made to feel inexpert and inferior. The ultimate sign of the student's professional coming-of-age is his capacity to emulate the jazzy language styles in which his psychiatric betters describe patients: "That one's flakey," the psychiatric intern says; "That one's an off-the-wall marginal," says the social work student.

One irony in all this is that while many students feel helpless, they do in fact have power; they certainly have more power than the clients who rebelled in the 1960s. Schools cannot operate without students. If students decide not to cooperate with the rituals called education, the schools will have to bend. If faculty ignore or evade the issues students raise, if the curriculum ignores students' ideas and experiences, they can boycott classes. When field work supervisors require students to record the intimate confidences of clients in official agency dossiers, they can refuse to do so. No faculty member can survive an empty classroom; no supervisor can satisfactorily explain collective resistance by a unit of students; no dean can suspend a student body. Schools need students, and that is the source of student power. What students need to see is that social work education is in large part a concerted effort to control their ideas, their perceptions, their emotions, and their behaviors. It is an effort made so much easier because students, imagining themselves defenseless, and unwilling to take risks, offer no resistance.

We must "change our situation," as one student remarked. In order to begin, we must undo some of the harm done by our professional indoctrination. We must re-educate ourselves about the social work profession, about the agencies in which we work, about the problems of clients, and, most important, about our own role in the agencies and with clients. Some of the major tenets of such a re-education follow.

The tenets for radical action

First, we have to break with the professional doctrine that the institutions in which social workers are employed have benign motives: that the purpose of hospitals is to provide health care for the sick; that the purpose of welfare agencies is to provide assistance for the impoverished; that the purpose of child care agencies is to protect children. We must break with such beliefs as matters of doctrine, taking nothing for granted, and, using our common sense and humanity, look at what agencies actually do.

Once freed from a belief in the benign character of the social agencies, we can free ourselves from a second item of doctrine that follows logically enough—that what is good for the agency is good for the client, that the interests of the agency and the interests of the client are basically identical. If the agencies were in fact benign, committed primarily to the well-being of their clientele, this might be true. But if we pay attention to actual agency practices, a very different reality emerges. That reality should make us constantly alert to the possibility that the agency is the enemy of the client, not only because it is committed mainly to its own perpetuation, but because its perpetuation is often conditional on the systematic neglect or abuse—material or psychological—of the lower class and the deviant. Thus agencies for the blind "cream" the more youthful and educable for rehabilitation in order to improve their record of "success." Public housing agencies try to reject "problem" families so as to enhance the image of the bureaucracy. Urban renewal authorities steal neighborhoods from the poor. Foster care agencies all too often keep children in foster care families or in institutions, refusing either to return them to their parents or to place them for adoption even when these are viable alternatives, because each child adds to the public subsidies they receive.

In other words, there is often a profound conflict of interest between the welfare of the agencies and the welfare of clients. But it is a fundamental object of professional education to deny this conflict, to teach students that the agencies of the welfare state are *their* agencies. In the countless field evaluation reports which we have read in our capacity as teachers, students are rated on the degree to which they have developed an "appropriate identification" with the agency. We have seen many evaluations in which students were faulted for failing to identify adequately with an agency, but we have never known a student who was criticized for overidentifying. By contrast, students are quite regularly given negative evaluations for "overidentifying" with clients—more often than not because they were seized by the sense that clients were being mistreated.

This emphasis in our socialization clearly serves the interests of our employers. We are, quite simply, being taught to identify with the prisons and asylums, with the welfare departments and the urban renewal authorities, and we therefore develop a "learned incapacity" to perceive our own interests or those of clients. It is a remarkable achievement, reminiscent of the achievements of the era of industrial paternalism and company unionism, when many workers were induced to identify with their employers. But assembly-line workers have since learned that General Motors is not "their" company. We have yet to learn that lesson.

Third, we have to break with the professional doctrine that ascribes virtually all of the problems that clients experience to defects in personality development and family relationships. It must be understood that this doctrine is as much a political ideology as an explanation of human behavior. It is an ideology that directs clients to blame themselves for their travails rather than the economic and social institutions that produce many of them. Students are measured both by their ability to "reach for feelings" in clients and by their ability to provide Freudian interpretations of those feelings. There is little professional literature that instructs students to reach for their clients' feelings about their lot in life, or to provide socioeconomic interpretations of those feelings. This psychological reductionism—this pathologizing of poverty and inequality—is, in other words, an ideology of oppression, for it systematically conceals from people the ways in which their lives are distorted by the realities of class structure. Many teachers, supervisors, and agency administrators are teaching students to throw sand in clients' eyes. And this ideology is all the more powerful because, thanks to the authority of the "helping" professions, it appears to be grounded in the "science" of Freudian psychology.

If many professors and employers encourage us to ignore the ways in which various socioeconomic forces contribute to the personal and family problems of our clients, it is for the obvious reason that clients might then become obstreperous or defiant—that is, they might become a serious cause of embarrassment to the bureaucracies. One student reported the following conflict with her supervisor over just this point. She was assigned to the special services division of a welfare department. Her general responsibility was to reach out to clients who appeared to have problems of various kinds, and to give help by providing liaison with other agencies and resources, as well as to engage in treatment. One of her cases, Ms. D., lived in a tenement rat-trap, with falling plaster and stopped-up plumbing. Ms. D. had refused to pay her rent for a number of months, and the student expressed wholehearted sympathy.

When the student informed her supervisor about the condition of the apartment and the action which Ms. D. had been taking to fight the landlord, he was outraged. The student was told, in no uncertain terms, that it was contrary to agency policy to encourage rent withholding by clients. "No professional would encourage such irresponsible behavior. What about her anger? Did you get her anger out? Your job is to help her express her feelings about the situation, not to encourage her to conduct a rent strike!" The supervisor then insisted that he and the student role-play, so that the student could learn how to help a client express anger. "And so we played that game about feelings," the student said. Students who are taught only to reach for feelings are taught to protect the bureaucracies, and by doing so, to protect important economic groups, such as rapacious landlords, on whose good will the bureaucracies depend.

But once we break with this third tenet of professional doctrine, we will become aware, and be able to help clients to become aware, of the multiple links between economic problems and the problems defined as pathology, as when men out of work grow discouraged and drift away from their families. Men who cannot earn a living have always deserted their families in our society, not because of problems originating in family relationships, but because the humiliation of not being able to support women and children erodes family relationships. When people do not have steady jobs or income, they are deprived of a chief source of self-esteem, which may lead in turn to the kinds of behavior we label personality deterioration—to the listless men hanging on street corners, to alcoholism, addiction, and to other forms of retreatism. In a sense these are psychological problems, but in a profounder sense they are the products of an economy that requires a chronically high rate of unemployment and underemployment, and that therefore denies many people access to a livelihood, and to the building blocks of self-respect.

In the same vein, it should be recognized that the mothers who turn out to be incompetent and irresponsible often have these deficiencies because of the overwhelming discouragement of trying to raise children alone, in crowded and deteriorated quarters, without the income to feed and clothe them properly. When these children reach the age of six or seven, mothers then watch helplessly as they lose them to the life of the streets. These women cannot be helped much by therapy. A small part of their tragedy is that often they cannot even turn to us for human sympathy and support without being stigmatized.

My supervisor only supervised us with reference to those cases which interested her. The clients had to have either interesting pathology or some secretive events in their lives. The cases she refused to discuss were those she considered "hopeless." For example, I was seeing a fifty-nine-year-old black woman whose husband was an alcoholic, whose son was on heroin and involved in a day program for drug rehabilitation, and whose daughter was in college. This mother was working as a salesclerk to support her family and to keep her daughter in college. She was also involved in many church activities, one of which was taking adolescents on trips out of New York. This was to give them a chance to see other things besides the "ghetto." My supervisor decided that this was a very "masochistic woman" and there was nothing I could do for her. She told me to let her ventilate and refused to discuss the family with me any further. I had to call friends in social work to get needed information—such as how to obtain disability benefits for her husband and job programs for her son. I felt alone with the weight of my client's problems on my shoulders. My supervisor further stated, when I pressed her, that this woman had "no ego." No ego! From my perspective, this was a woman who was keeping her family together precisely because she did have a strong ego.[4]

[4] Quoted with the permission of Debra E. Pearl.

What lower-class mothers in this society need most is the means to survive: the means to feed their children, to take care of them, in ways which allow women to recapture pride in their role as mothers and as people. Once we stop locating all problems in personality adjustment and family relations, it will become clear that adjustment depends in the most fundamental way on resources. This is not a surprising assertion, except perhaps to many members of the helping professions. In a sense, it is an unprofessional assertion, merely for being so commonplace. It runs counter to long-standing trends by which social work has tried to remove itself from the concrete and urgent needs of poor people, and has instead become preoccupied with psychological needs. These trends have their origins partly in our desire to gain status by elaborating our expertise in esoteric clinical methods. We should reject such professional opportunism and accept the burden of asserting the obvious. If a client has no food in the house, he or she needs money. If a client lives in overcrowded and squalid housing, he or she needs money. Money in American society is, quite simply, the root of all normalcy.

Ms. K. came to this country a few years ago from Puerto Rico. She was separated from her husband. She had just had her second baby and was trying to arrange for a friend to baby-sit so she could return to work. The babies were often ill, and that required numerous visits to clinics. Few baby-sitters were willing to undertake these chores. The clinics were also costly, and she had little money. Although Ms. K. had previously worked double shifts, she had used her money up during the pregnancy, and had been advised by a social worker to apply for public assistance. But no one had given her any help in dealing with the application process.

Anyway, Ms. K. didn't get assistance, and she came to the social service department of the hospital where I am in training. She was very upset; she always cried and appeared extremely nervous. She was diagnosed by the team as being a "depressive neurotic" and therapy was recommended. The case was then given to me by my supervisor.

During our early interviews, Ms. K. always cried; her hands shook nervously and she was constantly depressed. Her physical appearance began to deteriorate. Her clothes were dirty and she had extremely bad body odor. This is important, for when she was originally seen at the clinic she was described as being neat, clean, and attractive.

As I saw it, Ms. K. had a great deal to be nervous and depressed about. The world she had created for herself was gone. She had lost her job; her husband was gone; she had two babies that she could not care for if she were going to work; she had been evicted; and she had no money.

I soon realized that Ms. K. could not read English well. She was extremely embarrassed about this, and tried to hide it from me. This turned out to be one reason why she had so much difficulty with the welfare department. She didn't understand what they were talking about when they told her to get various documents, and she could not read the instructions given to her. She was illiterate in a bureaucratic society. Consequently, I gave Ms. K. a great deal of help with her housing and welfare problems.

I don't know what I think about the diagnosis of "depressive neurotic." Ms. K. certainly had all of the symptoms that the people on the clinic team pointed out to me. But a funny thing has happened. Now that Ms. K. has gotten public assistance and a place to live, her behavior has changed. She is now neatly dressed when she comes to see me, and she doesn't cry or wring her hands nervously any more.

Clearly, if there is any system of programs and agencies with which we ought to be intimately familiar, it is those that provide concrete benefits—Supplemental Security Income, Aid to Families with Dependent Children, Food Stamps, and the like. But we are not. And professional education is largely the reason that we are not, for the English Poor Law commissioners still haunt our classrooms. We no longer talk about encouraging immorality; instead we worry about encouraging dependency among the poor. The rhetoric has changed, but the pieties persist; it is the psychologically unworthy who must now be protected from their defects of character. Consequently, students are not taught about the world of the waiting rooms and the long lines, nor about how to help their clients deal with that world. The faculty members of the schools of social work generally do not know that world, and many do not want to know it. But a student can ask a casework teacher to describe the general differences between neurosis and psychosis and be quite confident of obtaining an extended answer of some kind. Students are taught "social policy"—those grand schemes defining how the world ought to be. Such knowledge is a source of academic and professional prestige. But if a student asks for a description of the differences in criteria of eligibility between Aid to Families with Dependent Children and Food Stamps, nine out of ten teachers of casework and social policy will stand mute.

Fourth, and finally, it follows from what has been said that we ought to become aware of the ways that "professional knowledge and technique" are used to legitimate our bureaucratic power over people. The professional dedicated to serving people will understand that his or her most distinguishing attribute ought to be humility. The doctrine that "we know best" must be exorcised; there is simply no basis for the belief that we who have Masters of Social Work degrees or other similar university credentials are better able to discern our clients' problems than they are, and better able to decide how to deal with these problems. In fact, we know next to nothing about the problems we claim to understand. A potpourri of dubious propositions drawn from the social and psychological sciences has been dignified as knowledge, when the most charitable thing to be said about them is that they are speculations.

None of this would be so important were it simply that we did not know very much. But thinking we know a great deal, we often ignore what clients say they need. Even worse, we invoke this witches' brew of "professional knowledge and technique" to brand people with horrendous psychiatric labels, and impose on them the loss of efficacy and self-esteem that inevitably follows. The ultimate absurdity occurs when we persist in stigmatizing people even when our own "diagnostic techniques" fail to disclose evidence of pathology. One student reported a case of a thirteen-year-old boy who was referred to a child development clinic for hyperactive children because of behavioral and academic difficulties in the public school. The psychologist examined the youngster first and reported:

He related in an appropriate manner ... did not display very much hyperactive behavior ... his approach to work was not impulsive. Rather, he tended to work persistently and was appropriately involved in the tasks even when they were difficult for him. Recommendation: James should be considered for our treatment program for hyperactive children.

Next the psychiatrist examined him and said:

James showed no hyperactivity either in my office or in the waiting room. He was not restless or fidgety. His attention and concentration were good, and he wasn't distractable. There was no evidence of thought or affect disorder. Recommendation: Acceptance for treatment program as well as pharmacotherapeutic treatment based on the diagnosis of hyperkinetic reaction of childhood.

Finally, the neurological examiner noted:

Throughout the interview there was a moderate amount of movement, both body and small hand movement, but this was never excessive nor was there any evidence of distractibility or decreased attention span. Diagnosis: Hyperactive reaction of childhood. Recommend admittance.

The final diagnosis and recommendation appear in the case record as follows:

Although James was not found to be excessively active either during psychiatric or neurological examinations, nor during psychological testing, he does fulfill the regulations, or to evade them. To do this, we must read the manuals, visit the intake offices, harass the staff, and continually invoke the appeals procedures. We ought to arm ourselves for this resistance with a special urgency now, for higher and higher levels of unemployment and underemployment are being defined by ruling groups as "normal" even while inflation has severely eroded the limited incomes of many families.

I called up the Gramercy Department of Social Services Center to inquire about Ms. R., a client of mine at the hospital. Ms. R. was concerned about what would happen with her welfare check which she said would be issued in several days. Previously, she had gone down to the Gramercy Center, signed for these checks, and then received them. She was justifiably anxious over the disposition of this next check. Her sister was at her home taking care of her six children. Also, Ms. R. had recently moved from the Bronx and had not as yet had her Food Stamps reissued. Lately, Ms. R. was unhappy with her apartment and desired help in finding a more suitable home.

After the phone at Gramercy had rung for fifteen or twenty minutes, a woman finally answered. She garbled something and I then tried to explain my purpose for calling. "My name is . . . . I'm a social worker from . . . ." "Oops," she interrupted me, and forwarded my call to "Group I," where another woman introduced herself with, "What's the problem," and I again proceeded. "My name is, . . . I'm a social worker . . . etc." Well, after I explained the problem in excruciating detail, she asked me to *repeat* almost everything I had previously stated. After this process was accomplished, she said, "Well, I'll have to call you back." I said, "Excuse me, I thought that I was referred to you because you were able to handle this matter." "I'm sorry, I'll have to speak to my supervisor; she's out to lunch." I said, "Could I speak to a social worker in your office?" She said, "I'm a . . . *specialist* in . . . ; we handle these matters." "But you just told me you *were not able* to handle this!" I decided to terminate this charade and said, "Well, I'd really appreciate your cooperation in expediting this matter. Can I expect to hear from you this afternoon?" She replied, "We'll handle this as soon as possible. I'll call you back today or tomorrow." "Thank you very much," I said, gritting my teeth in anger, but trying ever so hard to sound appreciative. It was not her fault that utter confusion seems to have enveloped DSS's already chaotic bureaucratic structure. I closed our conversation by asking, "By the way, could you tell me who I am speaking to?" "Mrs. Brown." "Thank you again, good-bye."

On Thursday, having failed to receive my return message from Mrs. Brown, I decided to call the main DSS office in Manhattan. I received a run-around and proceeded to call the Gramercy Center again. No one answered the switchboard for fifteen or twenty minutes and I simply lost patience and hung up. Pondering the dilemma, I felt rather useless, impotent, angered, frustrated . . . etc. I said to myself, "Maybe I'll just have to wait, mail a letter perhaps, or visit their office." Well, after a few more minutes of ambivalent nonaction, I decided to call the main DSS office once again. This time, after speaking to three or four nondescript know-nothings, I felt as if I was finally connected to someone in some position of authority and responsibility who gave me the phone number and name of the assistant manager of the Gramercy Center.

I then called the assistant manager and said I had been referred to her from the central office. I informed her of the problems I was having regarding Ms. R. and the noncooperative nature of Group I's efforts. I also decried the lack of response to switchboard calls and further informed her that the switchboard number is the only number available to the public. She was very cordial and assured me, "I will see to it that Ms. R.'s check is forwarded in the mail, and I will go over to Group I immediately." She explained to me the problem regarding the Food Stamps: "We do not handle the actual granting of these stamps; that is carried out by computer, and since Ms. R. recently moved, it will be a while before her case is transferred." She finally switched me to a man from General Services regarding Ms. R.'s housing problems.

This man was very cordial but quite devoid of helpful information. He decried NYCHA's bureaucratic ineptitude, while personally manifesting DSS's utter dysfunctionality in almost the same breath. "I really can't help you much with this, we really can't do very much. . . . I'd like to be of more help, sorry. I can give you the name of some real estate agent, but you know. . . ." I pumped him and did receive some valuable information regarding relocation, building condemnation, etc.

On Tuesday, I visited Ms. R.'s home and found that DSS had sent her a note stating that her benefits would be reduced due to her hospitalization. This form also said that any alteration of this reduction would only be made upon a personal appeal. Also, Ms. R. told me she received her ADC check, but failed to receive her rent check. Thus, upon returning to the hospital, I again called the Gramercy Center via the switchboard. After two or three minutes of ringing, I decided to use the direct number I had been given; unfortunately, no one answered. Then I called DDS's main office and received the phone numbers of another assistant manager as well as the hallowed office manager. The office manager was out, but the assistant manager was available. I opened up our conversation once again decrying (politely) the failure of the switchboard to answer incoming calls, the lack of response from Group I to my original call, etc. I was quite simply "setting her up." By illustrating her office's ineptness, I was hopeful that she would take matters "into her own hands" and help restore Ms. R.'s complete benefits. She assured me that she would immediately see to it that Ms. R.'s benefits were totally reinstated for her next check. She told me that Ms. R.'s rent check was one day late and that she should receive it by Thursday or Friday. She thanked me for my interest, I thanked her for her concern, and after all these thank-you's, we said good-bye.

I continued my contacts with the Gramercy Center through a man who seemed genuinely concerned with Ms. R.'s case. He helped expedite a $170 check to Ms. R., covering baby-sitting services rendered by her "aunt" while she was hospitalized. I had been working on establishing a "medical emergency" so as to expedite

Ms. R.'s acceptance into a NYCHA project. In this regard, all six of her children were sent for check-ups in our Pediatrics Clinic. Their cumulative physical condition was deplorable. I amassed seven or eight letters from doctors on Pediatrics and Neurology, as well as my own testimony and forwarded these documents to both Housing and DSS.

Eventually Ms. R. was interviewed by NYCHA and placed on their medical emergency list. However, the waiting period for this process was impossible to determine and could stretch out for years! From my inquiries, I struck on one other avenue regarding Ms. R.'s desperate housing situation. Henry Street Settlement ran a housing relocation program. They operated a group of furnished apartment houses used solely for emergency relocation purposes. A family residing in these received top priority for placement in a NYCHA project. However, they could *only* handle cases *referred* by DSS!

Thus, I recontacted Gramercy. Unfortunately, the housing person I had previously talked to informed me (of something I already was *well aware* of) that DSS could *only* refer relocation emergency cases. "Yes, I understand that, and I appreciate the position this places you in, but what about Ms. R.? I've contacted *every* agency in the city and each agency denies its responsibility in this matter. I fully appreciate the necessity for these regulations, but, hell, when will we move, when Ms. R. and her six children all end up hospitalized?" "Yes," he said, "I understand, but look, let me read you these regulations here. . . . " I said, "Do the regulations tell us what to do with six chronically ill youngsters and a mother who is suffering from severe headaches, dizziness, and vomiting, who are forced to live in a heatless rat-trap, with junkies living in the hallways, the ceilings collapsing, holes in the bedroom walls. . . ? Let me run down the report I received from the Pediatrics Clinic. . . . " Then he said, "O.K., O.K., look, I'll visit the family at home tomorrow, and recommend that the family be placed at Henry Street. . . . but, look, I know my superiors are going to reject my recommendation."

I fully appreciated his final remark. Thus, I called the office manager to solicit aid in this matter. She told me, "This is not within my jurisdiction. . . . " So I said, "There does not seem to be any regulation existing in NYCHA or DSS codes to specifically deal with a medical emergency exacerbated by poor housing. *However,* I've spoken to the people at Henry Street and they will accept this referral." "They will?" she replied. "Absolutely, so if they are willing, perhaps we can effectuate this approval from your end." "Well, I'll try. . . . " To be sure, Henry Street's "approval" was entirely irrelevant to this process, since they *had* to accept *all* DSS referrals, and *only* DSS referrals, but I said this to add a note of strength to my argument, especially when dealing with individuals steeped in a bureaucratic matrix. ("If Henry Street is willing to stick its neck out, perhaps you. . . . ")

Eventually, this request was rejected by a DSS supervisor. I immediately phoned him (supervisor IV–Director of Social Service) and he said, "I am sorry, but our regulations concerning referral to Henry Street clearly state. . . . " I said, "Are you then refusing this referral?" "I believe I am making that clear." "Thus, you are accepting responsibility for any medical deterioration in Ms. R.'s family?" He said, "The housing conditions for hundreds of thousands of New Yorkers are deplorable. . . . " "Yes," I argued, "but fortunately the heads of all these households are not suffering from possible brain tumors, all these children have not become *addicted* to eating lead chips and paint. . . . " "I appreciate your concern, however . . . regulations. . . ." I kept on, saying, "You really sound as if you are concerned. I have turned *every* corner, called *every* city agency. . . . We just cannot allow ourselves to be immobilized by perfectly sound regulations, when in a specific, unique instance, these regulations fail to satisfy the pressing needs of a family in real distress." "Look, I cannot do more than I have, however, I will refer you to our assistant director."

My conversation with the assistant director followed quite closely the above described narrative. However, I pushed very strongly the concept of accountability. He seemed to be particularly sensitive to this. Further, I consistently emphasized my appreciation of the difficult position he was placed in regarding this case and how overwhelming his job must seem when faced with the obstacle of a "seemingly" unmovable kind. He proposed we have a case conference. Thus, I journeyed to Gramercy and met face to face all those myriad voices I had come to know so well . . . all ten of them. Initially everyone was pessimistic and negative regarding the *possibilities* and *advisability* of such a referral. Then the assistant director said, "I really believe this case has real merit. . . . " (The rest of the staff quickly fell in line and soon *supported* my position.) Then he continued, "O.K., I'm going to ask you to write us *one more letter,* and I'll then give *my approval* for Ms. R.'s referral to Henry Street. . . . How is that?"

Ms. R. and her six children are now residing in one of Henry Street's apartments.[5]

Resistance is necessary in every social service setting. Social workers are employed in large numbers by hospitals, where they usually function to uphold the authority of the hospital, and of the doctors who are its unquestioned authorities. There is ample evidence of the malfeasance of American doctors, and of the criminal negligence of medical personnel generally in such simple but essential matters as accurate hospital records and lab tests. Social workers are used by hospitals and their medical rulers to appease anxious or dissatisfied patients, to cool out the mark. What we ought to do instead is to challenge the doctors and hospital authorities, and encourage patients to do the same.

My client, a thirty-eight-year-old, separated Puerto Rican mother of six adolescent boys has phlebitis of the right leg with possible thrombophlebitis. She has been

---

[5] Quoted with the permission of Lewis Zuchman.

hospitalized four times in the last two years. She is suposed to attend clinic once a month but often fails to do so. One of the things that we have decided to work on together is "why she does not go to the clinic." I accompanied her to the clinic on Monday. She was to be examined so that a form could be filled out and she could get a housekeeper, and she was to ask the doctor to clarify her medical status. After an interminable wait we were ushered into a booth and the attending doctor grunted, "Sit down." He said in a very condescending tone, "And what brings you here?" My client meekly told him about leg pains and trouble breathing. He glared at her, demanding clarification. She froze—and I had to draw her out on her complaints. Together we were able to get her problem across to him. He then waved her to the examining table and told her to take off her skirt. She did this and he proceeded to examine her in a very brusque manner. I felt humiliated just watching the procedure. He examined her legs, pressing repeatedly on a painful area. He then marched out of the room without a word, to look for a senior doctor.

As he was leaving, I asked him if it wasn't normal procedure to give a patient being examined a johnny coat or a drape. He glared at me and said, "Are you trying to tell me how to examine my patients?" I said no, I was simply referring to a matter of common courtesy. He said that he didn't know what I was talking about and stalked off. He returned with a doctor to whom he related the case, emphasizing the fact that the patient had not been to the clinic and that she had not been taking her anticoagulant for two months. The senior doctor did not seem to be agitated by this piece of information. He asked that Ms. Z. take off her pants so that he could examine her legs. Rather than addressing the request to her, he asked the intern to ask her! The intern said authoritatively that he only needed to look at the one leg; the other had no tenderness. The senior doctor responded that he wanted to compare the two. (This is something that even I knew and understood.)

As they were walking out of the room I repeated my request for a drape. The intern said they did not have one, and my client whispered to me, "It's O.K." I was fuming and even she was beginning to show signs of anger. The fact that she reacted at all is significant because she, like most welfare mothers, has been so beaten down that she has come to expect very little and demand even less. She is so used to this sort of treatment that she takes it for granted. She deserves it, there is nothing that she can do about it, and protesting will only make things worse. They returned, examined her, and left again to discuss the case. The intern returned and said that he was going to admit her. She became very upset, as she had spent last Christmas in the hospital, too. She and I talked a moment, and then she told the doctor that she would come in tomorrow, but that she had to go home and arrange things for her sons. He grudgingly agreed and she got ready to go into the waiting room and wait for the nurse to come and tell her about registration proce- dure. I told her that I would be out in a moment. She left and I turned to the intern and said, "May I speak with you for a moment?" He stopped writing in her chart. I said, "Listen, I know where you are coming from but . . . " He interrupted me. "The staff here are lazy, they're never around when you want them, they aren't there when you examine a patient . . . you don't know what it's like in here—it's like a stable. There is nothing that I can do." I said, "Yes there is, you could try being a bit more considerate, try thinking about how the patient feels. If I were sitting on that table I would have felt like a piece of shit." I was almost in tears, I was so angry and humiliated for my client. He looked at me and said, "You've made your point," and resumed his writing.

I turned and walked out. I sat down next to Ms. Z. and told her what I had said to him, and we discussed how she felt about it. During the examination I had asked if she minded that I spoke up and she had said, "Go on." She seemed to be standing behind me, cheering. We talked about why she couldn't say anything herself—her feelings about it doing no good, etc. . . . It was the way things are. After we talked to the nurse we went back up to Social Services to give the hospital social worker the form for the housekeeper. We related the episode to him, and this time Ms. Z. got involved and began to demonstrate her anger. The hospital social worker said that he would look into the incident to check on the doctor and on the lack of drapes.

The hospital social worker and I have discussed this matter since then and we are endeavoring to determine if this lack of courtesy is common clinic procedure. If it is, I plan to work on getting it changed. This may seem like a minor issue, but sitting nude on a table in a strange room with strange people wandering in and out places a person in a very vulnerable position. It's a small thing, but it means dignity.[6]

Obtaining medical treatment for people at all is often as much a problem as the way they are treated by medical personnel. The supervisor of one student placed in a hospital setting learned of a patient in the waiting room who was only nineteen, pregnant, and lonely.[7] She instructed the student to "let her ventilate her feelings." The student established contact, and learned that the young woman had been thrown out of the house by her grandmother because of the pregnancy, and was living with a friend who gave her twenty dollars a week to perform baby-sitting services. The student told her that she was eligible for public assistance as an emancipated minor, and inquired whether she had Medicaid. The patient replied that she had two letters, one saying she was eligible and the other saying she was ineligible. The student told the patient to go to the Department of Social Services and try to get things straightened out.

On the next visit to the hospital, the patient was in tears. She had been told that she was not eligible for public assistance or for Medicaid because

[6] Quoted with the permission of Susan Pinco.
[7] Quoted with the permission of Arlene Hagan.

she was an "illegal" (from a Latin American country). The patient was now upset both because she had "disgraced" her grandmother and because she might be deported, for the irate DSS worker had called the immigration authorities to report that an illegal alien was trying to obtain public relief. The student promptly called several legal defense organizations. She was advised to do everything she could to stall any action until the baby was born, since it was unlikely that a deportation proceeding would be instituted if the patient was the mother of a citizen.

The student then told her supervisor of her plan, and made it clear that the patient needed prenatal care even though she had no Medicaid card. Her supervisor became quite defensive, and expressed regret that she had assigned the case. She also insisted that the student prepare a written statement saying that the supervisor did not know the patient was an illegal alien, and said she doubted that care could be provided. The student expressed disgust, but made the necessary notation in the hospital chart. The hospital charged $1000 for a delivery, and the supervisor did not want to be responsible for a case of nonpayment. The student later learned from the financial office, however, that Medicaid provides coverage for thirty days in the event that an illegal alien is admitted on an emergency basis. Each time the patient came in for care, the student managed to get the admitting department to treat it as an emergency. On one occasion, she slipped the patient in by saying that she had lost her Medicaid card.

The patient then received a notice to report for a deportation hearing. The student told her supervisor that she was going to write a letter saying that the patient could not appear because of her pregnancy. "When I told my supervisor this, she was completely dumfounded, but she didn't know how to get out of the situation, so she had to go along." Luckily, the baby was born on the same day that the hearing was scheduled, and the student left the placement in May feeling that the deportation question had become moot. She planned to continue seeing the patient on her own, however, in order to be certain that the immigration authorities took no action.

In the criminal justice system, social workers have been made into something resembling the police agents of the state. In that role, we make life-determining decisions to revoke probation or parole and to place people in institutions. Ostensibly we make these decisions as social workers committed to rehabilitation. But do we really believe that penal institutions of any kind rehabilitate people? And if we do not, then we are permitting a lot of professional and technical mumbo jumbo to obscure the fact that we are incarcerating people, not rehabilitating them. In the juvenile courts, the banner of treatment flies even higher. Under the guise of treating

parents and the presumed deficiencies of their children, we have participated in the institutionalization of children for such behaviors as truancy,
incorrigibility, or sexual promiscuity. In effect, we have participated in the
criminalization of children for offenses for which no adult could be arrested
or confined. An important form of resistance is to use our discretion to
keep adults out of prisons and children out of the reformatories and "residential treatment centers" whenever we possibly can. If we use our
common sense, we know that children are almost always better off even as
runaways than in institutions.

A case was referred to the private counseling service in which I am placed. The
mother, Mrs. X., reported that her daughter Joan had gotten in trouble with the
police when she and a friend went into a truck and stole seventy dollars. Mrs. X.
stated that her daughter had been in trouble a few times in the past, and was
spending too much time with "bad girls." Both she and her husband felt that the
child was disrespectful to them, and they both spend a lot of time yelling at her.

Mrs. and Mr. X. are white, lower-class, and Irish Catholic. Mr. X. has been
hospitalized and is now medically disabled. He has been unemployed for some
time, and the family has had to go on welfare. They have applied for Supplemental
Security Income benefits. Mrs. X. used to be a domestic worker and she is planning
to resume that kind of work.

There are several stresses on the family in addition to the father's illness and
unemployability. They had to move to a cheap apartment, and of course they have
lost a lot of social status because of their poverty-stricken state. With these changes,
communication in the family seems to have broken down. Anger and disappointment seem to have taken over. I have been working with various family members
around these angers and communication problems, and I have also become Joan's
advocate in dealing with the courts.

I received a call from Joan's probation officer who wanted information about
the family, since she is making out a report for the judge. She said there were two
choices for Joan: residential treatment or some kind of continuing counseling. She
told me that if we could come up with a good plan, the judge could be persuaded
to keep Joan out of an institution. So I began to work on the case.

After I had seen Joan several times to talk things over, I got a call from her
mother that they were canceling their various sessions with me. The message also
said that their Medicaid eligibility had run out, and they could no longer pay the
agency's fees. I tried to reach them by telephone and letter, but they did not
respond. I then contacted the probation officer and explained the situation. She said
she would get in touch with them and tell them to call me. I felt strongly that the
reason they had discontinued coming was because they had no money. Mrs. X. is a
very proud woman.

A few days later, the probation officer's supervisor called me and bawled me out
for getting her supervisee involved in my problems with my clients. She said it was

perfectly obvious that Mrs. X. does not want any kind of counseling for her daughter, that she is resisting, and that the only answer for Joan is to put her in a residential placement. Since the parents can't control Joan, she said, the child needs "a structured setting."

I could not believe what I was hearing. Once I had calmed down, I told her off. I began by saying that she didn't know anything about the family and all they've been through because of the father's unemployment and illness. She finally backed down and said she would consider a plan if I could develop one. I figured I had won round one.

A few days later, Mrs. X. called because the probation officer had been in touch with her. It soon became apparent that the reason for her discontinuance was that her Medicaid card had run out, just as I had thought. With a little effort, I was able to get that problem straightened out, and then Mrs. X. agreed that the family would continue.

I then worked out a plan for Joan to have a "Big Sister," and I arranged to continue seeing various family members on a regular basis.

When I spoke to the probation officer, she was quite embarrassed. She explained that her supervisor always thought institutional placement was the best remedy for kids. She explained to me that she was a student in training and didn't feel secure arguing with her supervisor. We agreed to continue working together around the pending court appearance, and we both felt confident that the judge would listen to us. As it happens, he did. Things are going much better with Joan now, and with her family.

If we work in mental institutions or have dealings with them, we will dismiss treatment claims for what they are—doctrines that are utterly unsubstantiated. Mental institutions do not treat people, and they rarely cure them. With our heads cleared of doctrine, we can see that what hospitalization actually does is deprive people of ordinary liberties and of any vestige of self-esteem or competence. And we play a role in that process—as social workers in intake offices, as members of psychiatric teams, in discharge departments and in referral agencies. We can use the opportunities afforded by these positions to resist decisions to commit, to challenge capricious diagnoses, to question the stupefaction of people by drugs. We need to remember that while people may need counseling, mental institutions do not provide it. What they do provide, almost no one needs. No one needs stigmatization; few people need medication; and even fewer need institutionalization.

One student resisted his supervisor over the question of whether a veteran in an out-patient veterans' facility should be drugged. Mr. M. had been diagnosed as schizophrenic, but at the time the student began seeing him, he had obtained a job as a truck driver, was earning more money than ever before, and found the job enormously rewarding. He showed some signs of nervousness, however, and the student's supervisor suggested that Mr. M. be seen by the agency psychiatrist in order to obtain medication so that he "wouldn't fall apart." The student replied that far from falling apart, he was doing fine, and that medicating him would interfere with the performance of a job that had come to be extremely important to him. The student stressed that if this veteran lost his job, then he would indeed fall apart. Consequently, the student refused to refer Mr. M. to the psychiatrist for medication. Afterward, the student commented that he felt gratified about the whole matter, noting that the price he paid was insignificant—a sentence in his field evaluation saying that he was having difficulty with authority and that he had dogmatic views about drugs and psychiatrists.

The key decisions that lead to the institutionalizing of people occur in many settings where social workers are employed, or to which they are related—not just in the mental health agencies and the courts. The incarceration process can be set in motion in the public schools, for example.

Ms. A. and her seven children live in one of the most rundown sections of the South Bronx. The A. family moved to the United States from Puerto Rico in 1970. The case was referred to the Bureau of Child Welfare by the guidance counselor at P.S.____ because George was having serious behavior problems at that school. When the case was first transferred to me, the guidance counselor called me to inform me that George was a "recalcitrant" child who should be placed immediately in an institution. I visited the family and learned that Ms. A. was vehemently against placement for her son. A couple of weeks later, I received a call from the guidance counselor informing me that George had been suspended because he had been involved in a fight with a school employee.

I went out to visit the family again. George told me that the school employee had hit him over the head with a broom because he had refused to get out of his way when he had been ordered to do so. Ms. A. was furious with the school and threatened to sue.

I called a meeting to discuss with the school officials what could be done to help George. The consulting psychiatrist was present at this meeting, together with the school principal, George's former teacher, the guidance counselor, and some bigshot administrator from the school district. It became clear to me and to the psychiatrist (we became allies during this battle) that the school officials were not interested in helping George; they had only one objective—to get rid of him. The teacher and the guidance counselor repeated again and again that George was an "impossible" child and that the school could do nothing to help him. The school principal made it clear that he was mainly concerned with the school's image in the community. Because George had once cut his wrist in a fit of anger (both the psychiatrist and I doubt that this incident could in any way be construed as a "suicide attempt"), the principal talked about her concern that George might try to commit suicide in the school. Her concern was not for the child, but for herself. She mentioned at least five times during the meeting that she could already envision the "screaming *New York Times* headlines" if George were to kill himself in "her" school.

The meeting was tense. I flatly stated that BCW would not place the child unless the mother and the child voluntarily requested placement. The psychiatrist urged the principal to arrange for George to be placed in a "grade B" class which is a special, small class that caters to the needs of "problem children." The principal said that she could not guarantee admission to one of these special classes because there are so many "disturbed" kids in the South Bronx. But finally we won, and George was not sent to a residential setting. He got the special class instead.[8]

The way people are treated in institutions provides countless occasions for resistance.

I am placed in a residential treatment institution for field training. During the course of the year, I became aware of many instances of child abuse, especially by the cottage staff. Others knew about these practices, but everyone was afraid to take action. The chief victimizer of the children was the head of child care who was a former matron in the women's prison. She had hired several retired prison guards as cottage parents. Children were intimidated, demeaned, and physically abused. At first I was frightened—these were frightening people, and I was afraid for my own safety. Veiled threats were made. I also had doubts about whether it was proper to accuse another staff member. The doctor was also abusive. One of my clients thought she might be pregnant and wanted a test, which had to be approved. At first the doctor refused: "Miss Tureff, *I* am the doctor around here. This is a medical, not a social decision." Then the doctor asked, "Has your client been diagnosed? I find her behavior most age-inappropriate. I think she is more than just psychoneurotic, she is definitely pre-psychotic. How long has she been promiscuous?" I replied that she had been seen by a psychiatrist, but no label had been attached. I also said that she was not promiscuous, just sexually active.

As the weeks passed, I became increasingly concerned with reports of child abuse, especially physical beatings. Teachers in the school told me of children with bruised lips. Children told their natural parents about beatings. A number of children told me directly. And other professionals on the grounds had their own sources of information regarding such practices. One of the natural parents came in to complain to the director, after I had encouraged her to do so. But the director dodged the problem, saying, "Look Ms. J., there are some suspicions about the cottage parents, but I can't just run in there and fire them. I need concrete evidence. They are under surveillance, and that's all I can do for now."

[8] Quoted with the permission of Laura Nitzberg.

Fortunately, a new director was hired toward the end of the year. I had been talking with my supervisor about the whole problem. She knew what was going on, but she too was frightened. However, she spoke with the new director, and after some trepidation, agreed that I (and several other students in placement) could do the same. The director subsequently suggested that the children be asked to provide testimony, but the children were too terrified. By now the new director was concerned. He called a meeting of the child care staff and lectured them on child abuse. Someone had also anonymously informed the state board of social services, and an investigator had come to the agency.

Once things got stirred up, things began to happen. Several child care workers have resigned, the head of child care is going to be terminated, and everyone is more aware now that child abuse cannot always be concealed, so they are more careful. Although I (and my supervisor) were both afraid that she might lose her job because of what I had been doing, I think now that she is glad that I protested these conditions.[9]

In the struggle against agency practices, it is often necessary to bring external pressure to bear, such as organizing clients to protest or threatening litigation. A mother and three children were burned out of their apartment in the South Bronx. The mother desperately sought housing for several weeks, but could find nothing that welfare officials would approve and for which they would advance a security deposit. She then went to the public housing authority. When she was shunted aside, she began to scream and refused to leave the office until something was done to ensure housing for her and her children. The police were called, with the result that she was placed in a mental hospital, and her children sent for placement. The mother was promptly diagnosed as "schizophrenic—paranoid type," medicated, and involuntarily detained for several months. When she was released, she went to the child care agency to demand her children. The student assigned to the case had to tell her that the children could not be released until an appropriate apartment was found that met the agency's criterion of adequacy. To make matters worse, it turned out that the welfare department would not approve a rent allowance adequate for the family until the children were returned—a case of "catch 22."

When the woman flew into another angry rage, the student protested to her supervisor that the agency should help find housing for the family. "That," she was told, "is not our function." The mother subsequently broke down again, and was returned briefly to a mental hospital. The student again protested to her supervisor, saying that if the agency's

---

[9] Quoted with the permission of Susan Tureff.

housing standards were universally applied, there would be no children left in the South Bronx. The supervisor would not relent.

Because of the cost of visiting the children, who were in an upstate institution, the mother had difficulty seeing them, although she tried to do so as often as possible. On these visits, she screamed and cried and raged that she wanted the children back, all of which was used by agency personnel to discredit her emotional health and maternal "fitness." Her visits to the children became more sporadic and more enraged. The student was also enraged; she argued that the agency was receiving thousands of dollars for the care of the children, but still she could not persuade her supervisor to authorize payment for the mother's travel.

Finally, the student herself visited the children and reported that she could find no reason why they should not be returned to their mother. Her supervisor disagreed: where but in a professional child care institution, the supervisor said, could such children receive the best of clinical services and other forms of care? The student saw it differently; she saw an agency enriching and maintaining itself by kidnapping children.

Since all else had failed, the student decided to get legal assistance for this mother. She ran down a civil liberties lawyer who called and wrote the agency, making it clear that litigation would follow. There was quite a flap at the agency, but the student stood her ground. Finally, the agency director decided he did not want to go to the trouble and cost of a court action, and so the student was allowed to help the mother find housing, and the children were subsequently released.

This last case illustrates a number of the themes of this paper—from the pecuniary motives of the agencies to their stigmatizing practices to the infantilizing of students who have extensive experience. It also makes a crucial point: Resistance is steady, unending, frustrating work.

The agency in which I work is a community center in a ghetto. The children come to the center because their parents send them "for healthy, safe, recreational purposes." For many of them it is also a baby-sitting service in the practical sense, as many are working. The children come to have fun and because their parents make them. The group of eight-year-olds I am working with has six (out of eleven) so-called "problem" children—that is, they have functioned poorly in previous groups (some clearly are not "groupees"), and exhibit acting-out behavior or withdrawn behavior. Some are in private treatment; some are on medication therapy. The composition of my group was decided upon by the departmental supervisor at the request of my field instructor, Ms. N., who wanted me to have a "difficult group which would provide a good learning experience"—thus sacrificing the needs of the children. Ms. N. is Coordinator of the Mental Health Unit and sees everything and everyone (including myself) in terms of diagnosis and treatment.

From its original purely recreational focus, the center moved after the riots in the 1960s to develop a mental health component so that it could get mental health funds. The agency became "professionalized"—meaning that they now employ primarily MSWs and have shifted their emphasis toward mental health, i.e., preventive, socialization, and ego growth treatment. The state has just licensed the center and it is now able to receive mental health funds for "recreational services." The rub is that the children and their parents still view their participation in the program as purely recreational.

In order to get reimbursement, "diagnoses" have to be sent to the city. I objected to this vehemently at a general staff meeting, and was told that "our parents know that we care about each child and that we do more than pure recreation." The diagnoses, I was assured, would be of the broadest, nonstigmatizing variety—such as problems of adjustment to puberty, to adolescence, to school, to peers, etc. "Anyway," it was said, "who doesn't have such an adjustment reaction at one or another point in their lives?" Further, I was assured that no names would be sent in with the diagnoses; each client would have a number and the diagnoses would be sent in by number. It was said that the agency had received assurances from the city that a number would "never" be traced to the specific individual diagnosed; our agency would keep the names in locked files. However, I observed that clients were openly discussed by name in the lobby and in front of "non-professional" community assistants who became privy to snatches of the history and "problems" of center members. I was also told at the staff meeting, "We will not single out Medicaid clients, but all the children in the mental health groups will be given diagnoses, since this is only fair." Eventually all groups would fall under the mental health program. To begin with, only some groups (those led by MSWs or graduate students—three in all, including mine) were so designated because the service had to be offered by a person in training or a professional if reimbursement was to be obtained. It was also stated that if the city and state did not uphold their end of the confidentiality issue, our agency would use its full legal power to fight.

Meanwhile, no client had been advised of the agency's new mental health direction, or of the agency's intention of "cooperating with the appropriate city and state agency" by sending in diagnoses. This process had already begun, in order to collect fees. I raised strong objections, stressing the parents' right to be informed first and given an option to say whether or not they wanted their children diagnosed. It turned out that others had felt the same discomfort, but not my supervisor, Ms. N., since the whole mental health program was her "baby." I was told to deal with this in private supervision and that the administrative staff would seriously consider my objections. They did, and instructed Ms. N. to stop all procedures until parents had been duly notified and had signed an authorization to the effect that they understood the nature of the program and the meaning of our "cooperation" with "appropriate city and state agencies."

At our next supervisory conference, Ms. N. instructed me to explain all of this to the parents in the mildest possible terms. I objected. I also complained that each kid had a file in the agency and that my records on the kids were being used as the bases for diagnoses. She told me to sit down with her and make the diagnoses. I strongly objected to both the diagnosing process and to the use of my files for that purpose; that since the kids come here for recreation, it was unfair for them to be diagnosed; that when I send my own kid to camp or to the "Y" to swim, etc., I would be very disturbed about the existence of such a file; that people come and utilize services innocently, and then have a folder made up on them that can be damaging to them in later life; further, that it is presumptuous of me or anyone else to slap a diagnosis on someone; that this is what always happens to the poor, etc.

Ms. N. then told me that I didn't trust the agency. Why did I think the agency would not respect the confidentiality of its clients? I repeated my objections and reasons. Next she said, "You are a student in this agency and you better do as you're told." I said I knew my position, but students also have rights and feelings. I was then told that since I had been an agency director before entering graduate school, I therefore had difficulty taking supervision, that I don't understand the importance of records for continuity—"how helpful it will be for the next person to see how so-and-so functions; this is good social work practice." She added, "You are a very aggressive and argumentative woman and you come on very strong. As a student, you fail to understand that you are at the bottom of the totem pole and obviously you have never had to take supervision and have difficulty accepting the student role." I was told to think about that. I told her that I wasn't born a director, I had never before had difficulty taking supervision, that perhaps I was not as passive as most, but this had not caused me any problems and that I did not wish to be psychoanalyzed since we were discussing what was to me an important ethical issue.

She asked me what could happen to the clients that I was afraid of. I gave her countless examples of people who have been plagued and harassed in later life over just such "innocent, professionally well-intentioned" reports, and that I was particularly concerned about this happening to poor people all the time. She said I was not being realistic, that this was not so. We left feeling very angry and frustrated, and subsequently I learned that she called my faculty field adviser to inform her that we were "having a personality conflict."

At a subsequent meeting with Ms. N., she insisted on making diagnoses; she liked diagnosing. The tension was thick and I said I wouldn't join her. She then did it in my presence, discussing each case with me. Whenever possible, I pushed for "diagnosis deferred" or "no discernible problem."

This meeting occurred shortly before evaluation time; I soon received a negative report (two pages of repetition) on my inability to take supervision, my "need to learn from my own mistakes rather than following her suggestions," etc. My skills were perfect (great perceptions and sensitivity, etc.). We argued again on the personality issue and I told her that I was not going to watch my p's and q's (I had decided that no degree was worth selling myself for) and that I was open to reasonable objections, but that I had my feelings and personality and that I wanted these discussed only with respect to my direct practice performance. Again, I was told of my aggressive behavior, my obsessive-compulsive pattern, and how I misperceive everything she says. I asked her how it was possible that I could misperceive everything she said and be so perceptive and sensitive in my work. She said, "I'm your supervisor and I will exercise my prerogative by staying with my analysis." I said this was her right.

Several weeks later, I was asked by Ms. N. to write a special report on one of the kids who was acting out and whose therapist wanted to put him on drug medication although the kid's mother objected. The therapist needed corroborating evidence. I wrote a statement which generally focused on the kid's strengths and progress (since I had been asked to write a progress report!). Ms. N. called me on this and asked me to add a paragraph describing his tantrums in detail. I said that he wasn't the only kid who had tantrums, and that what I had written is how I see the matter and I wasn't going to add anything further. She reluctantly accepted my decision and the kid has not been medicated.

It is interesting to note a change in our relationship as the months have passed. After our confrontations, Ms. N. said to me, "One of the problems is that I am an aggressive woman too." She seems to respect my opinion more, although she still pumps me for "psychological information" about the kids. But I dole it out sparingly and cautiously. I still hear: "You are part of this agency and you better do what you're told." However, I go about my business, I voice my opinions, and I do those things I'm told that do not conflict with my ethical standards.

Even small victories require toughness and persistence.

Finally, a few words of warning are in order. Anyone who undertakes to fight for client interests must be prepared to be discredited. One of the main lines of attack mounted by the agencies is that their clients need no advocates; what is done to the client is for the best. Sometimes, when the evidence of abuse is too blatant to be dismissed—for example, when desperately needy families are summarily turned away from welfare departments—the line of attack shifts. Now the claim is not that the agencies are above reproach, but rather that the client is "dependent," for otherwise he or she would be able to overcome the obstacles generated by faults in agency practice. If one gives actual assistance—telephoning on behalf of the client or accompanying a family member to some agency, or whatever—the charge will be leveled that this help actually exacerbates the client's problems by inducing dependency. Presumably, clients should fend for themselves, the theory being that otherwise they will not acquire the competence to cope.

These assertions are designed, of course, to prevent agency procedures from being resisted or disrupted. To argue that clients can, one by one, successfully fight the huge, centralized, and powerful agencies of the welfare state solely with the weapon of their egos is, of course, to render them helpless while appearing to render them strong. By this sleight-of-hand, problems of power are converted into problems of personality: it is not the power of the agencies that needs to be fought, but the strength of the client's ego that needs to be buttressed.

Serious forms of retribution may also ensue, although we typically exaggerate the punishments that will be meted out if we run afoul of our superiors (these exaggerations enable us to avoid any action at all). Still, we have to develop tactics not only to defend clients, but to defend ourselves. Clearly, the more of us in any agency who are joined together and committed to mutual support, the stronger we will be, not only ideologically—although that is important—but because we will be able to counter bureaucratic efforts to discipline us with job actions of our own. Some of us will find ourselves too isolated to develop collective tactics of self-defense, and some of us may even be fired. But most of us can get other jobs. In any case, we delude ourselves if we think that any serious political action—in social work or elsewhere—is possible that does not entail some risk and sacrifice.

At best, if we seriously decide to resist on behalf of the poor and the victims, we are not likely to be rewarded with professional esteem, and we probably will not advance rapidly in the bureaucracies, simply because those who side with the sick and the deviant, the poor and the criminal, are not usually rewarded for their troubles.

But if we choose such a course, we will become social workers in fact and not just in proclamation. And we will accomplish something important. If we manage to get people who are hungry a bit of bread, or to protect the weak against the assaults of the courts or the mental hospitals, then we will have gone a short way toward redressing the wrongs of a harsh society. Which of us is so arrogantly unfeeling, or so confident of the prospects for revolutionary transformation as to think these small gains not important?

In the longer run, moreover, if we fight for the interests of the people we claim are our clients, then we will also be waging a struggle against the institutions of the capitalist state. There is a kind of tautological trick inherent in some Marxist arguments, to the effect that any actual effort to deal with the contradictions created by capitalism will produce reforms that paper over the contradictions. The trick is a professionally convenient one,

for it enables us to say that no action short of the final cataclysmic action
ought be taken. But revolutions are not made all at once. If we believe that
the maintenance of wealth and power in the United States depends in part
upon the exploitation, isolation, and stigmatization of the victims of capitalism by the agency of the welfare state, then our role is to resist these
processes, and all the more fiercely because we now understand that the
practices of these agencies are not accidental, but are central to the operation of capitalist society. If we believe our analysis of the welfare state, then
it follows that if any struggle is important, then so is this one, for it is a
struggle to make contradictions explicit, not to obscure them.

Radical Social Work

1
Introduction: Social Work in the Welfare State

Roy Bailey and Mike Brake

Social work has become a major growth industry in the last couple of decades in Britain and the United States. A recent government report on university grants in Britain has suggested that the expansion of higher education should stress vocation, especially the field of social work. Universities and polytechnics have had suggested a target of 4,000 graduate and non-graduate social workers a year, a figure accepted by the Central Council for Education and Training in Social Work. The professionalization of social work, in the training programmes and subsequent careers, has already created a differentiation between graduate and non-graduate social workers, and those who have postgraduate degrees in social work.

Social work, both as a body of knowledge and as a sphere of activity, has developed its theory and practice from other social sciences. The influence in particular of psychology has led to an over-emphasis on pathological and clinical orientations to the detriment of structural and political implications. Training schools have tended to defend traditional social-work practice, in particular the dominant mode of social intervention known as casework. Where critical debate has arisen, it has been reformist rather than radical, and has been concerned with method. The political, social and ideological place of social work has never been satisfactorily discussed, nor has its possible exploitation as an agent of social control been taken seriously.[1] Social work has consequently failed to develop the self-criticism of other established disciplines and practices. Social-work schools tend to explain away student criticism, robbing arguments of legitimacy by appealing to areas of the pathological, such as anxiety, authority problems or developmental inadequacy.[2] Consequently, in the professional literature, there is a wide gap to be filled in the need for a critical perspective within the profession. This collection of new essays is an attempt to bridge that gap, and to encourage

[1] Only such groups as Case Con have attempted serious criticism.
[2] See Cannan (1972) for an excellent critique of social-work training, and also Rosenburg. Most criticism is to be found outside professional texts and journals.

serious radical criticism within the training schools and the profession. We feel that the important contributions made by outside groups—Gay Liberation, the Women's Movement, Mental Patients' Union, Claimants' Unions and Tenants' Associations—reflect lack of confidence in social workers, usually with good reason.

Any understanding of the position of social welfare in our society requires an understanding of its history, and an understanding of the state. 'The state is founded upon the contradiction between public and private life, between general and particular interests. . . .' (Marx and Engels, *The German Ideology*.) Social welfare can be seen as an attempt to resolve contradictions between certain aspects of production and consumption. In western industrial society the state intervenes in attempts to solve problems intrinsic to capitalism: both the problems and the intervention are integral to the capitalist mode of production. Traditionally, under this system, the labourer sells his labour to the owners of the means of production. However, the market conditions under which labour can be provided are not simple. Any complex industrial society must have a pool of healthy labour, preferably docile and expendable, and a system of welfare benefits can of course assist the provision of this pool by mitigating the worst excesses of poverty and exploitation. The development of a well nourished and skilled working class occurs because, 'if a healthy literate working class is needed by the system, then there is an objective overlap of interests between sections of the working class, and the capitalist class. Furthermore even the most reformist trade-union leaders subscribe to the need for these "improvements" for their members. In situations where there is an extension of state and municipal control over education, housing and welfare, the trade-union leader can play an important (although structurally marginal) role in the decisions made by these bodies in the municipal-welfare state. They can do so without needing to change the nature of society.' (Pearce, 1973a.) Welfare can be allowed to develop with the cooperation of working-class movements, because it does not challenge ideologically the fundamental nature of capitalist democracy. This is not to argue that these benefits should be rejected as reformist, nor that the benefits gained in class struggle through the thrust of trade-union power should be belittled, but the development and success of welfare schemes within a capitalist society can only be understood if it is realized that, as long as the unions and others act as pressure groups within the state context, they tend to sustain rather than undermine the established situation.

Marx and Engels argue in *The Manifesto of the Communist Party* (1848) that 'the executive of the modern state is but a committee for managing the common affairs of the whole bourgeoisie.' The state executive not only controls the political and economic situation, but also the distribution of welfare schemes. Despite the fact that welfare is the result of a long history of political battles, and that it is executed by an administration separate from the interests of business, it is still used to subsidize industry and business. Supplementary income benefits, for example, are a substitute for a basic minimum wage policy, and allow profits to be reaped in what would otherwise become marginally unprofitable industries. Thus the latter may well owe their continued existence to indirect state subsidies. That welfare is used to serve ruling-class interests is illustrated by threatened withdrawal from strikers of social security payments. Industry would thus be given assistance to force the submission of strikers by starvation if necessary. Welfare lies at the centre of the class struggle, and this can be seen in the United Kingdom by the setting up of bodies like the Fisher committee. This was created to examine the abuse of social security, at a time when social workers were more concerned that the majority of those legally entitled to social security were being deterred because of the publicity stigmatizing welfare claimants. If one considers that

in 1948, the inspectors for the Inland Revenue claimed that half a year's revenue was awaiting collection, if evasion could be detected, and arrests vigorously pursued (i.e. at that time £743 million). In 1966, 11,500 cases of tax evasion were completed. A further 9,300 cases were deferred due to the pressure of work on the officials concerned. In 1969, 9,000 cases were completed and 3,100 deferred. Out of 115,000 known tax evaders, over the decade 1959–68, 176 were prosecuted. The Inland Revenue Staffs Federation have repeatedly asked for more manpower to tackle this problem. Instead Sir Keith Joseph instigated the Fisher Report, and the numbers of supplementary benefit special investigators were greatly increased. In 1971 there were over 9,000 *known* cases of tax fraud which cost the Exchequer nearly £12 million. In 1971, 5,753 claimants were prosecuted for abusing their benefits—the sum involved was less than £300,000. Even when prosecuted, tax evaders are well treated. In one case in 1960, for example, six jewellers who in ten years defrauded the Inland Revenue of £31,000 were, on conviction, instructed to pay back the money and given the *choice* of imprisonment *or* paying back. . . .' (Pearce, 1973b.)

the Fisher committee is revealed as an instrument of class bias.

The moral attitudes of certain sections of the British right wing to the poor can be seen in Sir Keith Joseph's speech at Birmingham (19 October, 1974), when in one statement he managed to attack rising incomes (among the working class), vandalism, drunkenness, promiscuity, left-wing students and academics while defending the family (provided it contained not more or less than two parents), Mary Whitehouse, national pride and patriotism.

This was the same minister who set up the Fisher committee, and later attacked the poorer sections of the manual working class for their low intelligence and their increased birth rate.

The historical development of social work

The industrial revolution was not only intimately related to basic changes in the economic structure of society—illustrated by the rise of the business oligarchy, and the decline of the landed aristocracy—it was also associated with fundamental change to the social and political superstructure. A healthy work force was perceived as necessary for maximization of profit, and, later, one capable of being trained for skilled and semi-skilled occupations. This, in turn, led to the working–class demand for the franchise to be extended, and then for education. Gradually awareness grew of the strength of working-class solidarity through the trade unions, which led to specific demands concerning access to economic and social rewards, not only in income, but in public health, housing and education. Feared growth of military expansion abroad was connected with the development of a military force at home—which had to be healthy. The discovery of the effects of chronic malnutrition among the working population meant that the interests of the ruling and working classes were complementary, but were necessarily developed at a pace set by the bourgeoisie.

London in the nineteenth century had a direct effect on development of charity and social policy in the rest of England (see Stedman Jones, 1971). The professional classes had become increasingly aware of the dangerous elements of the working classes inhabiting the rookeries. In order to reduce the poor rate and prevent the spread of epidemics to middle-class areas, roads were cut through slum areas which left waste large sites, driving the poor into the East End. One effect of the increased overcrowding in that area was the rise in rents for poor accommodation. The collapse of the Thames shipbuilding industry, bad harvests and severe winters led to militant political action by the unemployed and the poor in the capital. Such incidents as the Hyde Park Railings affair in the 1860s, and the riot of low income groups in 1867 resulted in the fear that the police would be unable to control the unemployed and the criminal class: 'How different is the London mob from the docile agricultural peasantry, or the orderly Lancashire operatives. . . . We must not conceal from ourselves the possibility of Londoners living from time to time under the rule of military.'[3] Stable

[3] Rev. Henry Solby, 'A few thoughts on how to deal with the unemployed poor with its rough and criminal classes' (1948), quoted in Stedman Jones (1971). The similar views expressed by Kitson (1971) are worth noting.

industries had collapsed and the increase in the casual poor, sweated labour, overcrowding and bad public health conditions presented a threat to all classes. The wealthier districts had expelled the poor, and the poor districts could not deal with the influx either as ratepayers or as inhabitants. The inept administration of charity was seen to be a major exacerbant: 'If you handcuff the indiscriminate alms giver, I promise you inevitable consequences, no destitution, lessened poor rates, empty prisons, few gin shops, less crowded mad houses, under population and an England worth living in.'[4] Against this background of social values, the Charity Organization Society was established in 1869. The middle classes were to instruct the working class in the virtues of thrift and self-help, and to administer public and private charity so as to reward the deserving poor and control the undeserving. 'The proletariat may strangle us, unless we teach it the same virtues which have elevated other classes of society.'[5] Guilt was uneasily allied to fear. In 1856 20,000 unemployed had rioted in Trafalgar Square, looted the Pall Mall clubs and attacked buildings in Piccadilly. Fortunately the 1869 Great Dock Strike was seen as evidence of responsible and democratic procedures by the respectable working class, unlike the riots of the 1886 bread strikes. The unrespectable poor became separated in the popular mind, and were seen as a large class of unemployables who could be detained if necessary in labour colonies.[6]

New imagery concerning crime developed in the nineteenth century. The Lombrosan model of the moral imbecile was replaced by the notion of the corruption of urban life. There was a growth of a rehabilitative ideal, rather than brutalization by poverty either as deliberate policy or as the indifferent results of industrial capitalism. The role of the professional social worker had its roots in the poverty relief administrators. Gradually the caring middle-class amateur, usually a woman, was used to teach the values of middle-class life to the poor, especially the delinquent young. Its results were a mixture of benevolence and sentimentality: 'Point out to the children all that is beautiful in nature . . . teach them to love mother, and the home and to hope for heaven. . . . Give the little fellows good companionship, decent comfortable quarters, clean beds, wholesome food. Smile on them, speak to them, and let sunshine into their souls. . . .'[7] Children were particularly selected as possible rehabilitation successes because they were, unlike the

[4] Dr Guy, 'The curse of beggars'.
[5] Samuel Smiles, 1885, quoted by Stedman Jones (1971).
[6] Charles Booth suggested this measure, admittedly as a form of rehabilitation, but Canon Barnett resurrected it as late as 1909. See Brown (1968).
[7] 'Suggestions by the National Prison Association, 1898', quoted in Platt (1969).

adults, socializable and malleable. Social reform began to become dominant in social work, but after the first world war, especially in the United States, this became suspect. Nationalism, racism and jingoism had created a moral climate in which the interests of business enterprise were dominant, and the struggles between employers and employed made social reform suspect as an aspect of communism. Skilled workers were leaving poor districts for better neighbourhoods and the newcomers were blacks and immigrants, both perceived as dangerous groups. Reformist movements were thus seen as subversive: settlement workers in particular suffered from this reaction. The discouragement of collective action in social reform meant that individual aspects of the causes of poverty were examined, rather than its social, structural and economic basis.

The way out of this dilemma for the new professional social worker was the development of casework as an occupational skill (see discussion in Borensweig, 1971, 161). Freudian psychoanalysis had been discussed since before the 1914–18 war. It was innovative and controversial, and it focused on the individual rather than social and economic structure, as an explanation for social problems. Psychoanalysis provided a skill which was rewarding to the social worker, who felt helpless before problems which were the results of political decisions and material deprivation. It encouraged a feeling that something could be done, and gave to the newly emerging profession a distinct skill distinguishing them from the layman and the amateur. Social problems became individualized, and the profession became immersed in an ideology which devalued collective political action. The poor and the deviants had progressed from moral inferiority to pathology.[8]

The growth of social work in the twentieth century took place in the context of considerable social change. The working class made demands on their elected governments through trade-union solidarity, creating problems for the state which was also under pressure from private enterprise. The political struggle between labour and industry in the depression often centred on the reduction of welfare. In Sheffield in 1935, for example, the National Unemployed Workers Movement organized a march of 40,000 unemployed to the city hall and insisted on the restoration of benefits to the unemployed which the government had cut. The mayor and councillors hurried to London and informed the minister they could not be responsible

[8] This is not to argue that casework has no place in the relationship to the 'client', who may well have suffered psychological damage from the abuse and oppression of an indifferent or hostile society. Casework needs, however, to be practised radically to help the recipient understand his alienation, to promote his autonomy, and to assist radical change rather than adjustment.

for the consequences unless the cuts were restored. The minister capitulated, the NUWM rallied demonstrations in all principal cities, and repayment of the reductions resulted. The background of this struggle had started in 1932 in Birkenhead. There a crowd of several thousands had forced the Public Assistance committee to telegraph the government to abolish the means test. The police were instructed to retaliate by carrying out sporadic raids on tenements. An eye witness, Mrs Davis, mother of five children, whose husband had been invalided out of the army after his lungs were affected by poison gas, gave this account:

The worst night of all was Sunday. We were all in bed at Morpeth Buildings and were suddenly awakened by the sound of heavy motor vehicles. Hordes of police came rushing up the stairs of the buildings and commenced smashing the doors. The screams of women and children were terrible, we could hear the thuds of the blows from the batons and the terrific struggles in the rooms below, on the landing and on the stairs. Presently our door was forced open by the police. Twelve police rushed into the room and immediately knocked down my husband, splitting open his head and kicking him as he lay on the floor. The language of the police was terrible. The children were screaming and the police shouted 'shut up you Parish fed bastards!' My eldest daughter aged nineteen tried to protect me and her father. She too was batoned. They flung my husband down the stairs and put him into the Black Maria with other injured workers. A picture of my husband in army uniform taken in India was in a large frame hanging on the wall and before the police left they smashed this to smithereens with their batons. After taking my husband to the police station and charging him he was taken to the General Hospital where it was found that he had six open head wounds, one over the eye, and injuries to the body.[9]

The second world war intervened, but it was obvious that the state had to act to prevent militant action. Welfare benefits were used to reduce the more obvious inequalities. Militant working-class action had provided the thrust for change but its effect was dissipated by the piecemeal nature of most of the reforms. The lowest wage levels were still near or below subsistence, and in no way was a policy proposed to eradicate poverty. The state still followed the principle of minimum interference in a profit-orientated economy, and maintained the anomaly of profits extracted at the expense of a comparatively low wage structure.

The post-war Labour government set up the basic foundations of the British Welfare State. In fact only the most severe problems of poverty were attacked. The literature on poverty and the welfare state is vast (those interested should consider Titmuss, 1962; Kincaid, 1973; Holman, 1970;

[9] Quoted by Cockburn (1973).

Townsend and Smith, 1965; D. Wedderburn, 1965), but this is not the place
to discuss it in detail. Briefly, it became clear that in Great Britain in the 1950s
something like 12 per cent of the population were living close to subsistence
level, and many of them were fully employed. Fringe benefits had assisted
the wealthy to remain as relatively well off as they were earlier in the
century. Impoverished groups remained, despite the welfare state,
especially the chronic sick, the unemployed, single-parent and large families,
and low wage earners. They lived and still live, in the worst housing
conditions, pay relatively more for accommodation, and send their children
to the worst schools. It must be remembered that it is against this sort of
background that social work is practised. Administrative reforms such as
those recommended by the Seebohm Report, and since carried out, may
solve over-use of agency work by replication, but they have not introduced
new concepts nor created new types of social workers.

The education of social workers

The education of social workers has changed very little in any real sense. For
most, social work is casework. Courses are divided into degree, non-
graduate, and postgraduate. There are a few higher degrees in social work,
and these seem to be a preparation for top management levels. Human
growth and development courses are filled with evaluative assumptions
about normality, rather than with explorations of cultural diversity. The
history of social policy is considered as a series of legislations: it rarely
involves an examination of class struggle and interests. The 'caring' aspect of
its vocational orientation is stressed, but at the expense of social control
aspects which are hardly ever confronted and challenged. Recruitment into
social work is still based on vague concepts, such as 'maturity', which are
outside the scope of measurable objectivity. This means that final assessment
of students may partly derive from judgements that come entirely from the
world view of the supervisor. The social worker is seen, as Cannan (1972)
suggests, not just as having special skills but as a special sort of person above
the political struggle. The use of criteria other than academic means that the
rebellious and the radical are in danger of being counselled out.
Undergraduate courses tend to attract and to retain the more sheltered
young person, whose conventional school life has not permitted a critique of
his or her mentors. Courses are unofficially compartmentalized into the
pragmatic (such as casework, psychology or human growth and
development), the quasi-legal (such as social administration and policy), and
a sort of liberal studies group including sociology. Casework remains the

dominant vocational subject, and suffers from being presented in an uncritical, rarefied way. There is no discussion of the creation of social reality by hegemony. No examination is made, for example, of the ways in which men define the world of women, heterosexuals define the world of homosexuals, whites the world of blacks. Lip service may be paid to interactionist deviancy theory—a liberal admission that deviants may have different perspectives. There are no real explorations of class struggles and the way in which oppression reflects ruling-class ideology. Social worker and client[10] relations are never explored in power terms, nor in terms of mystification or the negotiation of reality (see Scheff, 1968; Handler, 1968; Leonard, 1965; and Horton, 1968). At the structural level, courses seldom consider those elements of poverty, deprivation and injustice that function to maintain capitalism.

Can there be a radical social work?

Our purpose in producing this volume is not to discourage radical students from taking up social work, nor to depress those workers already struggling in contradictions which have not been created by them. Radical work, we feel, is essentially understanding the position of the oppressed in the context of the social and economic structure they live in. A socialist perspective is, for us, the most human approach for social workers. Our aim is not, for example, to eliminate casework, but to eliminate casework that supports ruling-class hegemony. To counteract the effects of oppression, the social worker needs to innovate a dual process, assisting people to understand their alienation in terms of their oppression, and building up their self-esteem. Despite the optimism of the New Left, psychological damage and social problems will occur even in a post-revolutionary society.

A radical form of social work must be developed. Social workers themselves suffer from economic exploitation (though far less severely than, for example, hospital workers), and development of a radical critique may mean their involvement in a programme of political action. They must distinguish their clients' material and personal needs, although for most of the working-class material deprivation lies behind many of their problems.

[10] A polite misnomer: the social-work 'client', unlike most other clients of the professions, cannot choose his professional, cannot easily change him, has no consumer association to protect him, and no market guide to help him select, where appropriate, value for money. Presumably the term gives social work a professional respectability, and maintains the pretence that services are provided in an egalitarian manner.

However, a consideration of the personal sphere must also remain—hating one's gender role, loving the same gender, hating one's occupation, disliking one's parents, spouse or children is not personal inadequacy. The danger of hegemony is that it may result in psychological damage to those who resist it. In this way casework may assist people to resist hegemony and develop pride instead of self-hatred. A framework of cultural diversity is more illuminating than an uncritical acceptance of the ideology of 'normal'.

Social work—adjustment or change?

Social workers now have in their ranks an increasing group who are becoming critical of the contradictions of their profession. Pressure groups such as Case Con for socialist social workers, and Child Poverty Action Group have made valuable contributions. The interests that militant groups have in community work (especially in Northern Ireland) suggests considerable dissatisfaction with traditional social work. Traditional approaches have wittingly or unwittingly clearly supported authority in local or national government. For the first time clients of social workers are taking a radical stance and even challenging the very conceptual apparatus of the profession, for example the claimants' unions, the tenants' associations, single-parent family groups, the Mental Patients' Union, the Women's Liberation Movement, the Gay Liberation Front and the Campaign for Homosexual Equality.

The following chapters are not intended either by the editors or the authors as definitive answers to the problems confronting radical social workers, but they do attempt in this initial volume to pose questions, to raise issues, at least to make the practitioners of social work uncomfortable. It is not intended to demoralize those social workers who are themselves conditioned and controlled by the very institutional structures in which they work, but to make them aware of the contradictions, and to assist them to develop critical action.

The first article by Geoffrey Pearson examines the problems faced by social-work students. He examines the ideologies of social-work approaches and suggests that radical social work needs to restructure the roots of the dominant social order. Pearson attempts to rescue the student from psychodynamic reductionism concerning his motivation, and to raise the debate to a valid place in moral and political discourse. Peter Leonard suggests a radical praxis for social work—the use of conscientization, a concept developed by Friere, as a form of liberating education which creates a critical consciousness. Rather than an appeal to internal drives located in clinical pathology Friere suggests a process where people 'not as recipients, but as knowing subjects achieve a deepening awareness both of the socio-cultural reality which shapes their lives and of their capacity to transform that reality.'

The misperceptions that social workers and clients have of each other create misunderstandings which may mystify either or both sides. Stuart Rees explores these and relates them to the wider structure in which this dialogue occurs. He suggests that social workers need to clarify their identity and to assert more independence. This means a better exploration in the education of social workers, of the clients' definition of the situation. It also means commitments from senior personnel in the social services as to their intentions and actions in terms of local social policy.

Stanley Cohen analyses social workers' reactions to the theorizing of sociologists. Nothing is more irritating to the field worker (especially in residential work) than to be subject to severe criticism by academics, who then drive off in expensive motor cars to comfortable suburban homes proud of having done their radical duty. Radical academics can contribute much in terms of analysis and criticism, but often this is done patronizingly by those who have never worked in or been at the receiving end of those institutions they criticize. However, this is no reason to stop the criticism, but to confront and develop objections from field workers. While Cohen schematicizes (admittedly simply) theoretical models, he does show the importance of maintaining short-term goals in a long-term programme. What clients need from academics is assistance and encouragement to build up sufficient material resources and psychological strength to fight their own struggles. Don Milligan illustrates this point by challenging the social reality resulting from a society whose hegemony is, in the sexual sphere, dominated by heterosexual monogamy. Only by raising consciousness and developing solidarity can atomized individuals come together in a collective struggle. Milligan shows that homosexuality, far from resulting itself from emotional disorders, is oppressed because it confronts male sexism and the machismo values in our society. Ultimately the gay community must be taught to take pride in homosexuality and to befriend and assist its gay brothers and sisters. Counselling for homosexuals, argues Milligan, should only be carried out by homosexuals or bisexuals.

Crescy Cannan looks at the welfare-rights aspects of social work. Many social workers, dissatisfied with casework, tend to emphasize material problems and poverty. However, welfare rights are not in essence radical at all. They subsidize exploitation through low wages, prepare social workers for the gradual merger of social services and social security, and can institutionalize the social worker into an agent for the distribution of discretionary benefits. Finally, Marjorie Mayo looks at what Cannan has called, in *Case Con*, another carrot for radicals—community work. By analysing the ideologies behind the United States poverty programme and the community development projects in this country, Mayo reveals them as an inexpensive anodyne for urban poverty and administration inadequacies. The Batley Community Development Project which recently received the resignations of its action team, after strike action, reveals that the contradictions have already manifested themselves. The Batley team supported a local grass roots organization, which it felt was in danger from becoming controlled by the local corporation. (See Edginton, 1974, for the full story.) This raised the issue of the conflict between managerial bodies and client groups felt by community workers, and the relationship between national government projects and local government planning. As an appendix we attach the Case Con manifesto. This raises many of the important issues in developing a human strategy for socialists concerned with social-work practice and education.

This collection of essays attempts, then, to point out problems and contradictions in the profession of social work. No easy solutions or glib panaceas are offered, but we hope that social workers and social-work students will find it useful to discuss the issues raised and the ideas put forward with colleagues and teachers. Finally, we hope that the recipients of social work will themselves oppose stigma and stereotyping, and resist all authoritarian attempts by the state to undermine their dignity.

2
Making Social Workers: Bad Promises and Good Omens

Geoffrey Pearson

This article is a critique of social-work education. It bases itself on certain kinds of evidence, and I must therefore say something about what this evidence is and the 'research methods' used to obtain it. This is a critique 'from the inside': for long stretches it runs on the inside codes of social work's professional culture—those pieces of professional knowledge, professional ideology and professional commonsense which are barely perceived (and certainly not literate) in the professional world of social work.

If I describe the main method of research as 'participant observation' the reader should not allow himself or herself to become mystified, as if what happens inside social science is somehow radically different from what happens in the everyday world of social work: the tools of this research project are the human voice and the human ear. My observations are also based on a small number (65) of 'semi-structured interviews' and 'structured conversations'. In an earlier phase of this project I also used a 'sentence completion test' to get a crude measure of the reasons for career choice among social-work students (Pearson, 1973).

But all this is not too important. What is important to note is that all research methods are versions of *literary* expression: they are different ways of 'making literate' experiences which are *lived* and *felt*. In anthropological fieldwork, for example, one lives with the subject in order to gain understanding, and so the anthropologist gains a very rich experience of the texture of life—even if he may retain blind-spots such as the economy and politics of imperialism. (See, for example, Goddard, 1972.) In 'civilized' social science—as opposed to anthropological social science which is geared to 'primitives'—the social scientist does not find it necessary to live with his subject. He invites him along to an office or a clinic; or he asks him to complete a questionnaire, a personality inventory, or even to submit to measurements of his galvanic skin response. It is a peculiar arrogance on the part of the social scientist: as if civilized social science had *made literate* as much of civilized society, civilized man and civilized thought that primitive anthropology has done for primitive thought.

These reflections on what it is we do when we say we do research require a certain humility. The reader must not assume that a piece of research such as this can say everything there is to say (and know) about social-work education. The anthropologist Lévi-Strauss remarked (1973), for example, that the sum of understanding which *his* deliberate researches gave him of primitive thought often seemed to amount to no more than a brief moment of recognition, or empathy, of the kind one might rarely get staring at a cat.

Given that kind of humility, we can also state a methodological requirement: people should write more about what they know (as opposed to what they have read about). And this defines the substance of my research 'methods' which are outlined above: simply—if one dare write 'simply' in this context—to make literate, and to unearth the ideological base of, some life experiences of myself and others who are involved in social work and social-work education in the United Kingdom in the 1970s.

In anthropological fieldwork the anthropologist takes the risk of getting too close to his subjects. Going over to the ther side is considered bad form in anthropology. It is also a problem in that the researcher can forget how to speak in his native tongue (see Castaneda, 1972; 1973a; 1973b). His research reports then make little sense back home, and he is considered less than 'objective'. When all this happens the anthropologist is said to have gone native. However, the subjects of this essay, like myself, have been native since our births. During that time we have all been members of various 'tribes'. And in that sense, this 'critique of social work education'—which is a piece of 'uncivilized' social science— is a literate rendering of the transition rites of the tribe of the social-work profession.

Why on earth do they do it?: the ideology of motivation

Social-work students and social workers spend a great deal of time scrutinizing the motives of their clientele. They also spend a great effort ruminating on their own: part of the folkways of social work is for social workers to chastise each other for wasting too much time in 'navel gazing'. Judged by the appearances of professional discontent and rumbling, however, the results of this introspective effort are as thin as the social worker's understanding of what clients are about. In terms of a secure, firmly grounded conception of one's place in the world, social workers lead their clients as the blind lead the half-blind: people at the bottom of the heap (although not all social-work clients are) 'know their place' in a more direct manner than professional 'men in the middle' who are tugged this way and that.

One way in which a person finds his way in the world is by the clues and recipes thrown up by the values and codes of his member groups. Work is a focal point in these codes, and through work (and socialization into the habits, routines and attitudes of work) men learn to place themselves in the world. In this respect social work is like other kinds of work, and its codes provide recipes for understanding what it is to be a social worker. A dominant motif of the value codes of the social-work profession is to contrast the social worker's dual allegiance to 'the individual' and 'society'. In one sense these codes of ethics, rule books, articles, essays and texts which express the principles and values of social work give a guarded literacy to professional experience in the welfare state. At the same time, however, these value codes do actually *reify* society and the individual into two separate 'things' which have entirely separate existences: as if individual clients did not live in society but somehow apart from it. Friere (1972a, 28) writes of a similar problem in attitudes towards illiterate men in Latin America: 'Educators would be benevolent counsellors, scouring the outskirts of the city for the stubborn illiterates, runaways from the good life, to restore them to the forsaken bosom of happiness by giving them the gift of the word. . . . These men, illiterate or not, are, in fact, not marginal . . . to the structure, but oppressed men within it. Alienated men, they cannot overcome their dependency by "incorporation" into the very structure responsible for their dependency. There is no other road to humanization —theirs as well as everyone else's—but authentic transformation of the dehumanizing structure.'

Social work does not see it this way: it prefers to talk abstractedly about 'accountability', 'responsibility' and its ambivalent mandate from a spectral, unspecified thing called 'public opinion'. Which is not to say that there is no moral content or political content in social work. On the contrary, there is every reason to suggest that moral-political issues are the very guts of social-work practices, and I will briefly state the main ideological perspectives which can guide an appreciation of social work. I will indicate, that is, how the activities of social work, which are so often discussed in professional circles as simply technical matters belonging to a special realm of professional judgements, hold a place in moral and political discourse. For example, a *conservative* social work (which appears to have a weak constituency) sees clients as deviants who are 'against society' and therefore in need of control, disposal or recycling. Herbert Spencer (1906, 501) put this view of social welfare precisely when he wrote that 'though certain waste products of social life do not return into the circulating currents, but are carried off by underground channels, yet other waste products are carried off along those ordinary channels of circulation which bring materials for consumption.' Bearing in mind that Spencer is pursuing his body metaphor of social life, he also describes (1906, 502) a conservative conception of social welfare when he compares some of the institutions of society to a 'liver' which 'separating certain waste products from the blood, throws them into the intestine as bile.' However, conservative social work rarely expresses itself directly (and certainly not in print) and the major source of this conservative spirit comes from *outside* social work and is *against* social work as such: we find it in complaints about the soft treatment given to prisoners, national assistance 'skivers', etc.; in appeals to bring back the birch, bring back hanging, or to 'get tough with the toughs'; or in attacks on the namby-pamby attitudes of social workers and other 'do-gooders'. We also find it in the modern Tyburns of the *News of the World*, the *People* and the *Sun*.

These responses come from outside social work, largely, one suspects, because the dominant constituency in social welfare is that of liberalism. A *liberal* or a *reformist socialist* social work sees deviants as products of a sick society, or as hapless inadequates who cannot make the pace of 'modern living'. Liberal-socialist social work urges care, rehabilitation and reform. It has an explicitly compassionate stance towards deviants, although it is actually more complex than that. Taylor, Walton and Young (1975, 11) describe how in the British liberal tradition there is always 'not only . . . the Fabian translation of utilitarianism but also the legacy of methodism in the early history of the Labour movement'. Methodism, they argue, 'has often been used as an ideology to castigate and segregate off members of local communities who persist in deviant or militant activities when others have desisted.' In this way it leaves its mark on the British traditions of criminology and social work, and liberalism can thus be compatible with a punitive spirit.

Another dominant tradition in the ideological contours of social work is that of *Christianity* and *humanism*. Often intermingled with other ideologies, it rarely finds such an explicit expression as in Biestek's statement (1961, 137) that 'the caseworker hopes that he is, in some small way, an instrument of Divine Providence.' It is inevitably compassionate towards deviants, always admitting the possibility, of course, that some interpretations of 'Divine Providence' can admit retribution, expulsion and punishment. It is perhaps one of the most difficult tendencies in social-welfare ideologies to place. One might easily, for example, put too much emphasis on the importance of Christianity in the traditions of social work simply because of the Christian leanings of so many of the founding fathers (and mothers) of social welfare.

And this amounts to a misreading of the history of social work because it ignores the extent to which nineteenth-century Christianity often masked the bitter political programmes and the fear of the revolutionary mob which informed so much of the origins of the welfare state. (See Pearson, 1975, chapter 6.) When one thinks of how Christianity and humanism influence the motives of social-work recruits, it is made all the more difficult to assess because students are taught to mistrust 'do-good' motives.

Finally, there is a *radical* social work, whose ideology reaches for a position close to that expressed by Paulo Friere—a restructuring, at the roots, of the dominant social order. Radicalism, or positions approaching radicalism, have a fitful career in the history of social work. In its contemporary mode the major dilemma of radical social work (and socialist social work) is how to give a practical expression to its ideological prescriptions. The depth of its problems can be judged by the fact that radicals tend to embrace community work (as opposed to casework) as the proper solution to social problems, even though there is nothing in the community approach *per se* to exclude the ideologies of humanism, christianity, liberalism or conservatism. If conservatism finds that it has an absent constituency in social work in terms of membership, radicalism is faced with the absence of a constituency in terms of practical accomplishment.

What I have described so far are the main dimensions of the moral and political content in social work. These ideologies provide the main guidelines which dictate any understanding of what it is to do social work, or to be a social worker. In its professional codes, however, social work goes about its business as if this arena of moral-political discourse did not exist. In another paper (1974a) I have shown how social work's value code is in fact empty of any content whatsoever: the abstract, reified individual is opposed to the abstract reified workings of society, and the social worker is placed in between these two false halves. The 'principles of social work' do not show how antagonisms of need, resources and priority arise, or are to be overcome. They only describe their presence and leave the social worker to get on with it, whatever 'it' is.

We must pose a question: is it too fanciful to imagine that social-work recruits (as men and women in a world in which social welfare has a place in moral and political discourse) do not weigh up and engage in these disputes? To read the literature of social work one would imagine that social workers are essentially unlike other men, that they are men who have been reared in a moral-political vacuum, and that their decision to earn a living in social work is not in any way informed by the ideological contours of social welfare. If the recruit turns to the literate expressions of professional experience in social work—if he turns, that is, to social-work texts—in order to begin the difficult task of placing himself in the world, he is left without bearings. Career choice is reduced to a whim or a personality quirk, and politics goes the same way (Pearson, 1973; 1974a).

When social workers do consider the motives which bring people (presumably including themselves) into social work they find a familiar pattern: just as social work has traditionally emphasized the personal and familial determinants of clients' distress and social problems (to the neglect of the determinants of social structure, class, inequality and power) its version of what motivates social workers abstracts personal whims from the realm of moral and political discourse. Thus people are reckoned to be interested in madness because they are afraid (or intrigued) by the madness inside themselves; recruits are judged to want to care for the downtrodden in order to satisfy some inner (psychological) need; they are thought to be interested in working with neglected children in order to work through some emotional complex of their own childhood. These notions of what it is which brings social workers to social work are not commonly made explicit, but in a recent (and unusually clear) statement of the matter Herschel Prins (1974, 42) has identified a number of motives which he believes insert themselves in the lives of social workers. Taken together these motives are supposed to provide a psychology of altruism:

The often stated 'wish to help people' may be the surface expression of a much deeper need, namely the creative urge to bring order out of chaos and the striving for harmony and control. . . . There is the motive of (not so) idle curiosity [and] one must be aware of the possibilities of obtaining vicarious satisfaction from the (prohibited) behaviour of others. Living vicariously is, I think, always an indication of failure of personal integration. . . . There are unconscious needs to punish, to be in control, and adequate in the face of the inadequacy of others . . . our own needs to make restitution for early destructive phantasies and aggressive feelings, and our needs to be omnipotent and to act as the defenders and the champions of those for whom we have a professional responsibility. . . . Linked with the need to make restitution is what some people have described as the 'Great Mother Complex'—an all providing overflowing Kleinian breast full of the milk of over-dependent kindness. I think the dangers are self-evident, and require no further comment . . . the need to solve one's own problems . . . has much in common with the behaviour of some very anxious children who tend to see other children as being more anxious than they really are, and who take unnecessary steps to reduce this anxiety.

This peculiar mistrust of helping motives is common in social work. Mayer and Timms (1970, 14) have written of the modern social worker that she (or he) 'is by training inveterately suspicious of appearances, and so she judges that the client cannot perceive clearly and without distortion the reality of the treatment situation.' They continue that 'the client's appraisal of the services offered (especially if negative) and his reasons for feeling as he does are apt to be viewed as epi-phenomena, as derivations of his underlying problem.' Equally, Prins's descriptions of the motives of social workers carry the same message, 'Be on your guard!': motives are not to be trusted, especially when it is the motive of wanting to do something direct and relevant in the lives of the poor, the sick and the outcasts of a highly stratified society. Social-work ideology accepts the norm of a society in which it is commonly believed that 'people in general' do not care for outcasts, and turns that into a reason for querying why some might want to care: a moral inversion which is necessary if, as Prins (1974, 62) puts it, one is 'to withstand the frustrations and disappointments that abound in this work.' What Prins does not say, of course, is that often these disappointments find their origin not in the psychological realm, but in the face of social inequality and social work's impotence in the face of this inequality; that it is more a collective, professional disappointment, rather than a personal one.

Here it is necessary to be particularly clear about the character of social work. On the one hand Herschel Prins's formulation of the matter speaks directly and accurately to a reality of social work (one often denied or forgotten by radicals) which is that many social-work clients *are* emotionally troubled and suffer from an unhappiness which is not washed away simply by the provision of material or economic help. And social workers who imagine that the god of materialism can resolve all human problems will suffer frustrations and disappointments. But the core of that crucial insight from social work's collective experience needs to be extracted from its profoundly conservative counterpart which holds that all social work's problems lie in the personal sphere and in the psychological sphere: that is, in the problems of the reified 'individual' as opposed to the reified 'society' or (to give it its even more banal form) the 'environment'.

I have posed two crucial issues in social-work education and its ideology: first the separation of the 'individual' from 'society'; secondly, the transformation of the social-work recruit's aspirations for a committed life in work into a criticism and a debunking of moral and political commitment as such. These two motifs are not at all unrelated. It is the same world view which informs both. For example, just as it splits off the individual client from the society in which he (like other men) lives—driving a wedge between the personal trouble of this particular client and the public issue of the deprived mass of clients which has been called the 'paupetariat' (Morgan,

1974)—in the same way it inverts the social worker's public confession of choosing to work in a committed professional activity into a private neurosis which is pledged only to inner needs. These inversions of the public into the private are typical of social-work ideology, and they provide a lopsided picture of the relationship between individual motivations of all kinds and social structure. Peter Berger (1966) puts the relationship between individual and society rather nicely when he says that man lives in society but society also lives in man. Thus a client's individual problems are not only an expression of his individual motivation and behaviour in society, but also an expression of how society defines his life chances in a class society. Equally, the decision to become a social worker must be read both as a personal statement ('This is the kind of person I am') and as a public confession ('This is how I choose to live my life in this particular world' and 'This is the kind of world I live in'). Career choice is thus a complex statement about commitment to certain human values, the nature of the world in which the chooser believes himself to be living, the kind of work available to him, and his assessment of the value of other kinds of work.

To state the question of career choice as a fully human, fully social issue—it is how each person chooses to place himself in this society; it is how he chooses a job in which he or she will feel in a proper relationship to the world. It is curious, however, that, in talking abstractly about a person called a 'professional' who exercises certain kinds of neutral skills and professional judgements, writers on social work have remained incurious about the person who chooses this particular place in the world. Why is he not designing motor cars, marketing tooth-paste, buying and selling shares, managing a chemicals factory, being an accountant, a schoolteacher, a civil servant, an engineer, or an administrative clerk: why this particular job? 'I didn't want to market cornflakes,' one social-work student put it ruefully.

The choice of a social-work job represents an often barely articulated form of commitment to certain standards of human value, and a curiosity and a compassion towards some aspects of the man-made world. It also provides a particular kind of experience of the world. Unlike someone in a business career, a social worker does not see the world through the fetish of price-theory. He also places himself in a direct relationship to a number of popularly obscured questions of social inequality, human difficulty and human error (both social and personal). However, social-work ideology—just as it neglects the public question of the client's personal trouble—obliterates the public confession of the social worker's career choice, and thus a vital dimension of experience is lost in both social work's professional culture and its training schools. As everywhere in its culture, 'society' and 'individual', 'public' and 'private', 'political' and 'personal' are pulled apart. When the social worker chooses his job he might believe that he is standing at the confessional, but he is being heard by teachers and colleagues who are more interested in listening to private troubles. Even Christianity, judging by my researches, has become a suspicious motive in the professional-technocratic gaze of social work. It has become a 'queer' reason for wanting to work with social outcasts. The abject material forces of a dehumanized society thus petrify everything which is not committed to the profit motive into the secular, inhuman quirk of a few 'oddballs'. Social workers have thus come to interrogate their own motives much as they question those of their oddball clients: in the reified professional world all men are equal (clients and social workers alike) before the anonymous public world of 'society' which is the groove and the rut of the great and the would-be great, and which was, and is, and will be evermore.

At root social work's ideology, its representation of itself to itself, rests on this false split between this 'thing' called society and these splinters called 'individuals'. And even when it questions that outlandishly crude juxtaposition of the 'society' versus the 'individual', the principles of social work and the professional codes which are said to guide practice indicate nothing more than the fact that there may be an opposition between some people's needs and the 'real priority' (or the 'limited resources') as defined by someone else. Someone else, that is, other than the social workers and the clients. Who is this 'someone'?: why 'society' of course. Professional ideology thus peeps out on the world from within a closed box of circular argument. It sees nothing of the world of moral and political discourse into which recruits step, and it is little wonder that, after a few experiences of the 'frustrations and disappointments' which Herschel Prins describes personally (but does not name publicly), social workers might ask themselves, 'Why on earth do we do it?'

'It's not like it says in the books'

When Prins (1974) and others describe the motivations of social-work recruits we do not, of course, actually hear the voices of recruits. We hear professionals speaking 'on behalf' of recruits. We hear professional interpretations of what recruits are imagined to be saying. We hear, in short, professionals describing an aspect of their world to other professionals and initiates of that world. Elsewhere (1973, 210–13) I have discussed how it is unwise to place too much trust in professional images of pre-professional motives: the problem is that professionals are socialized into a world-view which colours and distorts their perception of job motivation. Professionals learn, among other things, the right and proper way to understand what the job is and how to view the acceptable motives for doing the job. And this view does not necessarily bear any relation to the actual motives of raw recruits. Potentially, therefore, there is a clash between the professional view of a profession's activity and lay, pre-professional views which may be carried by its recruits. During the process of socialization to professional norms and standards the way in which the rookie understands his motives, the way in which he learns to define the job, what he thinks of as proper, rational and acceptable professional behaviour—all these things can undergo a transformation so that they conform more closely to how professional culture describes the world. The way in which a recruit's view of the job changes during professional training has been carefully documented for the nursing profession by Fred Davis (1968), and other researchers (for example, Oleson and Whittaker, 1968; Becker, 1961) have documented different aspects of this process for other occupations. We can state the general principle that professionals undergo a process which the French call *'déformation professionnelle'*, that is, a deformation of the self which might reach even into the character structure. It is hardly a well-understood process, but it is how professionals learn to see the world with 'professional eyes'. Thus between social-work teachers, supervisors and professionals and social-work students there lies the possibility of the most far-reaching antagonisms as to what social work is, and as to what a social worker is.

Research on socialization to professional habits, views and routines tends, however, to suffer from a major handicap. There is a tendency for professions to be seen as monolithic and unchanging, whereas professions and jobs do undergo changes. A specific problem in social-work education, for example, is that social work's professional structure has been undergoing some pretty massive changes recently, and these introduce a new dimension into how we must look at social-work ideology and the life of the social worker. It is a commonplace and everyday complaint of social workers that teachers and those who are at the top are remote from the realities of the field. It is not just, however, that people at the top forget that there are messy troubles in day-to-day social work, cases which 'blow up', office crises, etc. We can state the nature of these problems more usefully in historical terms, as follows. In the last few years both in the United Kingdom and the United States social work has entered a new and more direct relationship with the state. The rapid expansion of social work has not just involved 'more of the same'. Rather, it has forced a movement in the dominant spheres of interest away from psychiatric social work, medical social work and probation, and into social service departments in the United Kingdom and poverty programmes in the United States. It has altered the kinds of problems which social workers face and the basic organization of social work, involving a closer relationship with the police, housing departments and social security systems. These new experiences are barely voiced in professional ideology. The bearers of the dominant ideology—the people at the top—were recruited and socialized into a profession which faced a quite different world, and those who got their professional eyes in the earlier and later periods of social work's history do not see the world in the same way. Struggles over evictions, rents, bad housing, bad education and low incomes form much more of the social worker's daily work experience in this new period than one would imagine, say, from reading casework texts which are the literary embodiment of the earlier professional experience. The ideology belonging to the earlier period is perhaps best described by Paul Halmos (1965): political solutions to personal troubles are eschewed; the solution to social problems lies in love and care. But that 'faith' has undergone a series of convulsive movements, and a steady and persistent political rhythm has entered the experience of modern social work. Halmos's 'faith of the counsellors' has entered history, although it lives on as a ghostly fetish in the dominant professional culture of social work. And that fact is recognized by people engaged in the practice of social work: 'it's not like it says in the books.'

When social-work recruits without professional spectacles are given a voice, their ambitions are not at all what professional culture says they are, and their confession reveals their choice of work as a criticism of the society in which they live with their clients. In an earlier piece of research I found a very definite pattern behind their choice of work, a pattern which could be read as a critique of the 'affluent society'. Social-work students confessed to be scared of boredom, commercialism and the rat-race. They feared the professional deformation which other jobs might impose on them, and that work in the world of business would turn them into robotic, narrow-minded and prejudiced men and women. (Pearson, 1973, 213ff.) Their career choice was, however, exceptionally ambiguous: on the one hand it constituted a criticism of the 'good life'; but on the other it promised to be only a private solution to the public ills which they hoped their work-life would resolve. They defined social work as a more human and meaningful activity than other jobs open to them, but hardly recognized that it would also be the instrument which might lock other people (their clients) more securely into the 'good life': in the world of work they were entering, a successful action on a case would be one which delivered clients into the dehumanizing rat-race from which they were in flight. As a consequence of this it became necessary to ask who they were fighting for, their clients or themselves? (Pearson, 1973, 218ff.)

The crucial thing about this research was that it provided no empirical indications whatsoever that any of these recruits were choosing social work as a career because of a simply technocratic or intellectual desire to master the skills of the profession. Nor was there much evidence of a desire for personal, financial advancement. Here were moral agents exercising moral choices in the face of the world of work. And it is these moral-political choices, which become evident when the recruit is asked to speak, that are excluded from social work's professional consciousness and culture. They provide a motivational base which gives a critical edge to some aspects of social-work practice. What I now turn to is a brief exploration of how these moral choices fare in social-work training programmes and how they come to grief in the work itself.

Professional saboteurs and middle-class bandits

The following discussion of the nature of social work as work is based on conversations with 65 social workers. This cannot claim to yield a 'representative sample' of social-work opinion. Nevertheless, 65 accounts of social-work experience do enable one to begin to state something about social work which is commonly left only to commonsense judgement: namely, what is it like as a job?

My focus in these interviews (which are better thought of as 'structured conversations') was on social workers' experiences of their education and the difficulties they encountered in their work. It quickly emerged that social workers see their work as hard work, and that there was a disparity between what was taught on training courses and what was experienced in work. Particularly, there was a gap between the official aspirations of the social-work professional code and the actuality of practice. Social workers found that the conditions of their work made it impossible for them to do what they imagined they had been educated to do. Everyone mentioned the size of their caseload, the shortage of certain vital provisions (nursery schools, decent housing, adequate welfare benefits) and the antagonism between social work and other professional or paraprofessional groups in the welfare field. In this last area, although there were often quoted exceptions, doctors and psychiatrists were thought to be preoccupied with their own financial betterment, hard-headed and careless, while social security officials and the police were described as heartless. Where the police were mentioned I made the point of asking whether the social worker had any extensive experience of mental welfare and the compulsory hospitalization of mental patients. Where this experience did exist it seemed (this is very speculative) to ameliorate feelings towards the police: policemen had been found to be well-meaning and compassionate (and also somewhat bewildered) in this tricky area of decision making. But given important reservations such as these, the 65 social workers gave an account of a world which appeared hostile to what they understood to be the aims of social work.

The main interest of this research, however, was two-fold, concerning first, the rules of social work agencies and what social workers do with those rules; and secondly, the experience of education for social work, the transmitted values of the social-work profession, and what social workers do with these in practice. An area that emerged as being of primary importance, and where rules, training, values and action intersect, was 'industrial deviance' in social work—that is, the bending and breaking of rules and regulations by social workers in order to advance their work with clients, and the turning of 'blind eyes' towards clients who only seem able to 'get by' be 'getting round' the welfare system.

The most commonly mentioned forms of rule-breaking were in relation to social security benefit regulations. These include:

1   People who have undisclosed earnings in excess of the allowed amount while in receipt of welfare benefits. Usually these earnings were thought to be small amounts obtained from jobs such as washing glasses in pubs, part-time work helping out in a shop, house-cleaning or baby-minding.

2   Women claimants who receive benefits as single women, or divorced women, but who are nevertheless cohabiting or in a close relationship with a man.

3   Clients who attempt to fiddle the social security system through false disclosures, skilful pestering, emotional bullying and other forms of deception. These were commonly described to me as well-meaning rogues who knew their way around the system, although my impression was that much of what I heard was highly dramatized, and possibly even mythical.

Another main category of official rule-breaking concerned social workers who do not strictly enforce the conditions of probation orders, parole orders and care orders—neglecting, for example, the commission of offences or ignoring residence requirements. There was also frequent mention of clients on low incomes who tamper with electricity supplies or gas supplies—for example, people who reconnect their supply unofficially when it has been disconnected for one reason or another (usually non-payment). Two further areas of rule-breaking—which are in many ways quite different from the instances already mentioned—surrounded the Mental Health Act of 1959, and regulations concerning the frequency of supervision visits where these are dictated by legislation.

I will go on to elaborate the nature of this rule-breaking and its meaning in a moment. For the purposes of summary, the frequency with which this professional deviance was mentioned may be divided into the number of social workers who had *heard* of it; those who had *knowledge* of it (from their own work or the accounts of clients and colleagues); and those who admitted *complicity*. Table 1 summarizes the evidence, and although it cannot give any firm indication of the frequency of this type of industrial deviance, it does imply a high degree of tolerance of it by social workers.

Table 1   Social work and industrial deviancy

	Social workers who had 'heard' of it	Social workers who had 'knowledge' of it	Social workers who admitted complicity
Social Security: excess earnings	62	57	48
Social Security: cohabitation	65	51	47
Social Security: 'fiddles'	65	28	21
probation orders, etc.	65	28	27
gas/electricity supplies	57	41	31
supervision visits	65	61	42
Mental Health Act	65	62	56

Industrial deviance can take a number of forms, and it will vary according to the opportunities offered by the work situation. In factory work, for example, it can take the form of jamming machinery for unofficial rest periods; deliberately wrecking production to 'get back' at employers, relieve boredom or give vent to frustrations produced by the work; breaking 'red tape' rules in order to make the job more straightforward, often with the employer's agreement; or, in some instances, the sabotage of industrial processes to back up demands for better wages or working conditions. As an example of the last type we can point to the machine-wrecking of the Luddites and others in the early industrial revolution: Eric Hobsbawm (1964, 7) has called this 'collective bargaining by riot' by men and women whose lives and customs were being destroyed by the domination of the new factory system of labour and by mechanization. Sometimes industrial deviance must be understood, then, as a primitive form of trade unionism.

In an essay on the motives and meanings behind industrial sabotage Laurie Taylor and Paul Walton (1971) suggest that there are three distinguishable types of industrial deviance—attempts to reduce frustration and tension (type 1); attempts to facilitate or ease the work process (type 2); attempts by workers to assert some control over the work process (type 3). Their evidence is drawn largely from observations of factory work, but in order to clarify the motives and meanings of professional sabotage in social work we can usefully employ their classification scheme.

Social work's industrial deviance does not fall into the first category. Boredom and frustration in social work seem to be swallowed or 'talked through' with colleagues and do not appear to result in social workers taking it out on clients. Nevertheless, some of the accounts I was given of rule-breaking by clients implied approval or even expressed unconcealed glee on the social worker's part. I heard, for example, of an elderly couple who had done a 'moonlight' from a condemned council property thus evading the payment of rent arrears, but who had then moved themselves back into the empty house without the knowledge of the housing department. A senior medical social worker had blundered into this situation by asking the housing department if there was any chance of the couple being rehoused, only to learn that officially the area in which they were living had already been cleared of tenants. This social worker's account of the matter was rich in its expression of the difficulties of knowing the right thing to do. Her confusion was multiplied when she telephoned the electricity authority who were themselves very concerned about the old couple living in a house without a power supply. On a home visit on the previous day, however, she had talked with the couple before a blazing electric fire: the old man, apparently, was something of a wizard with gadgets and had plugged himself into a main supply some distance away. But although the medical social worker's story was full of confusion about where the limits of her obligations, responsibilities and confidentialities lay, her story was also full of excitement: she had clearly enjoyed her client's deviant ingenuity. In the event her decision was to ask the couple for a full account (which was to be given the status of full confidentiality) of their different dodges so that she could avoid fouling their pitch. And this decision was tinged with a sort of thrill—something which helped balance the more mundane aspects of her working life.

Many stories I heard were told with the same enthusiasm. However, the overall picture is complex and this kind of professional deviance does not fall neatly into Taylor and Walton's 'relief of boredom' category. Stories such as this conveyed a moral: people called clients will not be tied down, and their ingenuity and inventiveness (albeit deviant) was described to me as a fully human response to material hardship. In that sense the excitement which social workers felt about these actions came from the way in which they confirmed the social-work value code that all men (even the downtrodden) have an 'innate dignity and worth' which cannot be squashed. But there is an even more important way in which the social worker's complicity in law-breaking amounted to more than a sort of deviant kick. In the case I have described, for example, the medical social worker also felt that it was not her job to enforce the regulations of the housing department and the electricity authorities. For even if they were enforced, she argued, the problem would still remain: where were this couple going to live? Similarly, social workers told me that it was not going to help their clients at all if infractions of probation orders were reported to the court: and they added that they (as social workers) were there to help, not hinder. Many people, it was suggested, could not manage effectively on social security incomes and retirement pensions. Ignoring the cohabitation of women claimants, or claimants who had jobs 'on the sly', was thus justified on the ground that it might help to prevent family breakdown, illness or malnutrition because of an impossibly low income. The refusal to pay attention to rules and regulations, therefore, is seen as a way of doing the job more effectively: a complex motivation which might both ease the work process (type 2) and redefine the purpose of the job (type 3). Taylor and Walton (1971, 232–4) argue that for large bureaucracies to function effectively sometimes workers must ignore and break bureaucratic rules. Can we then describe the actions of this medical social worker (and the others) as *good* social work? In order to answer that question, of course, it would be necessary to state unambiguously what the goals of the welfare state are. But the whole point of this type of professional deviance is that it does not just facilitate a more 'effective' accomplishment of the given goals of the job, but also involves a struggle over the control of work and the definition of what the job is.

This complex picture can be clarified if it is set against two areas of professional rule-breaking which more clearly involve the rearrangement of work and the facilitation of the job at hand (type 2). These two areas are where social workers ignore rules about the frequency of supervision visits when these are regulated by law, and the operation of the United Kingdom 1959 Mental Health Act. In the first it seems quite common for social workers to find that because of pressure from other cases they cannot comply with statutory requirements concerning visits to 'supervise' clients and families. They therefore 'fiddle their books' and case-records in order to comply 'officially' with official requirements. If we simplify matters a little, we can describe this as a rearrangement of work so that social workers can spend more time with those who need their help, to the neglect of clients who are thought not to require the same intensity of work. It is a comment, as much as anything else, on the high caseloads which social workers carry, and the ways in which bureaucratic rules can be remote from day-to-day pressures. This problem of how to act according to professional (or semi-professional) judgement, or how to present a show of professional judgement in a bureaucratic organization, is one of the most general in social-work practice (Scott, 1969a).

In the case of the Mental Health Act a rearrangement of inconvenient bureaucratic rules is once more at issue. However, professional deviance in relation to the compulsory hospitalization of mental patients much more obviously challenges the spirit, ethos and goals of the 1959 Act, so that it merges with professional sabotage. Put very simply, and perhaps a little too simply, the guiding spirit of the Act is to encourage 'informal' (that is, voluntary) admissions to psychiatric hospitals, while providing safeguards for people who are judged to be a danger to themselves or others and who can be compulsorily detained in a mental hospital for a period of treatment or observation. These are the moral-political grounds of the existing mental health legislation in England and Wales. Under normal cirumstances a patient can be removed against his will to a mental hospital on the strength of two medical certificates and the agreement of the nearest relative or the mental welfare officer (who will be a social worker). In an emergency, under section 29 of the Act, only one medical opinion is required, but the guiding spirit of the Act makes it clear that 'emergency admissions' are only to be used in difficult circumstances. The role of the mental welfare officer (the social worker) in all these instances replaces the functions of the magistracy under older legislation: it provides, that is, a lay-cum-legal-cum-social constraint on the freedom of medical judgement.

My enquiries confirm what is already a suspicion in professional circles: namely, that section 29 of the Act is abused as a short-cut to hospitalization. It was felt by the overwhelming majority of social workers that this section is frequently used in circumstances which are not an emergency, simply because it does away with the problem of arranging for two medical opinions to be given. Section 29, that is, makes the job easier.

This practice constitutes an infringement of the rights of mental patients—although I have heard it defended on humanitarian grounds because it supposedly makes the business of hospitalization less distressing for the patient's family. Another feature of compulsory hospitalization that attracted comment was the sham nature of many 'informal' admissions which were informal merely in the sense that a formal, shaming and stigmatizing compulsory hospitalization was used as a threat. I also noted disquiet about the way in which family troubles might be by-passed, housing problems 'dissolved', or old people quietly smuggled 'out of sight' on pseudo-psychiatric grounds. Social workers frequently complained that they were forced by the intractability of economic and housing difficulties into using psychiatric detention as a 'solution' to their clients' problems. And feeling powerless in the face of powerful and legitimized psychiatric opinion, social workers often went against their own judgement in arranging psychiatric detention. 56 out of the 65 owned up to abusing the strict legal definition of the 1959 Act, but only two had actually gone against medical opinion and refused to sign an application for compulsory detention, even though it is in the spirit (and letter) of the 1959 Act that social workers should oppose medical opinion if this is in the interest of the patient. It was easier in the long run to comply, it was said, and in any case often nothing else could be done without a massive change in the attitude of the welfare state. Behind so many of these complaints and worries about psychiatric justice was the feeling that modern psychiatry provided a false hope and not the real solution to many clients' difficulties. Some of the more 'radical' social workers argued that there was no such thing as mental illness. These were very few, but when this did happen (on eight occasions) I argued that there was a crucial distinction between the fact that some problems are wrongly defined as 'illness' and the fact that madness, nevertheless, exists.

Thus we may see that when social workers try to rearrange their work, in order to perform it with greater ease (type 2 deviance), their efforts involve a redefinition of what the job is (type 3)—that is, an assertion of professional judgement against bureaucratic and legal definitions of what the job is. In the case of the Mental Health Act this assertion appears to involve a restriction of the client's freedom and a dehumanization of the law. In the other areas, however, and much more commonly, the professional challenge to bureaucratic rules, which is implicit in social work's industrial deviance, emphasizes the client's freedom, providing an informal correction to official standards of bureaucratic and legal social controls. This is what social workers mean, I suppose, when they talk of their job as 'oiling the wheels' of the machinery of the welfare state. But 'oiling the wheels' also means here 'bending the rules', so that the machine runs in a new direction.

When professionals become saboteurs they do more than 'put a spanner in the works'. A 'go slow' or a 'work to rule' by professionals, or bureaucratic or semi-bureaucratic officials, has the effect of jamming up the works. But professional deviance which is not a work-to-rule can (and does) actively challenge the purpose, direction and meaning of professional work. In the case of social work, industrial deviance amounts to a small-scale restructuring of the welfare state on a day-by-day, extemporized level. It is a restructuring (and not just a destructuring) which supports the little man against the big machine, and it is informed by two levels of experience—first, the ordinary sense of concepts of equality, freedom, justice, human rights which any citizen might pick up in his daily passage in the world; secondly, the rather specialized sense of these concepts which a social-work apprentice obtains in his professional training.

It is to this relationship between the transmitted values of social work and industrial deviance that I turn in the next sections. But before doing so I must admit to a few qualms about publishing these findings, largely because they are as ambiguous as the industrial deviance they report, and because in some ways they constitute a dubious form of exposé social research. One could interpret the findings almost at whim and arrive at any number of conclusions about what kind of action they suggest. It might be thought, for example, that these findings are shocking, in showing how devious men (even respectable men) can be. Or they might be thought to show how a small group of semi-professionals are heroically engaged in a dogged, rearguard action on behalf of poor people, sick people, old people, unhappy people—a sort of guerilla welfare.

There are two ways of interpreting these findings which I wish to set to one side before going further. This study should not be read, first of all, as a piece of disinterested research by an academic who sits on the edge of the action, occasionally commenting (in print, of course) on 'how things are out there'. A reader may find my conclusions not very promising in terms of their practical implications, but that is another matter. Secondly, this evidence of industrial deviance in social work might be taken to show how badly trained social workers are nowadays, and might lead to demands for more effective bureaucratic controls on social workers in order to curb their activity. That sort of interpretation is only valid, however, if one insists that social work's industrial deviants are themselves in need of treatment or correction; that one should attend only to their behaviour, rather than to the motives, meanings and moral choices which inform that behaviour. If we are to understand the meaning of the behaviour, however, we must attempt to understand the structure of the social worker's experience of education and work, how he tries to connect up in *his* life the disconnected threads of welfare theory and welfare practice. And that, it seems to me, is the necessary human and critical response to this subject: neither idle scholarship, nor witless law and order will help us to understand this feature of disorganization in the welfare state.

I suggest that social work's professional sabotage should be understood as one of the products of its culture and ideology, that it is both an attempt to implement in action some elements of that professional ideology, and an aspect of the professional deformation of self which any passage through occupational rites can be seen to involve. And to the extent that social-work thinking is governed, and flawed, by the false division of the 'individual' and 'society', social work's sabotage can be seen as a continuation of, rather than a departure from, professional consciousness. In its current crisis of identity social work rushes to one side or the other of this false split, either to defend 'the system' or, in acts of primitive, bandit-like industrial deviance, to protect 'the individual'.

A brief comment by Wilensky and Lebeaux in their book *Industrial Society and Social Welfare* can set the scene (1965, 321–2). They focus on the problem of a member of a profession which is pledged to humanitarian values and works within a bureaucracy. They point out the potential 'clash between humanitarian values and agency and professional norms' for, while social work is motivated by humanitarianism, 'in some agencies and programmes . . . humanitarianism is not the controlling philosophy.' They go on to say: 'In such circumstances the worker will often break agency rules in order to treat the client humanely—the probation officer will knowingly permit infractions of curfew, the relief worker will advise recipients to keep beer bottles (and boy friends) out of sight. But any worker who tries to be a good humanitarian and a good agency representative at the same time is in for a torment of conscience.'

This torment of conscience is at the hub of industrial deviance in professional social work. But we need to elaborate on it a little. It is not only the torment of individual conscience. It is also the point at which we can illuminate the struggling conscience of the troubled, collapsing world-view of social work as a whole.

The feel of education: bad promises

We can state two major themes in the education of the social worker—*criticism* and *redemption*. On the one hand he is instructed in some of the critical concepts of social science. The welfare state is interrogated with a view to its improvement. Class, social inequality, power, poverty are said to exist still within this curriculum. Urbanization and industrial complexity are located as major sources of personal and social dislocation, while small-scale ventures which rescue the individual out of the swamp of complexity—the family, the neighbourhood, the village, the settlement, a 'community' which cares—are described as the solutions to social problems. The emphasis on client 'participation' accentuates the alienation of the common man. The damage done by stigmatization and 'labelling', by the careless bureaucratic machinery of bad welfare organizations, is spelled out. Psychiatric and penal institutions, the practices of the police and the court, housing policy, the social security system, and social work itself—each is questioned in turn. Everything points to the fact that there is still a job to be done by social workers. An essential requirement of any profession's self-perpetuation and self-enhancement must be a consciousness that its own existence is a burning necessity in the world. And in social work that means that human troubles receive their due emphasis. In social work's educational programme the world is not seen as a happy place.

This state of affairs causes Brian Munday, a social-work teacher, to cry out in pain. In an article entitled 'What is happening to social-work students?' (1972) he complains that the major emphasis of the social-science contribution to social-work training is troubling and disconcerting, even 'ominous'. In particular it is sociology which, he thinks, inspires student discontent. The student is exposed to 'general attacks on traditional beliefs in society', and he is overrun by 'a variety of academic material that is threatening, undermining and often downright depressing.'

However, Brian Munday is wrong on at least two counts. It is not only sociology that encourages a critical appraisal of social problems. For example, the use of case-study material in social-work teaching (and the supervisory process itself in fieldwork) encourages self-criticism and questions the effectiveness of social-work methods. The other weakness in Munday's account of social work's troubled conscience is that it is not only pessimism and criticism which can depress the spirit of the social worker, or any other man. A much more potent source of grief is failed hope. And this is the second major motif in social-work education, for on the other side of its criticism of what is lies an optimistic promise of what might be. It is a promise, however, which is vacuous in the world of practical accomplishment. The experience of social-work education from the viewpoint of the recruit is thus punctuated by a series of bad promises. Social work holds a professional vision of a promised land of social welfare before the eyes of its recruits which is shattered in the world of work. Social work, although its view of the world around it is gloomy, is not unstinting in its praise of itself. It promises a version of redemption, and these two sides of its educational programme—its critical stance towards the welfare state, and its optimistic stance towards its own role in the welfare state—are the things which justify social work to itself.

Paul Halmos has in recent years sung the praises of the welfare professions. According to his version (1970) of what history holds in store for us, the growth of the personal service professions is the germ of a positive advancement in capitalist society. It will lead to a dissemination of the caring ideology of the 'counsellors' among the powerful institutions of society, producing a 'moral reformation' of political and industrial leaders, guiding us away from the domination of price fetish and profit motive into a 'personal service society' where human priorities will become the unifying principle of social life. This is undoubtedly an optimistic picture, and Halmos goes to some lengths to justify it in social theory. In his reckoning social science has become skewed in the opposite direction, always frowning, tough-minded and austere. Halmos thus invites upon himself a crusading task which he admits fills him with 'a not inconsiderable apprehension', for 'the role which I have assumed [is] the role of one who is to correct this pessimistically self-critical method' (1970, 6).

Halmos's manner might lead us to think his predictions for social welfare somewhat exceptional. But in fact the opposite is the case: his style of argument is a mere commonplace in social-work thinking and writing. Harriett Bartlett (1970, 218) writes, for example, of how social work is moving towards 'a kind of service not yet perceived or offered in Western civilization'. Olive Stevenson (1974, 2) has written that 'those who commit themselves to social work contribute, in my view, to the *sensitization* of society.' In the 1930s Bertha Reynolds (1934, 127) described social work as the '"personnel department" of the community of the future'. Carol Meyer sets social work a similar task, although now that the community of the future may already have arrived and is not-so-hopeful she looks backwards rather than forwards: 'the primary purpose of social work practice,' she writes (1970, 3–4), 'is to individualize people in mass urban society.' More specifically, she defines the job in the following terms (1970, 106): 'the primary aim of social work practice is to enable people to command their own lives and destinies to the greatest extent possible in the light of the isolating, technological, hopelessly complex world in which we live.' Many other examples could be given of such grandiose ambitions. Meyer writes (1970, 13) that much of the trouble in social work has been produced by the fact that 'social workers in the past have somewhat pretentiously made some promises they could not keep.' If so, then Meyer's own prescriptions for social work—and those of so many others—are a continuing act of bad faith.

W. H. Auden cannot have written much about social work, but when he did (1964, 22) he judged all this kind of thing to be mere conceit. He was writing about how to write and how not to write: 'Writers can be guilty of every kind of human conceit but one, the conceit of the social worker: "We are all here on earth to help others; what on earth the others are here for, I don't know."' But although social work may take itself too seriously, its conceit also preserves certain positive values of compassion, tolerance and community in a society where these are in short measure. And more than that: sometimes social work's celebration of the value of the individual citizen could almost be read as an incitement to disregard the bureaucratic rules of the welfare state. Helen Harris Perlman, for example, defends casework against its political critics (1973, 9): 'Man runs his short life span in six or seven decades. He should not have to wait—suffering, struggling, withering, as the case may be—while the wheels of social justice grind out social change, or, even when reform is swift, until that change makes its way through the labyrinth of policy–programme–process to affect him at weary last.' It is casework, she says, which enables the social worker to cut past the tangle of legislation and her highly emotional appeal even seems to imply that casework might dissolve social inequality itself. Perlman does not say how casework is to achieve all this; social work's industrial deviants provide the missing pieces in their practical demonstration of what happens when the idea becomes real. Of course, their way is necessarily sporadic and relatively unimportant (even impotent) when set alongside the social change which would attack inequality at its roots. Perlman seems to be saying that perhaps casework is the only way to support the individual in the face of the massive structure of social inequality. And, just like social work's bandits, she equates casework with the little man (or, as she calls him, the 'diminished man') who is crushed by the power of 'the system': 'To cut out casework from social work would be tantamount to a denial of the worth of the individual man.' (1973, 9; see also 1970.) When we look at the motivating sentiments, in fact, 'straight' social work and 'deviant' social work are not all that different.

This spirit of hopefulness and betterment, although often soured by a kind of pessimism which views anything modern and urban as morally flawed, pervades the ideology into which social work's recruits are inducted. The recruit is given a prepacked work problem by his training. Professional ideology preaches the redemption of social ills: all men, even those men known as 'psychopaths' in the hard-headed world of psychiatry, can be reached by the exercise of the principle of 'acceptance'. But this professional ideology also preaches criticism: the practice and organizational development of modern social service departments appear to be a villainous candidate into which criticism can bite.

In one sense social work has been overcome by the hardening of organizational arteries: the grounds on which to exercise the hopeful practice of social work do not exist, and even appear sometimes to be receding. Social-work departments are instead experienced as a mad rush, a helter-skelter of crises and troubled lives. This sometimes leads to the argument that professional education should be more 'realistic'—that is, a 'training' for the job rather than an 'education' for the promised future. On the other side, some educationalists argue that the student should be stretched in his education, preparing him for the El Dorado where 'real' casework (or 'deep' casework or 'intensive' casework) is a practical possibility. Others tread a middle path and advance 'new' techniques—brief therapies and crisis intervention techniques—which are supposed to make 'professional' work possible in the 'real' world: many of the innovations in social-work method can be seen as attempts to resolve the problem of social work's redemptive scheme. Meanwhile the social worker is left with a headache—a personal problem which is also a political problem, namely, how to act on the ideals of social work in the less-than-ideal world.

Commenting on her general experience of work, one social worker summed up what a great many said to me in their different ways. 'It'd be all right if you could do the job properly. I get sick sometimes. . . . I just had to take time off the other week, things were so bad. It's not the work itself—I enjoy that—it's just always knowing that you're scratching the surface.' She went on to complain: 'You're always having to get on at the system, as if you didn't have enough problems—you know, with clients. It's always the same. You can see what should be done, but . . . well . . . it's not like it says in the books.'

'Doing the job properly' was something which these social workers took very seriously. And one way in which a social worker could do the job properly—do the job, that is, for which he was prepared by his education to believe that he was paid and trained to do—was through the breaking and bending of the rules of the welfare system which would not allow him to do the job properly, rules which were antagonistic to the profession's redemptive scheme. Having described to me how he did nothing to discourage women claimants who had secret men friends, another social worker said: 'After all—what's all this "acceptance" rubbish about if you don't do that?'

The politics of social work: good omens

We must try to be clear about what social work's professional deviance signifies. My argument is that it must be understood as part of the more general crisis in social-work ideology, but that is a very general statement with no specific moorings. In the first section I described the enormous range of moral and political belief systems which can be contained within the field of social welfare. One cannot easily generalize in such circumstances, nor move from the specific to the general (and back again) without a certain amount of guesswork, and without making it clear that conclusions must be regarded as provisional and possibly mistaken.

When reaching for a formula to describe the motives which inform rebelliousness in social work, I have often found it useful to describe them as a 'political soup'—mixed out of Christianity, reformist socialism, snatches of Marx, visionary utopianism, nostalgic references to simple forms of pre-urban living, 'commonsense' reasoning, and a heart which beats in the right place most of the time. To go further requires a detailed appreciation of the complex traditions of British social welfare, and how these make themselves felt in the present time. One need only think, for example, of the very specific relationships between methodism and socialism in British welfare history—themselves only a tiny particle in the greater whole—to see the complexity of possible motivating ideologies in social work. If social work's rebelliousness is a political soup, then methodism and socialism mix Chapel Bibles, utilitarian factory discipline and trade union banners. Or, take the nostalgic flourishes in social work's literature which suggest that it is big towns, factories, the city, the suburban ghetto (and the down-town ghetto which lies within it) which produce the problems which social work must combat. I describe elsewhere (1975, chapter 7) some of these pastoral conventions in social-work thinking which deplore urban-industrialism, the breakdown of community, and the pace and jumble of 'modern' living. They have a persistent continuity throughout social work's history, but whether one should (or could) do anything about the broad structure of urban life, or whether one should just bow down before it in a sort of fatalism (which would also guarantee the continuing existence of social work) is not clear.

Here I have described broadly only two of the many motivating ideologies which jostle for a place in social work's consciousness. Social work's rebelliousness is not the fault of 'mindless militants': it is because social work is itself in a political soup. I have used the phrase 'social work as a whole', but one must really question whether it *is* a whole. Social work neither understands itself, nor instructs its recruits in the light of any coherent political philosophy of community, freedom, economy and society. Compared with the lavish care spent on helping students to develop casework and relationship skills, there is minimal effort to help them to relate to the complex personal, moral and political force-fields of social welfare. Social work is in a primitive political condition and its professional rebels are consequently pre-political primitive rebels.

'Primitive rebels', as Eric Hobsbawm describes them (1971, 2), are those who wage a blind, groping campaign against social injustice. Specifically, 'they are *pre-political* people who have not yet found, or only begun to find, a specific language in which to express their aspirations about the world.' The forms of 'primitive rebellion' which Hobsbawm describes include social banditry of the Robin Hood type, secret associations (such as *mafias*) which although they oppose the public authorities are often bound up with them, and millenarial movements which promise an end to the unhappiness of the humble man, various types of anarchism, as well as the labour organizations one finds before the emergence of mature trade unionism (for example, religious labour sects, the loom-smashing Luddites, Captain Swing and his followers who destroyed threshing machines and burnt hay-ricks, or Rebecca's daughters who broke toll-gates in rural Wales) (see Hobsbawm, 1971; 1972; Hobsbawm and Rudé, 1973). Hobsbawm's characterization of these movements as 'pre-political' is not meant to deny that they are forms of social agitation which act on real political grievances. But they are primitive forms of agitation, and although their place in the history of the struggle for justice for the common people is far from marginal, these movements appear to represent a phase of transition towards more effective and articulate political strategies. Sometimes this primitive rebellion amounts to no more than a sporadic attempt to right individual wrongs, to save a smallholder's farm from a grasping landlord, or to release an unjustly imprisoned man. At other times it can amount to an alternative system of law, power and justice which opposes that of official rulers. The fact that in the English-speaking world it is Robin Hood and his merry men who provide the most widespread image for primitive rebellion might lead us to think of its primitivism as utterly archaic, rustic and medieval. But this is not the case: it is typically a phenomenon of the eighteenth, nineteenth and twentieth centuries, it finds its specific political object in the dislocation of community, and we can best think of it as a form of 'community action'.

Banditry is perhaps the most primitive form of social agitation, and I do not describe social work as such as a mere rhetorical flourish. I am trying to establish an organizing concept which can further our understanding of social work's politics and its industrial deviance. We can show that 'social banditry' is the best available source of political imagery to help us tie down the political character of contemporary social work, even to the extent that many of the *official* ways in which social work goes about righting wrongs can be best described as a form of banditry. Of course, social workers are not bandits in the commonly accepted sense, but there are nevertheless a number of crucial similarities between social work and the activities of the bandit or 'noble robber'. The first of these, obviously, is that they are both on the side of the downtrodden, and that they are prepared to offend the law in his defence. However, the life of the bandit-social worker is hard, and some are inclined to sell their services to their rulers and become not-so-noble robbers of the poor. Prison inmates describe prison reformers who make a name (and a living) out of social reform as people who 'ponce off crime'. Social workers have been described in similar terms as people who 'ponce off the poor' (Priestley, 1974). The bandit always has his rich cousin—a sort of highwayman for whom misfortune is a trade. In terms of the modern bandit wars of colonial liberation, of course, his cousin is the mercenary. Secondly, although bandits and social workers are against injustice, they have no clearly articulated political creed. On the contrary, they rely on rough utopian promises which are often quite unintelligible to outsiders. Thirdly, both are frequently associated with millenarial beliefs, for example that even the climate will change with the coming of the 'new world'—as was the belief of some Sicilian pre-political rebels—and, in the case of social workers, that chairs, tables, telephones, offices, social workers, home helps and funds will somehow fall from the sky, reduce caseloads at a stroke, and make the casework dream a reality. Fourthly, they oppose injustice not by struggling for the defeat of injustice, but by getting around the edges of it, trying to ignore it, or by making crude efforts to bring back the good old days. A fifth point of identity is that this kind of primitive politics is the response by men and women whose way of life and traditions are threatened by change which they do not understand—whether it is why Calabrian villagers are driven into American coal mines, or what it is that drives on the growth of welfare bureaucracies. They struggle against these changes in an improvised and make-shift manner. Sixthly, very often their activities are geared towards re-establishing the eroded traditions of community and charity, thus working against modernism. Finally, they suffer in common an uneasy tension between demands for piecemeal reform and revolutionary (or millenarial) enthusiasm. For as Hobsbawm describes them the revolutionary aims of the social bandit will be subordinated to the immediate relief of suffering. And it is here that we find the most direct comparison with the restlessness in contemporary social work: 'It protests not against the fact that peasants are poor and oppressed, but against the fact that they are sometimes excessively poor and oppressed. Bandit-heroes are not expected to make a world of equality. They can only right wrongs and prove that sometimes oppression can be turned upside down. . . . The bandit's practical function is at best to impose certain limits to traditional oppression in a traditional society. . . . Beyond that, he is merely a dream of how wonderful it would be if times were always good.' (1971, 24–5.)

To describe social work's rebelliousness as banditry, then, is to describe it as an inarticulate and primitive form of social agitation. Equally, it is powered by a rough and ready sense of justice, although the specific form of justice which it sponsors is fashioned by the way in which social workers are manufactured in training schools. Sometimes it may appear to anticipate legal and social change. For example, the cohabitation rules concerning women claimants have been recently debated in the House of Lords where they were described as a primitive form of injustice directed against 'fallen women', chastity being a requirement for public relief. Whether or not those regulations will be changed, it is unlikely that social work's banditry will be the instrument which brings about that change. Although social work's industrial deviance is pledged to certain moral-political ends, it keeps itself well hidden. It is done on the sly, it does not risk confrontation, and it thinks little about what constructive tactics might be used to advance its own defence of common people. Inarticulate protest thus mirrors barely audible protest by clients and claimants against their life conditions. It does not raise the client's voice to a level of political discourse where the necessity for social change might be perceived, so that the client would no longer need to live 'outside the law'. As a form of banditry social work can probably only be a *refusal* against unjust laws. As long as there is injustice there will probably always be banditry, and if social work follows the pattern of true banditry it may recede in importance as more mature political challenges to injustice emerge. We must therefore consider whether social work's rebelliousness can break out of its chrysalis.

All that can be said with confidence is that if social work's banditry is set alongside other troubles in modern social work, then it provides a further indication of how the profession is struggling in a changing world. There is a great deal of restlessness in social work at the moment, and not all of it belongs to 'radicals'. It shows itself not only as banditry, but also as confusion, cynicism and a sort of professional melancholia. These must be understood as symptoms of two deep sources of trouble in social work's consciousness: the first is its tattered theoretical framework.

I have already mentioned the fact that social work's redemptive scheme contains the two antagonistic sentiments of *hope* and *criticism*. Social work has been able to ride this antagonism only to the extent that a compelling *paradigm* of professional action could hold it together. The earliest paradigm to hold this organizing function within social work was probably the bourgeois conception of charity—a charity, that is, which does not threaten bourgeois privilege. We cannot go into the reasons for its decline here, but the gap which it left was filled by psychoanalysis, or some other version of a motivational psychology. Psychoanalysis—in the bowdlerized form which has been popular in social work—contained the same compelling qualities around which social work could organize itself professionally and conceptually. A professional paradigm which successfully compels its members can appear to make all problems soluble. Psychoanalysis, for example, appears to reconcile the utilitarian urge to return society's waste products to utility with compassion, usually Christian compassion. In terms of classical political philosophy, it reconciles the Greek notion of freedom —which is based communally on the *polis*—with the Christian notion of freedom which is based on the individual and his salvation. But now social work has suffered another paradigm collapse. For many reasons—usually the wrong ones—psychoanalysis has been pelted with criticism and has suffered badly. And there is nothing at the moment to replace it. Most, if not all, 'radical' criticisms of psychodynamic casework have done little more than increase fervour for redemption—although this time it is phrased in quasi-political terms. 'Systems theory', which has been thrown up by the crisis, tries to bandage the wounds of social conflict by showing that conflict is not 'real': that it is only *this* 'subsystem' against *that* 'subsystem', the two comprising an allegedly unified, integrated and systematic whole (see Pearson, 1974b). All that is left is the chatter of encounter groups. No compelling paradigm has emerged which can organize the sentiments of professional social work: this is the first element in social work's unhappy consciousness.

The second feature of social work's current crisis concerns the developing organization of the welfare state. In Great Britain the Seebohm report was seen as the glorious culmination of social progress which would provide the organizational grounds for the practice of 'generic' social work. It was associated, of course, with the unification of social work's scattered professional bodies: here again was another thread in the movement towards social work's promised land, and it has proved to be another bad promise. Whether it is seen as a deterioration of professional standards, or as the progressive bureaucratization of the welfare state, the observable results are the same. As Ron Baker (1974) has put it: 'Those of us who fought for years to establish, maintain, and enhance sound casework practice see a marked deterioration in the service clients receive and are appalled by what can be peddled out in the name of casework nowadays.' Baker wishes to defend casework against its critics. 'Radicals', on the other hand, take the circumstances which Baker describes as a further reason to bash casework, for casework is judged to be a con.

But here what passes for radicalism is misguided. It is not radical criticism which is destroying casework, but a day-to-day onslaught in social service departments that appear to be governed by nothing more than managerial efficiency and the puzzle of the inequitable distribution of short resources. If radicalism, in short, continues to bash casework, then it does no more than join forces with the dehumanizing spirit within the welfare state which presses for organizational efficiency at the expense of the individual. However, there are good omens in these developments: principally that what radicals criticize in organized social work, and what those committed to traditional methods criticize in organized social work, might be converging. Social work's industrial deviance is not committed solely by the radicals. The vast majority of the social workers I have talked with could not be described as 'radicals' in any useful sense. They were critical of social-work organizations and of the impoverished welfare state, but their criticisms were only very rarely couched in any recognizable tradition of radical politics—other than that of primitive banditry.

If these omens are not false, then we can anticipate a reduction in the futile squabbles between radicals and liberals, and a growth of collective awareness within social work. I suggest that there is much more shared ground than the two sides may realize between 'radical' emphases in social work and those provided by liberalism and Christianity. But these convergences will not come about automatically. The links must be found and nurtured in order to further social work's programme of social justice. These will not be the links that soothe and suggest there is really no problem in social work, but those which can tease out and blow apart the false humanisms of social welfare. It will require a defence of what is right in social work—rather than a blanket condemnation of all social work as a con—together with an unswerving criticism of what is wrong. Above all, it will require that in social-work education there is a commitment to the political education of the recruits of a profession which in political terms may be sometimes a rebel but is also something of a dunce.

Conclusion: a warning, a rumour and a jester's joke

This essay begins with a critique of social-work ideology which rescues the recruit's choice of work out of the clutches of a psychodynamic interpretation of his motives, and places his motive to help (and the helping process itself) in the world of moral and political discourse. But this should not tempt the reader to imagine that there is no such thing as a psychology of motivation, or that there are no relationship skills involved in social-work practice. Immature radical and political movements in social work have often suggested as much. In their revolt they have made a fetish out of reversing the mainstream assumptions of social-work ideology. If the latter emphasized work with individuals the former directed themselves to community work. If social work stressed the skill of relating to a client, then radicalism insisted that there was no more skill to it than knowing 'how to get on with people'. If social work said that clients were emotionally broken, radicalism countered by diagnosing material deprivation. And so on.

However, to reverse an assumption is not to overcome it. It may be true that casework skills have fallen into a blind allegiance to something called 'normality' and 'conformity' without enquiring what it is that the normal man is conforming to; but it does not follow that there are no relationship skills in social work. A social worker may become irritated by the fact that when he is doing work with individuals and families, the broader problems of community, class, material hardship and social inequality constantly intrude. But if he abandons casework for work with communities, he will find there that the irritating factor is the individual and that he is faced with the problems of how to manage relationship difficulties effectively and of what to do about troublesome members of the community. Social workers urgently need an education in how to place themselves in the world of politics. But they still require an education in how to relate to clients whose lives have come unstuck. When social work does not do that, and only mouths slogans about 'clients in general', it is no longer doing social work.

The question of how to connect a general awareness of social injustice with a specific instance of practice constantly reappeared in my conversations with social workers. It becomes crucially significant at a point in the development of capitalism where another economic recession seems very likely. Under such conditions the advancing coalition between social work and the state might bear its full fruit, and under such conditions the practice of the social worker could easily atrophy into that of a high-status social security official. So-called radicalisms which reduce social-work practice to an abstract formula of welfare rights and material provisions, and which forget the human dimension of the problem, are no defence against such encroachments. Radical bandwagons such as 'welfare rights' might even be a premonition of things to come in social work: helping clients to get their rights when they have no rights.

The future of social work is clearly at issue. But the future of social work has a personal as well as a collective dimension. Many social workers talked to me of the problem of personal survival in the hurly-burly of social-work departments. One survival strategy was to aim for promotion to senior positions and management posts, to lift clear of the 'firing line'. Another possibility was simply to get out of social work because the job was too demanding, too stressful and too hopeless. There is even a rumour circulating that social workers are already deserting the job at an alarming rate. I was told that social workers were only staying in the job for an average of two years. I do not know where the figure comes from, but I was told the same story on more than twenty occasions in different parts of the country and I have also heard it from students on a number of training courses. I suspect that it is just a rumour, but the fact that there *is* a rumour indicates and enhances an inner hopelessness in the world of social work. If there is an inner hopelessness then it must find its origins in social work's world and in its education.

One story I picked up is particularly illuminating. It described a social-work teacher who was faced with a group of students who were troubled by their experiences of social-service departments and wanting to know how to change them. The teacher's reply is quite intriguing in its refusal to take the question seriously: 'Well, you can vote every five years, I suppose.' This story was given to me as the truth, I accepted it as gossip, and I pass it on as a jester's joke. The function of a jester's joke is to make the ruling sovereign laugh at his own pomposity. It tickles him, and it causes him to reflect on the precarious nature of his power. It exaggerates the truth in order to make the truth plain. For the truth is that social work is elastic enough to contain students who would ask that question, and a teacher who might give that reply (or say nothing at all). But a jester's joke is also intended to indicate the truth either directly or ironically, and in this way it can puncture a lie in social work's self-awareness. According to this particular lie, social-work apprentices are all radical activists, whereas their master tradesmen are all downright conservatives and psychoanalytical bullies. In this essay I have documented something of the malaise among social-work practitioners, and said something about the hope among social-work recruits, but I have said nothing about confusion among social-work educators. It would be wrong to assume that it does not exist. The government training councils can change their names as often as they like, gather reports to gather dust, raise the dust (and then complain that they cannot see), and turn somersaults in the air: but the test of social-work education is going to be whether it can own up to its own confusion and make a critical contribution to the defence of the weak. Meanwhile, we can only wonder whether it is making, or breaking, social workers.

3
Towards a Paradigm for Radical Practice

Peter Leonard

Introduction

The history of social-work education and practice is, in part, a history of massive ideological distortion. Examination of the philosophy and theory of social work reveals a degree of commitment to bourgeois values and capitalist models of social welfare of which most social workers have themselves been unaware. Conceptualizations about social work are primarily social products and reflect the particular socio-economic base upon which social-welfare institutions have grown. At the same time, the oppressive functions of these institutions are best served by concealing their ideological foundations and political purposes not only from the recipients of social welfare, but from the practitioners of social work itself. Thus the proclamation of humanist social-work values, including the commitment to client self-determination and individual dignity, is on the one hand largely fraudulent in that it prescribes goals within traditional approaches to social work which are impossible in a capitalist system, and on the other hand mystifying and confusing in that it attracts the allegiance of social workers who have a deeply-felt commitment to these values (Pearson, 1973). It is not necessary to see this process of ideological distortion and mystification in terms of conspiracy—rather it should be seen as the outcome of a deep contradiction within social-work systems under capitalism which enhance human welfare and negate it within the same process.

It is because of the power of the dominant ideological formulations in social work and the implications in their practice, that it is important to develop alternative radical perspectives on practice. It is not sufficient to undertake critiques of existing social-work activity, important as these are; if there is a radical function for social workers, then the systematic formulation of the objectives and methods of radical practice is crucial. Such a formulation must distinguish clearly between the *description* of the present activities of social workers and the exploratory *prescription* of what activities might be undertaken by social workers within a radical paradigm. The lack of a distinction between description and prescription has been an important source of confusion in the traditional formulations of social work.

Many radical social workers, especially those engaged in community action, have little taste for theory and are deeply suspicious of the mystifying and divisive effects of theorizing. As an activity theorizing can become debased into mere verbalism in which radical rhetoric accompanies oppressive practice. However, if dominant and influential theory in social work is to be combated and radical activity to become more than mere unreflective activism, then developments in theory and practice must go side by side in accordance with Lenin's proposition: 'Without a revolutionary theory there can be no revolutionary movement.'[1] The goal must be the emergence of a radical *praxis*, where theory and practice are unified through the binding together of reflection on the world and action to transform it. Only by struggling to overcome the dichotomy between theory and practice can we hope to develop radical social work (Gouldner, 1974).

This paper will attempt to sketch some of the features of a paradigm for radical social work based upon three elements—a radical social-systems theory; a unified approach to work with individuals, families, groups, communities, residential institutions and organizations; and an approach to the development of critical consciousness.

Social-systems theory

The development of systems theory generally in the West in recent years (see Bertalanffy, 1971) and the work of Talcott Parsons (1951) and his successors in sociology in particular are having a substantial effect on thinking about social work, especially in the United States. Such systems approaches and the conceptions of social work which spring from them are generally founded on conservative consensus-orientated ideologies. Much emphasis is placed on the interdependence of variables in social systems, and in the analysis of social institutions it is either asserted that the variables are indeterminate, that no one factor is of greater importance than others, or that the value elements are marginally the most significant. In either case, the intention is to avoid too much stress on economic variables and, in line with the reliance on value-consensus as the rationale for the particular features of a system, to emphasize the importance of normative elements in social structure rather than material ones. Gouldner (1971) has provided a penetrating analysis of Parsons as a systems analyst which shows the way in which his theoretical development was both a specific reaction against Marxism and a general defence of North American capitalism.

[1] V. I. Lenin: *What is to be done?* Oxford: Clarendon Press, 1963.

It is because systems theory has been recently so tied to the defence and maintenance of existing systems that radical social workers have given little attention to its possible uses. It would be more profitable, however, to rescue systems theory from the grasp of the apologists of existing institutions and to use it for the purposes of understanding and changing these institutions. There is no doubt that radical social work needs an overall framework within which to grapple with an enormous range of individual, group and wider environmental variables, and a revised form of systems theory could provide this. To begin with, it is important to stress that viewing social structures in terms of systems is not necessarily a means of justifying them. Gouldner, for example, argues that '. . . it is unmistakably clear that Marx *did* think of societies as social systems whose elements mutually influence one another. Marx did, after all, invent the concept of the "capitalist *system*".' (1971, 230.)

A generally Marxist approach to systems which is the background to this paper, acknowledges the mutual interconnectedness of social systems, asserting the dialectical relationship between a range of variables, including the fact that the 'superstructure' of political and social institutions and the ideologies which justify them interact with the 'infrastructure' of economic production. This interaction, although a mutually influencing one, is weighted in favour of the economic infrastructure. Thus in any social-systems analysis based on a Marxist perspective we would expect to find that economic variables have a preponderant influence on the system. Whereas the more traditional systems model begs the question as to which are the *determining* variables because they are all seen as mutually interactive, a radical systems model attempts a precise identification of cause and effect and thus provides a better guide to the action which the social worker must take.

The present approach to systems identifies the differential distribution of power and interests within social systems of various kinds—families, communities, organizations, societies—and the consequences of this type of differentiation for the whole system and for its parts. Thus instead of the assumption that consensus normally governs the life of social institutions, it will be assumed that the differentiation of power and interests within most social systems leads to various kinds of conflict. This in turn implies that systems are often in a state of continuous strain caused by the striving for 'functional autonomy' of elements within the system and the controlling, coercive and legitimating efforts of the more powerful 'managerial' elements (Gouldner, 1971, 231).

Fragmented approaches to social work

Social work in Britain has grown primarily as one element in social-welfare and educational institutions that were developed in substantial measure to ameliorate the harshest consequences of capitalist production and to ensure the delivery to the market of an effective and disciplined labour force. The role of social work in this has been to identify, respond to and control the individual casualties of the economic structure and of the material, physical and emotional pressures which living in a competitive society produces. But if we are to avoid an over-simple view of the growth of social work, we must take account of other, contrary, even conflicting, purposes which revealed themselves. Even the theoretical reliance of social work on a psychoanalytic model has carried with it a certain ambiguity, for the model itself has potential as both an oppressive and a liberating perspective on individual development (Laing, 1967). Concern with individual needs and problems, however arbitrarily and sometimes oppressively defined, carried with it, in many instances of social-work practice, a commitment to increasing the individual's ability to overcome the damaging effects of intra-psychic family and other social determinants. To see social workers, in short, *simply* as the willing henchmen of the ruling class in its exercise of social control is to take an undialectic view. It overestimates the rationality and monolithic nature of the capitalist state in its ability to determine in detail the activities of an occupation: elements of social work have always demonstrated a degree of ambivalence to the bourgeois values to which it is especially exposed by its class position. This ambivalence is one source from which a radical practice can develop.

The contradictions and ambiguities of traditional social work not withstanding, the overall result of capitalist ideological influences has been to produce a perspective on practice which is highly individualistic. This perspective, based on a model of individual and family pathology, still dominates social-work practice and education, in spite of the growth alongside casework of group, community and, more recently, residential work, which has not substantially altered the pathology model of practice. Community work, for example, is still usually seen as a means of tackling the problems which exist within a community, *its* pathology, and gives a less systematic account of the 'pathology' of the wider economic and political structures. Even so, the newer developments have proved difficult to incorporate into the classical paradigm of social casework. Given the early reliance on psychoanalytic models of treatment with their emphasis on technique, we can understand how conceptualizations of social work have grown around the idea of separate methods—casework, group work and community work. Distinctive methods were what bound a group of activities together, and ultimately more attention was given to methods than to purposes. The striving for professional status in social work reinforced this trend, for what was seen as professionally acceptable practice centred more on the appropriate means than on the ends.

The outcome of the attempt to develop discrete methods in social work has been to fragment further social-work perceptions of the links between the individual, the collectivity and the wider social context. In practice the separation of methods has been difficult to maintain and social workers have found themselves responding more flexibly to situations than the methods-fetishism of traditional theory allows. The boundaries between work with individuals, families, groups and community organizations have been impossible to demarcate, especially since the development of newer social-work strategies concerned with advocacy, welfare rights and the promotion of consumer groups. In social-work education, the dominance of the methods-typology has meant that the primary focus of courses has remained firmly on social casework, with teaching and practice in group, community and residential work, added to an already overweighted curriculum.

The failure to reconceptualize social work from the ground up and the continual addition of further elements of practice to a fundamentally casework base, have had a peculiarly similar effect on both the traditionalists in social work and on some of their radical critics. Among both groups a simplistic notion has developed that social work with individuals and families must operate within a framework of acceptance of the status quo, while community work is essentially equated with radical action for social change. Many radical critics, while acknowledging that community-work activities can be as oppressive as any form of individual work, fall into the trap of assuming there can be no radical individual practice outside the provision of information about welfare rights, and that radical action must be centred on collectivities of various kinds. To accept such an assumption is to accept the dominant definitions of social work with individuals and families which centre on the goals of adjustment and resocialization, rather than confronting such definitions and struggling to change them.

Social-welfare organizations encounter individuals and families who are suffering severely from the effects of an oppressive social system. These effects are experienced at a personal level; they involve people's feelings about themselves and others. Many people are badly damaged individually by their experiences, often both physically and emotionally, as, for example, some of those who are physically ill and handicapped. Although the oppressive and dehumanizing elements in the capitalist system affect every facet of our lives, some experiences of pain and suffering are inseparable from human life, including those associated with loss, bereavement, ageing and death. A radical perspective which ignores or argues away the psychological effects of experience and the need at times to respond to these effects individually, as well as through group, community or organizational action, is in danger of failing to consider others as whole persons, of perpetuating in another form, a fragmented, dehumanized view of men and women. Radical social work must therefore encompass direct work with individuals and families as well as with the wider groups and collectivities to which they belong, and must seek to relate organizational and individual action.

Integrated approach to social work

Those who wish to develop radical social work must formulate a model of practice which both includes a wide range of social-work activity and avoids the fragmentation that the traditional adherence to distinctive methods— casework, group work and community work—was bound to encourage.

Just as we can use a revised systems approach to map out the variables within which social workers operate, so we can also build an integrated model of radical social work on the basis of a critical evaluation and reformulation of some of the current work being undertaken by non-radical social-work writers. In particular, the recent efforts of Pincus and Minahan (1973) and Goldstein (1973) to develop integrated approaches may be seen as paving the way for more holistic conceptions of social work, and are likely to be extensively used in social-work education in the future. As long as radical social workers are critically aware of the dangers involved in using, albeit in changed form, the work of non-radical writers, there is no reason why they should not do so.

We shall begin with an overall critique of this current work and then move on to sketch some elements of a radical paradigm for social work based on this critique and on the work of Paulo Friere.

Although the approaches of Pincus and Minahan and of Goldstein differ from each other in a number of respects, including their degrees of theoretical sophistication and empirical relevance, they both rest upon a systems model that is governed by unacknowledged assumptions about the nature of society. Thus Goldstein reveals his reified and consensus-orientated view of 'society' when he asserts that 'the final measure of a profession's identity lies in the explicit character of what it does in fulfilment of a societal need.' (1973, 3.) Likewise, Pincus and Minahan demonstrate a combination of sociological naïvety and conservative ideology when they argue that 'some societal systems have been granted the authority to serve as agents of social control for people whose behaviour deviates from societal laws and norms and to protect people who may be harmed by the behaviour of others.' (1973, 32.) None of these writers seriously questions the use of the term 'societal' in this monolithic way: their lack of a class analysis of society reveals itself throughout their work and accounts for the poverty of their explanations at the macro-sociological level.

However, in spite of these writers' rather limited views of social systems generally, we can use their more detailed work on social-work functions and processes in the context of the radical systems model outlined earlier in this paper. The usefulness of the approach of Pincus and Minahan lies in its emphasis on the focus of social-work practice as 'the interactions between people and their social environment' (1973, 9). This enables them to identify a number of 'resource systems' with which people interact in order to cope with the environment. These are *informal* resource systems, including family, friends and neighbours, *formal* resource systems, including membership organizations, associations and trade unions, and *societal* resource systems, including schools, hospitals and social-welfare organizations. Although the stratification and power distribution within and between these systems and their often controlling and oppressive role is largely unrecognized, attention is given to problems of interaction with resource systems, including schools, hospitals and social-welfare. Social-work activity is designed to enable people to use their own capacity for effecting change, to establish linkages between people and resource systems, to enable change to take place in the systems themselves, and to enable people to carry out roles within the system. While the socialization and 'pattern-maintenance' functions of some of these activities is clear, they also include the potential for more radical activity designed to confront or resist resource systems.

Within the limitations imposed by its overall ideological perspective, the Pincus and Minahan approach achieves some success in shifting the focus of attention from individual or group pathology to that of interaction. Thus 'problems', they assert, are not attributes of people, but of social situations: therefore a problem involves a social situation, the people who are evaluating the situation as problematic, and the reasons for their evaluation. Again, in identifying the four basic systems with which social workers interact—change agent, client system, target system and action system—they widen the potential focus for social-work activity. The target system—that is, the people or structures which have to be influenced or changed in order to achieve specific social work goals—may be the clients of welfare services, or other groups, or may be the social worker's employing organization (the change agent) or other organizations. The action system comprises the social worker and the people he works with in order to effect change, including the client system or other individuals or groups of people. Much of this conceptualization of practice, inadequately sketched here, involves a somewhat simplistic view of the nature of social control and of the power of the social worker, especially in its discussion of the need to establish 'contracts' between social workers and clients. However, once again the positives of this approach are also evident—the emphasis on the organizational context of social work as a potential target for change, and on the cooperative effort which is needed in the action system if change is to take place. Finally, discussion of the concept of *relationship*, that dreaded idol of traditional social work, involves consideration of a wide range of interactions with a wide range of systems, including collaboration, bargaining and conflict.

Goldstein's approach, similarly based on a systems analysis, is interesting in that it emphasizes the provision of a context for *social learning* as the major objective of social work. In Goldstein's work, social learning is seen primarily as socialization and adaptation, but it could equally be seen as learning about the oppressive nature of the social structures which define and produce 'problems', and about the strategies needed to combat them individually and collectively. Understanding as a basis for action and change must be at the root of radical social work, with change emerging from changes in both clients' and social workers' consciousness. Within a radical perspective, Goldstein's view of the enabling function of social work, with its emphasis on learning in relation to change, has much to recommend it. He writes that 'although interim purposes may be directed towards emotional, attitudinal and perceptual factors, social work is essentially concerned with how persons actively deal with their relationships and environment within their social existence . . . social work provides a way . . . that persons may use to find a solution to or alternatives for a disruptive condition . . . social work does not solve problems or change conditions [it] is a means, not an end in itself.' (1973, 6.)

Conscientization in social work

Before we try to make use of an integrated approach to social work for the purposes of radical practice, we will turn briefly to the work of Paulo Friere (1972a; 1972b) in the field of education and its possible applications to social work. Friere has been concerned to develop a form of education for the masses in Latin America which is essentially liberating. It is an educational process which is designed to develop *praxis*, critical reflection on reality and subsequent action upon it. The development of critical consciousness is essential to his educational scheme, for this is what will enable the masses to transform reality. This liberating education, *conscientization*, confronts existing traditional education which is based upon what Friere calls a *banking model*, a model that reflects an oppressive social structure: 'In the banking concept of education, knowledge is a gift bestowed by those who consider themselves knowledgeable upon those whom they consider to know nothing. Projecting an absolute ignorance into others, a characteristic of the ideology of oppression, negates education and knowledge as processes of inquiry.' (1972b, 46.) The development of critical consciousness cannot take place where the oppressed are treated as merely empty vessels to be filled with a 'liberating' ideology: critical consciousness develops from an acknowledgement of the existing consciousness of the oppressed, however fatalistic it may be, and from mutual dialogue between all those concerned with the task of liberation.

In Latin America the concept of conscientization is having a profound effect on social-work practice and education (Alfero, 1972). A reconceptualization of social work is taking place. At the ideological and philosophical level conceptions of the relationship of man to the world have been changed to allow social workers to be fully involved in Latin American liberation movements. Such a change in social-work objectives can be illustrated by an extract from a 1971 report of a seminar of Latin American Schools of Social Work in Ecuador:

Social work will be able to contribute to the transformation of the present situation only so long as it commits itself to man and society in the social change process.

Social work implies talking in terms of a reflexive, horizontal, dynamic, communication which will dialectically feed back into action.

In spite of the fact that reality conditions man, we conclude that he is capable of influencing and transforming his reality. Even under conditions of oppression, man is capable of seeking his own liberation.

Social work should place itelf within an ideology of liberation. This should get its start from the deepest causes that have subjected men to oppression and underdevelopment.

The social worker will contribute to form this free man, preferably through an educational function which will be enabling and conscientizing. (Alfero, 1972, 80.)

From overall objectives such as these, social workers in Latin America are trying to develop techniques to operationalize conscientization in the specific circumstances that confront social work in these countries. In general social-work techniques within the conscientization approach must encourage the development of awareness in the human being, both the people with whom social workers are involved and social workers themselves. 'Once conscientization becomes incorporated into social work,' Alfero writes, 'we must keep in mind that we, as professionals, cannot conscientize others if we have not reached a specific degree of conscientization ourselves.' (1972, 81.) The operationalizing of conscientization for radical social work in Western capitalist countries is a major task for the future.

Elements in a paradigm for radical practice

Having identified some possible conceptual bases for radical social-work practice—systems analysis, integrated methods approaches and conscientization—we can now proceed, finally, to identify some of the elements of a framework within which radical practice can be located. At this stage, such a framework can be no more than a partial agenda to be developed by social workers in education and practice: it needs, particularly, a mass of recorded practice in order eventually to provide a substantial basis of knowledge and skills to which social workers can turn in order to develop radical practice. The framework takes the form of a number of propositions, some descriptive, and some prescriptive, concerning the context, aims and methods of radical practice in social work.

The context of radical practice

1 *Contradiction* In capitalist society, social work operates as part of a social-welfare system which is located at the centre of the contradictions arising from the dehumanizing consequences of capitalist economic production. Social workers, although situated in a largely oppressive organizational and professional context, have the potential for recognizing these contradictions and, through working at the point of interaction between people and their social environment, of helping to increase the control by people over economic and political structures.

2 *Dialectic of people and systems* The relationship between people and the various systems which comprise their social environment is a dialectical one. 'It is as transforming and creative beings that men, in their permanent

relations with reality, produce not only material goods—tangible objects—but also social institutions, ideas and concepts. Through their continuing praxis, men simultaneously create history and become historical-social beings.' (Friere, 1972b, 73.) Although it is true to say that men both create and are created by their social world, the context of social work provides an opportunity for enhancing the creative, determining, potential of people.

3 *Systems: oppressive and supportive*   The social environment with which people interact and which is the focus of social-work intervention, can be seen as consisting of a number of systems which are the source of both oppression and support. In capitalist society these systems—the family, the neighbourhood, the trade union, the school, the factory, the hospital, the social-welfare agency and others—all carry to greater or lesser degree the marks of economic exploitation and the cultural hegemony of the ruling class. The oppression of women in the family, the fatalism of people in a neighbourhood when faced with planned cultural elimination, the socialization of children in school to the demands cf the labour market, the alienation of factory workers, the elitism and exclusiveness of trade unions, and the bureaucratic, controlling and dehumanizing features of hospitals and social-welfare organizations, are all examples of this oppression. At the same time, these very systems can also be the source of support for people in order to maintain their identity, secure material resources, and at times resist the consequences of oppression. Social work has the potential of enhancing the supportive features of some of these systems in the interests of people.

4 *Individual consciousness*   The understanding of the interaction between people and systems in the social environment must include a recognition of the individual's own consciousness, of what social situations mean to him, and of his pain and suffering, hope and despair. In social work an understanding of the effects of past and current experiences on the consciousness, intentions and behaviour of individuals is crucial. Appreciation of these effects on the social worker himself, as well as on other people, is of vital importance to the development of radical practice. 'Discovering himself to be an oppressor may cause considerable anguish, but it does necessarily lead to solidarity with the oppressed. Rationalizing his guilt through paternalistic treatment of the oppressed, all the while holding them fast in a position of dependence, will not do. Solidarity requires that one enter into the situation of those with whom one is identifying; it is a radical posture.' (Friere, 1972b, 26.)

The aims of radical practice

1 *Education* While in general terms the aim of radical social work in capitalist society is both to mitigate individual suffering caused substantially by the consequences of economic production and to engage with others in the struggle to resist and overcome an oppressive social system, the *key task* of radical practice is an educational one. This role aims at contributing to the development in people—especially those suffering most profoundly, such as the clients of social-welfare systems—of a critical consciousness of their oppression, and of their potential, with others, of combating this oppression. In Chile before the military coup, a school of social work saw one of the objectives of social work as being: 'To raise the level of consciousness of the deprived classes and to promote in man a critical and reflexive consciousness so that in fulfilling his ontological vocation, man can overcome the contradictions operating in our society and assume an effective role in the structural transformations that it is imperative to achieve.' (Alfero, 1972, 79.) Of course, such an objective was formulated when a socialist government, committed to structural transformation, existed in Chile; the strategy involved in pursuing such an objective needs to be developed specifically for each concrete situation.

2 *Linking people with systems* In focusing on the interaction between people and various systems in their environment, radical practice aims to facilitate the linkage between individuals and those systems which might serve their interests. In some situations this involves joining with consumer or community action groups, and in others support and advocacy for individuals attempting to secure their welfare rights from official organizations. Such linkages cannot, however, be simply a matter of 'fixing' things. The radical social worker often strives to accompany these connecting operations with action directed towards the social relations involved in interaction. This activity aims at developing among those involved, including himself, an increased awareness of the unstated assumptions behind these social relations—dependence or interdependence, hierarchy or equality, indoctrination or dialogue. In the often limiting context of residential institutions it is especially important that this reflection takes place. In his work in linking people with their own families, for example, in situations where conflict, pain and despair have characterized their human relationships, the radical social worker aims to encourage each member to reflect on the distribution of power in the family system, who gains and who loses from this distribution and the extent to which the

family's internal structure reflects the imperatives of the external economic structure.

3 *Building counter-systems* Facilitating linkages between people and various informal and formal systems, even if accompanied by conscious reflection on the relationships involved, is frequently not enough. One aim of radical practice will be to help in the building of counter-systems either within or outside the existing systems. Such system-building aims to develop a power-base from which some changes in existing systems can be achieved, or from which in the short or long term such systems can be radically transformed or abolished. Within the family, for example, a counter-system may be established consisting of the social worker and an adolescent son or daughter where the aim is to shift the balance of power in the family or to provide a supportive system while the adolescent separates from the family. In residential institutions, it may be necessary to build counter-systems in order to ameliorate the effects of and ultimately to change an authoritarian regime. At organizational and community levels, the building of counter-systems may involve trade-union or pressure-group activity, or the establishment of facilities—counter-information services, or community workshops designed to encourage neighbourhood opposition to official planning policies, for example—which require continuing maintenance and the input of specific expertise by the social worker.

4 *Individual and structural responses* Radical social workers in capitalist society experience intense pressures similar to those experienced by other radicals in professional or semi-professional occupations. These arise from being part of the 'managerial' and controlling elements of the wider social system. What should be the aim of radical social work within existing social-welfare systems? The aims of education, systems linking and counter-systems building account for much of the activity of the radical worker, but we must also identify the aims involved in providing those direct services—material, psychological and sometimes coercive—for which the official welfare system was developed. In providing some of these services, especially those concerned with material and psychological support, the radical social worker must acknowledge that his activity is at best short-term ameliorative intervention which tacitly supports existing structures. Even though human pain and suffering demands an immediate individual response from the radical worker, his main ideological justification for this work of adaptation is that it is accompanied by activities designed to further the critical consciousness of the recipients of these welfare services and to build power

bases from which to achieve changes in the services themselves. Professional work in the state services—health, education, social welfare—involves varying degrees of participation in coercive and controlling structures; while capitalism remains the radical worker has few feasible alternatives to working both *within* and *against* these structures.

Methods in radical practice

1 *Dialogical relationships* If the key task of radical practice is education, then the method by which it must be achieved is through the process of conscientization by dialogue between the worker and other people. Paulo Friere has written extensively on the problems involved in developing dialogical relationships to replace the authoritarian and oppressive relationships which characterize the contacts existing between most professionals in education and social welfare and their 'clients'. While the oppressive nature of traditional educational and social-work transaction can be seen fairly clearly, we have to recognize that the cultural domination of 'banking' approaches to education and controlling approaches to social work infects also those who attempt more radical interventions. Radical change can only come from consciousness developed as a result of exchange rather than imposition. Mao Tse-tung (1971) writes: 'There are two principles here: one is the actual needs of the masses rather than what we fancy they need, and the other is the wishes of the masses, who must make up their own minds instead of our making up their minds for them.' Some radicals, however, seem to imagine that they can achieve liberation by using the methods of oppression. 'Unfortunately,' Friere writes, 'those who espouse the cause of liberation are themselves surrounded and influenced by the climate which generates the "banking" concept, and often do not perceive its true significance or its dehumanizing power. . . . Those truly committed to the cause of liberation can accept neither the mechanistic concept of consciousness as an empty vessel to be filled, nor the use of banking methods of domination (propaganda, slogans—deposits) in the name of liberation.' (Friere, 1972b, 52.) For the radical social worker the struggle to develop dialogical relationships is often made especially difficult by the official power which he holds in relation to the 'client'. Nevertheless, work on phenomenology in the study of deviance and mental illness (see Phillipson and Roche, 1974) enables us to pay increasing attention to the subjective meanings which people attach to their social world. Exchanging our perceptions of the social world with others can be the beginning of dialogue.

2 *Group conscientization* Working with people ('clients' and others) in an 'action system' to achieve change will, for the radical social worker, be a major method by which critical consciousness can develop. The group is central to such work, for conscientization cannot be undertaken by one individual on his own. Group support helps to carry the tensions and anxieties which a developing critical consciousness and the liberating action that must follow are bound to create. The development of a critical consciousness, by which the demystification of political structures and economic relations takes place, enables a group and the individuals within it to assert their own humanity and to confront dehumanization systems. By working in group situations, the radical social worker has available a range of strategies which he shares with the group. The strategies of campaigns, collaboration, and confrontation are to be used by the action system in relation to the target of intervention, according to a careful political assessment of concrete situations, and a calculation of the consequences for the action system and others of any particular strategy. The radical worker needs a range of skills to enable him to make such assessments and to use flexibly a wide repertoire of interventions designed to promote change. The radical worker is not so limited in the methods available to him that the action accompanying and following group conscientization must always be, for example, dramatic confrontation. The radical worker may be relatively protected from the consequences of any particular action (for example, a rent strike) compared with the other members of the action system, and must take this into account.

3 *Organization and planning* If radical social workers are to work effectively, whether with individuals, families, groups, in residential institutions or with large organizations, then they must develop a range of organizational, administrative and planning skills. Building and maintaining viable counter-systems, for example, demands working with others in the systematic analysis of problem-definitions, the assessment of available resources, the formulation of feasible goals within specific time limits, the monitoring of subsequent activity and the evaluation of the results. Whether the radical worker is working with individuals or groups of any kind he must be able to collect relevant data, negotiate working agreements with those involved in the action, use his expertise appropriately, and plan and carry out, in a way most beneficial to the people with whom he is working, the termination of his contact. Radical ideology does not replace the need for a range of skills in the effective organization and planning of the work.

Conclusion

I have attempted to highlight some of the problems involved in developing an overall analytic and prescriptive framework for radical practice in social work. It will be clear that radical social work is a long way from being able to formulate a coherent paradigm of theory and practice which could assist its development in the field and in social-work education. However, in identifying some of the possible elements in such a future paradigm, I have aimed to contribute to the promotion of critical discussion so that the work of building a paradigm can involve as many radical social workers in the field and in education as possible, and through them the oppressed and exploited on whom we depend for our livelihood.

4
How Misunderstanding Occurs
Stuart Rees

This chapter[1] is not concerned with aspects of client–social worker exchanges in long-term relationships but, for the most part, with the potential for misunderstanding which exists even before the parties meet and in initial meetings. For example, social workers are employed to provide personal assistance to members of the public who seek help or who are referred to them by other laymen and professionals. But social worker and potential client probably live and have lived in different worlds. They may have different interpretations of resources, objectives and the means to attain them. What is a routine matter to one may be an unusual and intolerable experience to the other.

To focus on misunderstanding does not imply that shared points of view about problems and the service required are a prerequisite to obtaining help. People may share one another's points of view yet do nothing about each other's problems. Misunderstanding may be associated with what each party eventually considers to have been a useful outcome. Yet some people who might benefit from a social worker's help never seek it; some who are referred never become clients; some 'drop out' after initial meetings, and others are entered as clients on agency records but are not aware of this fact and seldom if ever meet the social worker concerned. These are some possible outcomes of misunderstanding, the product of client's and social worker's orientations to problem solving, such as their different assumptions about people's predicaments and about the social worker's role, and the differences in their power to conduct and control the content of interviews.

[1] Some of the data used in this chapter are derived from my research into client/social worker perspectives, a project sponsored by the Social Science Research Council. In some instances the data have been included in unpublished papers and a reference is given. Where this research material has not been used previously, and is published here for the first time, no numbered reference is given.

Clients' orientation

Knowledge and beliefs

The general public and new clients' knowledge about social work includes a range of ideas and expectations stretching from confessed ignorance to a certain amount of informed guessing. Social workers may be clear about their terms of reference but such clarity is matched by public confusion.

The British public, including potential clients and those who might refer others, know little about the recent reorganization of social work, or about the functions of the personnel who staff the new agencies. In a sample of 65 Scottish clients newly referred to a voluntary and local authority agency, no one knew about the amalgamation into one department of the previously separate child care, probation, health and welfare departments, even though the reorganization had occurred four years earlier. Only one of these clients said they had ever heard of the legislation, the Social Work (Scotland) Act 1968, which brought these changes into effect (Rees, 1973). This one person, a widow of 77, said, 'I think it's another form of allowance like security. I just thought I'd get to hear of it if it was something for me.' A similar picture of public ignorance following the reorganization of social work services in England and Wales has been reported by Glastonbury *et al.* (1973, 194).

Ignorance about social work seems partly derived from confusion about the all-purpose label. Recently, and in the past, there has been familiarity with some forms of social work but not with others. In a survey of the perceptions of a random sample of 385 families in south Wales, respondents were found to have wholly or partly correct knowledge of the functions of the probation service, the NSPCC and Citizens' Advice Bureau, but less than half were able to give even a brief and incomplete description of the work of the three new components of the new social service departments (Glastonbury *et al.* 1973, 193–4). Twelve years previously Timms's findings were similar. In a pilot study of knowledge about social workers held by people of different age, sex, marital status and occupation, the best-known social worker was found to be the probation officer, of whom only 2 per cent had not heard, whereas three-quarters of the sample knew nothing of psychiatric social work and little more than half had heard of a child care officer (Timms, 1962).

In Britain and elsewhere, the social worker has no clear image. He tends to be associated with income-maintenance, with charity, with general notions of officials in positions of authority. Glastonbury (1973, 201) reported that in contrast to clear-cut references to social security and to doctors, the public have difficulty in relating problems to social-work agencies. In a study of the expectations of 141 mothers closely resembling the population of married women who might make use of a multidisciplinary casework centre, Maclean (1973) gave a similar picture of limited knowledge about the social worker's job when compared with that of more familiar figures such as doctors, health visitors and the police. Similar accounts of the imprecise image of social workers and of the vague assumptions about their roles may be seen in studies of the perceptions of the clients of United States family service agencies (Bolton and Kammeyer, 1968) and of a random sample of the general public in Holland (see Mayer and Timms, 1970, 181–2).

The public image of agencies often persists long after the personnel have changed their functions. A voluntary agency in which the staff prided themselves on providing casework services was widely regarded by people who had recently been referred to it and to other agencies as a place of last resort to be used only when entitlements to social security and other benefits had been exhausted. It was also regarded as a place where only women sought help (Rees, 1973, 4). Those respondents in this sample who had not been dependent on supplementary benefits confused the local authority social-work department with the income-maintenance functions of central government agencies. Many people, in particular those over 50, referred to social work as the UAB, even though the income maintenance agency which existed under that name ceased to exist in 1940 (Rees, 1973, 5). There is reason for such confusion: social workers have some financial resources and providing money is an easily understood and explained form of help. Maclean (1973, 5) reported mothers' beliefs that a local casework centre was a source of money and that such beliefs were bolstered by experience of its workings.

In the minds of prospective clients, social work is also associated with officialdom. In one instance where social workers were in a new multipurpose office block along with almost every other local authority employee, clients assumed that they were something to do with the council, and that their job was to check on standards of care related to age group. Old people thought social workers would see if the aged were being cared for, mothers that they would ensure children were not maltreated.

The all-purpose label 'social work' may reflect a professional concern with almost any social problem but it also blurs separate tasks and reinforces the expectation that all officials work together, sharing information and purposes of control. People with housing difficulties have said that they were reluctant to go to 'the welfare' (social work) because they thought that such people worked with the council (the housing department), an authority to be avoided if possible and appeased when necessary (Rees, 1973). Young people have been found to have a tendency to lump together indiscriminately the functions of various agencies—such as police, health visitors, probation officers—irrespective of their own experience of such personnel: each official is regarded as likely to tell all the others whatever he knows, so that clients asking for help from one would risk putting themselves in bad books with the others (Goetschius and Tash, 1967, 127).

Stigma

Even though knowledge is imprecise, there is a pattern in the assumptions and feelings associated with social work. The most widely held belief is that it means 'welfare'. Welfare has deep-seated historical connotations. It re-awakens beliefs about the Poor Law, about 'something for nothing', about places where the feckless receive handouts. In order to avoid the stigma of these associations, prospective clients endeavour either simply to avoid contact with 'officials', or to defend their moral worthiness by emphasizing the value of independence and the distinction between the deserving and undeserving.

Several authors have shown that one of the greatest deterrents to seeking help is that past experiences of receiving aid—in particular financial entitlements—have been unpleasant (Gould and Kenyon, 1972; Marsden, 1969). Although such unpleasantness is not part of a general policy, it is in some respects inevitable because of the values which society attaches to 'success', 'independence' and 'work' (Land, 1969). Social work involves the acknowledgement of dependence: it is confused with social security and charity, with being in trouble with officials and also bears connotations of stigma.

Studies of the public's perceptions of social work and attitudes to defining and solving problems show an underlying theme of distinguishing between the deserving and undeserving (Glastonbuty *et al.*, 1973, 197; Morris *et al.*, 1973). Those who have felt humbled by being dependent on supplementary benefits in Great Britain and on welfare in the United States are keen to define themselves as 'deserving' in relation to undeserving welfare recipients (Rees, 1973, 9–11; Briar, 1966). Until and unless they receive different treatment from 'social workers', some prospective clients believe that to ask for help is to risk being turned down, to risk being regarded as undeserving, while the real undeservers, the 'winos', the 'dropouts' and other deviants, are 'known' to be always seeking help, and getting it. In my own research (1973), the only respondents who denied feeling some sense of shame or guilt at being referred to a social worker were either those few who had been in contact with social security officials for years and had resigned themselves to their situation, or those who had sought advice or help with difficulties —such as applications to become adoptive parents, or for aids for the disabled—which did not reflect on their position in the social structure. They were people who had other sources for self-respect, such as their jobs or the support of family and friends, which more than compensated for any temporary feelings of dislike or shame at meeting a social worker (Rees, 1973, 7–8). But people without such sources of self-respect have to make other adjustments in situations that may appear as potentially stigmatizing and as likely to undermine their feelings. They may avoid seeking help, such as the thousands who do not take up means-tested benefits. They may delay seeking help until there is no alternative. When they eventually meet a social worker, they may, initially at least, slant their presentation of need to meet their perception of the agency's terms of reference. This may often not match the social worker's assumptions.

One purpose of the reorganization of British social-work services was to produce umbrella agencies to reflect the interdependence of family and community needs and resources. In the public's mind, however, social work is still inextricably linked with the history of the social services in general. The feelings of stigma associated with social work are an obstacle to the implementation of new philosophies and strategies and to the development of new resources: although 'less eligibility' and 'deterrence' have officially vanished from the statute book, their ghosts still haunt the consciousness of the British people (Pinker, 1971). From whatever frame of reference these assumptions derive, whether or not people have had personal experience of being humiliated, the authentic facts of their subjective feelings are more likely to influence behaviour than the officially defined aims and traditions of service (see Pinker, 1971, chapter 4).

Responses to authority

The use people make of their own authority and their response to that of others is a feature of their life style, partly a reflection of their personal resources and the degree to which they are dependent on certain officials or professionals. Prospective clients' responses to the authority of others are features of their general orientation towards defining problems and seeking help.

Social workers' clients are often referred to them precisely because they have few resources such as money, accommodation, the advice or support of relatives and friends, health, or knowledge of their rights and entitlements, or of ways to use the services of experts. The absence of such personal resources, writes Davies (1968, chapter 1), is often more likely to force people to seek local authority help than are bad social conditions. The manner in which people are referred to social work agencies illustrates their lack of personal resources and something too of the manner in which they are treated by and may perceive people in positions of authority. In a sample of 65 British clients (Rees, 1973), who were under no form of statutory or compulsory supervision, only between 8 and 12 per cent were self-referred whereas 19–29 per cent were referred by other professionals or officials without their prior consultation or consent, including four who were referred by neighbours or relatives. These people first knew of the social worker's involvement when they received a letter from him or when he arrived on their doorstep. In the United States those referred to social workers are not always told why: 'doctors most often recommend the Family Service in much the same way they do a medical prescription. The patient is simply told that the service would be good for him and something may be said about fees.' (Bolton and Kammeyer, 1968, 52.) Past treatment by officials perceived as having various forms of power and influence will colour future expectations. A characteristic response to authority is submissiveness. This may be particularly true of people who are poor, who are dependent, who have things done to them. They have, says Coser (1962), an essentially passive trait which is both a characteristic of them and their social structure. Of poor people in an area of Nottingham, Coates and Silburn (1970, 149) wrote that cheerfulness and optimism found an almost exclusively private expression, that the overwhelming majority failed to have any broad social expectations almost as though they had learned that such expectations were beyond their reach or control. Morris *et al.* (1973) showed that often people did not seek help from the legal services because they felt that nothing positive could be achieved by taking action of any kind and that, with regard to social security benefits and the Department of Employment, people approached their problems with a feeling of acquiescence and resignation. Passive traits in social workers' clients have also been reported although not labelled as such. McKay *et al.* (1973) expressed surprise that even people with particular expectations of the help they wanted regarded themselves as satisfied even if their requests were not met. Old people in particular were submissive and easy to please.

If people have only vague expectations about the help they might need, and if previously they have been treated by other officials with indifference or perhaps with rudeness and hostility, they are likely to be easily consoled and 'cooled out' by social workers' civility, their willingness to listen without interrupting, although such treatment may not be accompanied by any other form of service. People suffering a variety of personal and social problems are seldom their own best advocates, neither do they use very demanding criteria by which to assess a social worker's performance. In a study (Rees, 1974a) of the exchanges between 60 clients and their social workers over six months, there was only one recorded instance of a client complaining about the nature of the service from a social worker. In this case a complaint was made to a senior about the reception into care of a mentally handicapped daughter, although two families had written letters to the newspapers about their general circumstances and in two cases a letter to the Queen and Prime Minister respectively. Of relationships between clients and their respective caseworkers in the United States, Macarov (1974) reports that it seems to be a rare client who 'breaks cover' and indicates disagreement with the worker's leads, saying something like, 'Let's not talk about my kid anymore. Let's talk dollars and cents.'

In commenting on prospective clients' submissiveness to authority one must avoid giving the impression that people merely do what they are told, or that they are and always have been treated in an authoritarian way by officials. However, there is evidence that certain of the population, in particular lower-working class groups, have a marked tendency to expect authority to be used in a directive manner and in some circumstances consider prescription as both appropriate and useful (Lipset, 1963). These expectations are in direct opposition to traditional assumptions of social-work practice. Clients who sought social worker's advice and direction regarding the behaviour of others have been described as confused by the social worker's neutral stance, his non-interventionist approach (Mayer and Timms, 1970, 65–80). Clients of probation officers and other correction workers and the clients of family service agencies, both in the United States and Great Britain, have wanted their social workers to give direct advice and opinion, and the frustration of these expectations is reported to be the feature of the service which they most disliked (Gottesfeld, 1965; Reid and Shapiro, 1969). Sometimes those with 'authority' are characterized as people who may have a quick solution. Morris (*et al.*, 1973) suggests that quick solutions may often be needed because the seeking of help has been left until matters have reached crisis proportions, and that when people are then faced with refusals, referrals elsewhere or delays while action is taken on their behalf, they form a negative view of the helping process.

Social workers' orientation

Decision-making procedures in the social services are seldom visible and potential clients may have to guess at what the social worker does. But in many respects there will be grounds for their assumptions, and their guesses may be accurate. The procedures by which social workers distinguish certain groups as more worthy of attention than others, and the circumstances under which they exercise authority, match aspects of potential clients' expectations.

In various agencies, professionals are involved in selecting from a large 'eligible population' a smaller number of 'appropriate' clients. Of young people referred to United States juvenile courts, only a proportion were processed as delinquents (Emerson, 1970). Although blind welfare services are available for all sightless persons in the United States, Scott found them to be concentrated on blind children who were educable and the non-aged person thought to be employable (Scott, 1969b). The same selection process occurs in social work in Great Britain. In spite of social workers' official and utopian terms of reference in the promotion of social welfare, only a small number of people referred may get beyond intake interviews to be allocated as cases and of these even fewer may receive the social worker's sustained attention, as not only eligible but also as capable of being helped.

As a result of training, experience and association with colleagues, professionals of all kinds adapt to the demands of their jobs by the application of abstract systems of ideas—ideologies—which influence both their manner of interpreting societal demands and client needs. For example, Zimmerman (1971) has described how in the United States welfare receptionists tried to satisfy themselves with what was reasonable compliance with 'rules' in order to avoid difficulties and to get on with their work. Attempts to introduce patient government in psychiatric hospitals are regarded as dependent on the prevailing ideologies of professional groups at any one place or time (Strauss et al., 1964). Smith and Harris (1972) argue that in order to understand the organizational procedures of social-work departments, it is important to pay particular attention to the sets of meanings which social workers assign to their work and to the organization of which they are a part; they found that procedures for allocating cases were attempts, varying in degrees of success, to implement a number of need-ideologies at the operational level. These trends can be illustrated by examining how social workers determine priorities.

Establishing priorities

Time is a resource. One way for a social worker to use it carefully is to select by a system of priorities those cases he will take on at allocation and those to which he will pay most attention once they have become part of a caseload. The sense of priority will be expressed through preferences and interests, sometimes by a sense of moral concern and sometimes in terms of expediency.

Interest potential becomes a resource for the client. The social worker is more likely to find time and facilities for cases in which he is interested. Some cases are less interesting than others. A survey (Neill *et al.*,1973) of the attitudes of 69 area-based social workers in a new English Social Service Department showed a marked preference for working with cases involving relationship problems and children, least preference being expressed for work with the physically disabled and the elderly even though these latter made up the highest proportion (62 per cent) of the department's clientele. A voluntary agency, with more apparent control than a local authority over the people it selected as clients, specialized in work with single-parent families, although it was often only by accident that clients or referral agents could discover this policy. The agency had established a weekly social gathering for the mothers of single parent families. A social worker expressed how her interest matched agency policy: 'I take on a lot of these one-parent families. I have an interest in them because I think they have all sorts of problems which we can try to cope with and help in different sorts of ways apart from the social-work relationship.'

Often, the particular case in which the social worker is interested reflects the type of case he would like to be known by. It represents the most desirable label of his occupation, his preferred professional image. A social worker in a local authority, interested in the case of a recently separated mother referred for support with financial and other difficulties, illustrates the point: 'I think it's a case people are interested in. Most people I find are interested in work with families where there are children. Not everybody, but I think it's the type of case I could discuss with my colleagues.'

Priority is also established by a sense of moral concern. Decisions are taken to prevent other situations occurring. Those who can project themselves or their situations as having a certain moral character, says Goffman (1969, 24), place a moral demand on others, obliging them to take certain kinds of cooperative action. When social workers perceive cases as 'crises', situations of this order are likely to occur. A senior social worker expressed her point of view regarding crises: 'I think a lot of clients are very demanding and manipulators and you need to watch this. Some of them would have you running every minute of the day and you have to make sure you don't fall into this trap. While others, if they 'phoned me and said, "Look, would you come out"—there's one woman, I had only seen her once and I knew there was a real crisis when she 'phoned and I would go.'

Certain cases, such as those involving unmarried mothers, are often regarded *a priori* as having crisis characteristics, whereas cases which appear to involve applications for old people's homes or 'straightforward aid type things', may be regarded as something which can wait, 'because they are easier, they don't demand so much, you are not going to get the same crisis with them.'

Some priorities are determined by matters of expediency. Social work is sometimes visible and public involving the scrutiny of outsiders. Cases involving compulsory supervision, sometimes referred to as 'the statutory work' are of this nature. So too are those cases in which other agencies and professionals seek the social worker's cooperation—housing departments threatening to evict, courts expecting reports, doctors wanting a follow-up of patients they've referred. Although occasionally resenting such pressures, the social worker may feel obliged to respond. The sense of having to give some priority to visible work affects the social worker's rationing of time, and time given to such cases will not be available to others.

The influence of theories

Social workers may have to trim their time to meet the pressures of outsiders. But they may also tailor their theories to match particular expressions of need. Ideas and theories derived from training provide a basis for ideologies, and a means of communicating, often in a taken-for granted way, with immediate colleagues and interested outsiders, such as doctors, psychiatrists, health visitors and other social workers including the staff of residential institutions. Two theoretical assumptions are inherent features of social workers' training and seem likely to affect their orientation to their job, first that social work is part of a process, and secondly that problems may be understood and perhaps resolved through establishing and understanding interpersonal relationships.

The assumption that social-work help is a process is derived from casework theories which stress the value of making relationships, of establishing some interdependence between social worker and client, and of shared but different activities aimed at the attainment of a common goal. In some circumstances this may be a relevant and useful notion. But the client, argues Kuhn (1962), may see an interview as a single act whereas the social worker defines it as a process involving a sequence of interviews, the establishment of a relationship and the controlled termination of that relationship. Different assumptions about the significance of any one interview often contribute to misunderstanding between social worker and client about subsequent arrangements to meet. Many prospective clients—in particular those with few personal resources or those who have lived with some irrevocable difficulty, such as the parents of a mentally handicapped child—may have become used to a series of regular if brief meetings with a variety of 'caretakers', such as health visitors, educational welfare officers, the representatives of housing departments and supplementary benefit offices, credit and insurance collectors, gas and electricity men, doctors, ministers of religion, other social workers and perhaps even researchers. These meetings have been described as 'contacts' which sustain a pattern of life rather than change it, which are brief and taken for granted, which sometimes create more problems than they solve, which frequently deal, not with a client's difficulty or feelings, but with an official's needs to carry out some activity (Rees, 1974b). To many clients the social worker's identity is blurred by such previous encounters. Initial meetings with social workers are not necessarily perceived as different from those with other passer-by-officials, the 'caretakers' who are part of urban life, whose task is also to give some attention, however cursory, to various aspects of families' needs, their difficulties or obligations.

The uninitiated will not know that in first discussions about their situations, in which they are often not present, they are being assessed, not only as to whether they can be helped, but also whether they should become part of a caseload and perhaps too whether they should be considered long or short term cases. Even having become clients, it is often not known who is to take an initiative for further action, if any, and whether or not a case has been closed. In some departments and for some social workers it is policy that once a client, always a client. People are kept on the books, partly as a mark of concern and partly on the assumption that the process of problem solving is interminable (Rees, 1974a; Waldron, 1961). Clients may not know if they will see the social worker again and often assume that the matter is over. McKay and her colleagues (1973, 490) reported, 'A number of consumers were not clear as to whether they were in contact with the department and their perceptions did not always coincide with recorded information. Ten per cent of the consumers who thought they were in contact with a social worker were in fact sampled as "closed cases". In contrast two thirds of those who thought they were closed were in fact active cases.'

However simple or complex a case may appear, whatever someone's prior knowledge or the route of referral, the social worker will be involved in interpreting the problem, the service required and the resources available. On some occasions his response may be routine, relatively automatic. On other occasions he may feel that he has neither the knowledge nor experience to cope, or he may be faced with a conflict of interests, or he is expected to do x and y when he only has resources a and b. In each of these situations the social worker is likely to rely on those models of explanation with which he is familiar. In this respect theories become a source of influence; they raise certain questions in the minds of practitioners and make it difficult to raise other questions, to seek other answers (Rees and Edwards, 1973).

In view of the recent attention given to the welfare rights movement, to community work, to de-clienting social work, it is perhaps becoming hackneyed to repeat the criticisms of Wootton (1959) and Sinfield (1969) that social workers have concentrated too much on theories of interpersonal relationships instead of examining the social, economic and political sources of problems and developing alternative, relevant strategies and ideologies. But the theories attributing certain forms of social pathology are still a feature of many social workers' education and may contribute disproportionately to their subsequent sense of professional identity and general orientation.

For these reasons it should be helpful to underline that the manner in which problems are defined may be a causal factor as well as an outcome of behaviour. In a study (Taber, 1970) involving 35 Canadian social-work agencies, teachers, parents and social workers disagreed considerably in identifying problem children. The very process of discussing with the respective parties who were 'the problems' lead to changed interpretations, or the disappearance or stimulation of the behaviour that had caused complaint. A similar study (Shepherd et al., 1966) involving child guidance clinics in Great Britain found that many so-called disturbances of behaviour were no more than temporary exaggerations of widely distributed reaction patterns.

The pressures of outsiders

In their concern to understand behaviour, social workers may often fall back on a trained tendency to consider family dynamics as causal explanations. But the social worker is not a free agent. He is not always able to choose with whom he will work and how. He has been and is being used increasingly by other agencies to control circumstances and behaviour, as a regulator of conflict. He will be under pressure from various agents—such as elected councillors and courts, housing departments, schools and police—to take certain forms of action, to encourage repayment of rents or the acceptance of a transfer of accommodation, to find money in order to avoid gas or electricity being cut off, to encourage children to attend schools or adults to accept a 'need' for support or supervision. In allocation meetings, at least, the social worker's notion of social need may merely reflect the way in which it is utilized by other professional groups (Smith, 1973). In his assumptions about what is possible and desirable, the social worker may be partly influenced by his and his colleagues' theories and their interpretations of rules and resources. But he is deflected or even directed towards many clients, not by the people themselves, but by the representatives of other established and often powerful institutions and professions.

The first meeting between social worker and client is an inherently unequal bargaining situation because the former, like other professionals in similar contexts, can control the agenda by giving or withholding information and by deciding which resources are available and relevant (Scheff, 1969). Such influence is compounded, both by clients' probable submissiveness and because in many situations people are referred precisely because they are already in conflict with the considered authority of other agencies. The latter may significantly influence social workers' terms of reference and their interpretation of problems.

Miller and Paul described such a tendency in the United States. Their warning is worth repeating. When defining the social problems of the lower class, they wrote, it is vital to distinguish between what really are problems in the lower-class community and what appear to be problems because of an implicit comparison with features of middle-class culture. They concluded that there was perhaps not so much pathology in lower-class life as had been commonly supposed, and that social workers therefore needed to clarify the cultural sources of 'pathology' and to indicate more directly the nature of feasible treatment goals (Miller, 1959; Paul and Miller, 1965). Such clarification in the present circumstances would involve examining the relationship between characteristics of clients' assumptions and social workers' activities. In the immediate future and in individual cases the social worker may find that his allegiance is not with forms of 'local authority' but with those who are advancing different ways of interpreting behaviour, who are trying to develop other resources to represent less powerful people. He may wish to support and make use of community and tenant groups, the national pressure groups representing the interests of categories of dependent people and, in certain areas and situations, the neighbourhood law firms and the free schools.

Concluding comment

The discussion above suggests three ways and areas in which social workers might be enabled to clarify their identity, to assert some independence and to reduce present features of misunderstanding. They concern the content of social-work education, some redirection of agencies' resources and interests and, in the light of this, some attempt to change public beliefs.

In education and training, students should become familiar with what has been referred to collectively as the clients' orientation, their knowledge and beliefs, their possible feelings of stigma and responses to authority and also with the often unwitting manner in which social-work practice feeds some people's suspicions and assumptions, even though social workers might consider them 'incorrect'. Unless this is done, training will be an idealized form of experience, the notions of the classroom bearing little relevance to the exigencies of the job.

The new managers of social-work services, perhaps in association with those who sit on the boards of the private agencies, or the elected personnel on social-work committees, must clarify their alliances and say in what ways they will act independently to influence the objectives of local social policy. For example, front-line social workers often resent that they are asked to intervene by housing departments in cases of impending eviction. But they find little evidence that senior personnel either wish to change such a policy or are aware of its implications—namely that what appears to different local-authority employees as reasonable cooperation on a family's behalf looks like collusion to certain sections of the public.

Some general education is required to increase and to clarify public knowledge so that there are fewer mysteries, less fear and confusion about the social worker's job. Unless attention is paid to this and to the other proposals, then a policy of employing more social workers to deal with social problems may merely increase the volume if not the variety of the present potential for misunderstanding. It will do little to disturb the historical momentum of beliefs that social work means a place of last resort, or is just another arm in the alliance of officials, despite the fact that neither assumption matches the intentions of recent social-work legislation, nor some social workers' redefinitions of their roles, nor any newly acquired radical stance.

5

It's All Right for You to Talk: Political and Sociological Manifestos for Social Work Action

Stanley Cohen

I would like in this essay to deal with certain aspects of the relationship between sociology (the sociology of deviance in particular) and social-work practice. The aspects I have chosen have been suggested quite specifically by my personal experience and that of my colleagues in our contacts with various groups of social workers, especially those in probation, community work, youth work and residential institutions. In these contacts—as we trail around the country, serving on study groups, examining on training courses, or simply talking to captive audiences at the inevitable weekend conference by the sea—the most familiar reaction we encounter is encapsulated in the phrase (often quite explicitly used): 'it's all right for you to talk.' The implication is that, however interesting, amusing, correct and even morally uplifting our message might be, it is ultimately a self-indulgent intellectual exercise, a luxury which cannot be afforded by anyone tied down by the day-to-day demands of a social-work job. This reaction is especially pronounced when our message is supposed to be 'radical' and our audience includes self-professed 'radical social workers'.

I am still surprised, even on occasions hurt, by this reaction because I continue to think that those areas of sociology which interest me should be relevant to social workers and also because I selfconsciously avoid presenting ideas in a style that could be pejoratively termed 'academic'. Yet the negative reaction still comes up, either in an extreme form which is accompanied by manifest hostility and defensiveness ('we've got to do your dirty work', 'what right have you got to stand up there and judge us?', 'you've got no idea about our problems'), or in a weaker version which allows the validity of the sociologist's claims but is genuinely perplexed about their practical implications.

Our responses to such attacks or queries are invariably feeble. We either resort to a simple-minded role theory—poor social workers are trapped in their professional roles and cannot detach themselves enough to see what is to be done—or else the only slightly less simple-minded political variants of this theory couched in the rhetoric of 'working in the system', 'tools of the state', 'bourgeois individualism'. Such responses are not only patronizing, not only intellectually inadequate but also downright useless to most social workers. They only serve as self-fulfilling prophecies for the 'it's all right for you to talk' position and further reinforce the social worker's feeling that we don't take their problems seriously.

I want here to take the social worker's reaction to us at its face value and to examine some of the models for action which we appear to be offering. For present purposes, this means taking for granted the familiar sociological and political critiques about the limitations of social work as an agent for radical social change. I would not want to question the validity of such critiques —dealt with elsewhere in this volume—which continue to stress the macrosocietal contexts of race, class, inequality and power in which social-work practice in contemporary industrial societies must be located. But such critiques—as social workers correctly perceive—might have marginal, contradictory or ambiguous implications for day-to-day work. In this sense social workers are correct in saying that it's all right for us to talk, we don't have to do the dirty work.

And this perception is becoming increasingly urgent as social workers themselves become swept along in their own self-generated rhetoric (that is, unaided by the platitudes of sociological tracts) which demands radical changes in the professional role. This revolt from the 'agents of social control' or 'morality enforcers' (to use the by now familiar labels) might of course come from a right- rather than the more obviously left-wing political position. Witness the power, for example, of prison guards who refuse to go along with liberalizing changes in penal policy. But more importantly it comes from the whole cohort of radicalized social workers who are increasingly resisting definitions of themselves as functionaries of the social-control apparatus. Such definitions are especially painful in settings not like the prison or the courtroom but in mental hospitals, community organizations, child-care agencies and other institutions officially designed to further well being but increasingly perceived by workers and clients alike as disguised forms of punishment or repression. As Lee Rainwater (1974, 335) nicely puts it 'The dirty workers are increasingly caught between the silent middle class which wants them to do the work and keep quiet about it and the objects of that work who refuse to continue to take it lying down.'

These new cohorts of dirty workers are now looking for some theoretical reference point outside their immediate work situation which would legitimate the sense of activism and commitment they have brought to their profession (see Pearson, 1973; 1974a). If Freudianism is the god that has to be seen to have failed, then Marxism became the correct and only god, but unfortunately it seemed a god a little too far away and a little too harsh in its judgements. It was bad enough for an ordinary bourgeois individualist to fight the good fight, but it was so much worse if one were actually employed as an agent of social control, a tool of the welfare state, a weapon of pacification. What was needed was a middle-range theory which would make these judgements less severe, which would bridge the gap from mundane work to a revolutionary theory of society and allow one not to sell out. This need was met in some perfectly justifiable but also in some perverse ways by the new deviancy theory. This, and the more orthodox Marxism, are the major radical models being offered.

The promise of deviancy theory

In the last decade or so a liberal view of deviancy percolated through into social work under such rubrics as interactionism or labelling theory. The basic premises of this perspective are simple enough and involve little more than recognizing the deviants' right to present their own definition of the situation, a humanization of their supposed process of becoming deviant and a sensitivity to the undesirable and stigmatizing effects of intervention by control agents. Much heavy weather has been made by some sociologists about the higher theoretical intricacies of this view (see especially Taylor, *et al.*, 1973) and these critics have been particularly insistent in pressing the charge that interactionism presents a picture of the deviant as an innocuous creature clumsily mismanaged by middle-level caretakers. The deviant—this by now familiar critique argues—is portrayed as a passive victim of circumstances beyond his control, a creation not of the old pathologies of positivist criminology but of intervention by control agents. This tends to deny intentionality and consciousness, particularly of a political variety.

This is not the place to engage with these critiques which, to say the least, are overstated. The main point is that in pushing their particular political and epistomological line, they had to downgrade the possible implications of deviancy theory. They have argued correctly that the endless series of ethnographies of deviant groups and control agencies are dead-ends in themselves, but surely social workers can—and have—derived considerable benefit from this sort of work in simply sensitizing them to such matters as the deviant's own account of the world. And if one does not take too doctrinaire a line about the desirability of short-scale reform (an issue I will return to) then the policy implications are also not to be dismissed too easily.

It is of course true that labelling theory doesn't get directly at the roots of inequality and human misery, but it seems absurd to write off all the many reforms that are consequent on its position. We find the following in *Case Con*,[1] the 'revolutionary magazine for social workers' which has enjoyed such a wide success and which I will take as representing the radical position in the United Kingdom: 'This means that labelling theory really goes no further than being able to reform the ways we deal with deviance, so that we don't create deviant "careers" and don't amplify social problems.' (Cannan, 1970.) As radicals we would obviously want to go much further, but would it really not be a significant social change if we could reform our 'ways of dealing with deviance'? The indictment of labelling theory is not so much that it goes 'no further' than this, but that it hasn't been too clear about how to get this far.

Later in the same article, Cannan talks about how the rapid absorption of labelling theory into radical social workers' critique of the welfare state will only change the state's methods and not the whole power structure. No doubt. But where, five years after this article was written, are the signs of this rapid absorption? And again, the self-styled radical social workers (and the sociologists and criminologists who feed them their theories) need to be reminded that there are some clients, deviants and dependants who are indeed victims. They have, objectively, been exploited and victimized, railroaded and stigmatized, punished and excluded—and they see themselves like this. Most of them would prefer the 'methods' with which they were handled to be changed and would presumably not want to hang around until the power structure shifts for this to happen. More later about the revolutionary solution.

To repeat: the indictment is not that the solutions have been only at the middle level, without an explicitly political programme, but that these changes have not been made clear enough. The worker in a residential institution who reads Goffman wants to know how institutionalization can be dealt with; the community worker hearing about deviancy amplification is interested in how this spiral can be checked; the caseworker wants to operate without further stigmatizing his clients. The reason why these matters have not been spelt out (and here I agree with the radical critique of interactionism) is because of the laissez-faire, hands-off attitude behind the new theories. As Young (1975) correctly states. 'New deviancy theorists have been stridently non-interventionist.' They have often done little more than ask the middle-level managers of the control apparatus to leave deviants alone.

[1] The Case Con manifesto is printed as an appendix to this volume.

That this defect is not simply an oversight which will eventually be dealt with, is shown by the recent attempt by Edwin Schur (1973), a successful apologist for the theory, to dignify non-interventionism as a preferred solution to certain policy matters. I want to consider in some detail his recommendation of non-interventionism in the deliquency field, because this solution points to both the appeal and some of the weaknesses of this particular strategy.

Radical non-intervention: the liberal answer?

What Schur does is construct three ideal types to cover the dominant societal reactions to the deliquency problem. These are: *individual treatment, liberal reform* and *radical non-intervention*, the first two accounting between them for most current research and policy in delinquency. The individual treatment model is based on psychological theories assuming the differentness of offenders: deliquency is attributable to the special personal characteristics of delinquents. It favours clinical types of research and treatment, directs preventive measure towards identifying 'pre-delinquents' or at individualized casework and counselling programmes and favours the individualized justice approach to the juvenile court. The orthodox stream of casework and social reform in this country would probably lean towards this model, directing efforts, for example as it has in recent years, towards a welfare type of juvenile court and the introduction of more school counselling services. The *liberal reform* model is the more sociological variant on the treatment theme focusing as it does on factors at the social class and community level. It sees the immediate sources of delinquency in structural or subcultural terms, uses such theories as anomie and status frustration, directs prevention to the street gang or community level, advocates piecemeal social reform such as the increase of educational opportunities for the underprivileged and directs juvenile courts and correctional institutions to be more socially aware. One could identify this model here with the more sociologically rather than psychologically trained generation of probation officers and with such movements as group work and community work.

Schur then proceeds—plausibly enough for the most part—to show the many problems which have arisen in implementing both the treatment and reform models. The treatment model lacks anything like a sound empirical basis in the demonstration that deliquency can be accounted for by psychological differences: its favoured methods of intervention, such as prediction and early treatment, are theoretically and empirically suspect; the results of various traditional counselling and community treatment programmes have been uniformly disappointing while new ones such as behaviour modification raise uncomfortable ethical problems. Juvenile institutions—yet to resolve the conflict between treatment and custody —have not been notably successful.

Schur's critique of the reform model is somewhat less convincing. It is no argument against class-based theories such as anomie, status-frustration and blocked opportunity, to show that a few neighbourhood street projects, community organization schemes and programmes to widen educational and employment opportunities haven't worked particularly well in actually reducing delinquency rates. Nor are the theories necessarily undermined by the ritualistic repetition of the unrecorded delinquency studies which suggest that rates are more widespread through the class structure than the official statistics suggest. There is no way of knowing that the liberal prescriptions for reduction of socio-economic inequality and racism are 'correct' or not—simply because they have not really been implemented in the American context. Where the rgument against the liberal reform model is most telling is in showing the relative failure of the reformed juvenile court, and probation and juvenile correctional institutions in materially affecting the delinquency problem.

Schur then spells out the third alternative: *radical non-intervention*. Its assumptions are clearly based on the new deviancy theory, incorporating concepts derived from labelling and interactionism. The stress is on stigma, stereotyping and societal reaction, together with a somewhat more radical reformist position than in the older liberal version. Delinquents are seen not as having special personality characteristics nor even being subject to socio-economic constraints. They suffer, rather, from contingencies: they are the ones who have been processed by the juvenile justice system. Delinquency is widespread throughout society: some juveniles drift into clearly disapproved behaviour and are processed. This drift allows slightly more free choice than the constrained picture of the first two models, a position termed clumsily by Schur as 'neo-antideterminist'.

The focal point of attention thus switches from the individual delinquent to his interaction with the social-control system, and policy is directed towards changing the system: there should be voluntary treatment, decriminalization (particularly in regard to crimes without victims), a narrowing of the scope of juvenile court jurisdiction and its increased formalization rather than relaxation towards a welfare model. There should also be an unmasking of euphemism: an end to the use of rhetoric of treatment and rehabilitation in juvenile courts and correctional institutions to negate or disguise the reality of punishment. The differences between the models can be seen in the example of the school: the treatment model might advocate early identification of the delinquency prone and suitable counselling programmes; the reform model would suggest the widening of educational opportunity for school leavers; the non-intervention model would advocate an end to policies which label and stream trouble-makers.

Behind such specific reforms, the non-intervention model implies a policy to increase societal accommodation to youthful diversity, with the basic injunction: leave the kids alone wherever possible. Even further in the background, lies a vague commitment to radical social change in structure and values rather than piecemeal social reform. It must be said that the model is very appealing, even without Schur's concession that he is not completely rejecting some policies stemming from the other two. Social workers should endorse any programme which would take them away from the seductive powers of the treatment model. They would also be well advised to support non-interventionist tactics particularly in those areas where the legal system has extended too far and conversely where the legal model has been eroded by moralistic busybodies under the banner of welfare. They should certainly take up Schur's call for an end to euphemism and should stop trying to resolve the contradictions between their dual commitment to welfare and control by pretending that the control element does not exist. But beyond this, the non-interventionist argument peters out: it is painfully weak theoretically and it offers very few prescriptions to resolve day-to-day problems. Specifically:

1   Schur correctly notes how the sociological model has undermined the notion of individual pathology, but he suggests an alternative which rejects all notions of constraint. He complains, for example, that '. . . the reform outlook to a large extent rests on the notion of structured variations in the freedom of individuals to shape their own destinies.' (1973, 83.) Now no social worker can get through an hour of his round without being aware of precisely such 'structured variations' and it would be absurd to expect him to be convinced of a policy which suggests otherwise. This applies to problems of mental health, housing and child care as much as to delinquency. But again the defect of 'neo-antideterminism' is not so much that it is incorrect—it has been a crucial antidote to the over-determinist legacy of positivist criminology—but that its implications for practice have not been spelt out. It matters a great deal theoretically to show, say, that a female shoplifter acted intentionally and with some degree of choice rather than from some obscure condition called kleptomania or menopausal

depression, but *how* this may matter to the probation officer dealing with her is not at all apparent.

2 When it comes to the argument about the over-reach of criminal law[2] the non-interventionist case rests primarily on the pragmatic grounds of the law's sheer inefficiency in controlling certain areas of undesirable behaviour. When principles are cited, they tend to be little more than a restatement of traditional Wolfenden-report rhetoric about the existence of realms of private morality which are not the business of the law. Now both pragmatic and principled arguments are all very well in areas of normative dissensus and crime without victims. It is clearly desirable for any selfrespecting radical social worker to devote energy—through pressure-group politics and campaigns—to change certain laws in such areas as drugs, abortion, homosexuality, prostitution rather than simply to mop up the casualties of the law. But there are two inbuilt limitations to the decriminalization argument: the first is a self-admitted one that only a small proportion of offences are suitable candidates for this treatment. The vast bulk of offences— property crime—plus other obvious areas such as personal violence will remain criminal. This is not to say anything of the other areas of social-work activity—in regard to poverty, homelessness, mental health—where the criminal law has little significance.

The second limitation is less often admitted. Once an area of deviance stops being criminalized, it still has to be policed by some other form of social control. And more often than not, this form derives from the individual treatment or the liberal reform model. Now it might be preferable for all sorts of reasons to treat, say, drug-taking within a medical or welfare rather than a criminal model, but someone still has to man the control machine.

3 This leads to the third problem with non-interventionism from a social worker's point of view. The stress on the control system—how the raw material of rule-breaking is fed into the machine, processed and recycled—is valuable. It may be quite in order to talk of organizations producing deviants and to say that 'from an organizational standpoint the problem of delinquency is to some extent one of management' (Schur, 1973, 130). Statements such as these might justifiably give rise to sociologists' concern that the deviant is forgotten as the whole problem is transformed into one of mismanagement. But for the moment my

[2] For a more comprehensive but not particularly radical argument about this over-reach of criminal law, see Morris and Hawkins (1970) and Schur (1965).

concern is that the preferred system of management—and as long as social workers exist, management is where they will be—remains obscure.

4   Finally, there is a more disturbing aspect of the non-interventionist case to be considered: its argument against treatment and reform rests quite correctly on a fundamental questioning of the taken-for-granted assumption that delinquency is a problem about which something must be done. But to combine this question with the actual evidence that current delinquent policies are unworkable and even harmful, in order to justify a theory of accommodation to diversity, is empty without some guidelines for establishing just how this accommodation is to take place. Moreover, although some aspects of delinquency problem—and indeed many other social problems as defined by the powerful for social workers to deal with—can wither away, the structural features of society which both create real problems for certain members and then exacerbate these problems by dealing with them unfairly, will not. Non-intervention can become a euphemism for benign neglect, for simply doing nothing.

At this point we can return to the critiques of the new deviancy theory itself. For some of the problems in non-interventionism can indeed be traced back to the peculiar mixture of liberalism and romanticism inherent in the original theory. For what was sometimes implied—although not perhaps as unambiguously as some critics suggest—was an image of the naturally good man who was interfered with by state busybodies. If he was left alone, his problems would disappear. Leaving philosophical speculations about the nature of man aside (where they should be left by sociologists) clearly this picture cannot be held against the day-to-day experience of social workers. The man threatening to drop his baby from a window ledge, the alcoholic suffering from withdrawal symptoms, the pregnant schoolgirl kicked out of her home, are all doing things which call for help. The help (or control) hasn't yet come to interfere with them or change their natures. This of course has always been recognized by the more sophisticated deviancy theorists, most notably Matza (1969) in his warnings against romanticism and sentimentality: he is quite clear about the deviant being something more than the product of the control apparatus.

But another type of romanticism was to emerge. With the rise of militant and aggressive deviant groups, some of the new theorists—particularly those of us in the United Kingdom associated with the National Deviancy Conference—started (and some have never stopped) celebrating such deviance and claiming it as evidence of a new found political consciousness. Virtually any anti-social activity became elevated in this way. Young (1975) correctly detects the contradiction in this version of the theory: 'Now the message of the deviancy theorist to official society was "hands off you'll only make matters worse" but *at the same time* the implicit ideology was "believe and hope that the new deviant constituencies do represent a genuine threat to the social order."'

Those like Young who became disenchanted with this position—because of the idealism which advocated alliances with deviant groups and the unmasking of conservative control ideologists as the only tactics to adopt—moved in a position somewhat different to mine. They argued for a social base—specifically in Marxism—which would somehow resolve the weakness of the idealist position. But when their solution appears as a set of guidelines for social workers, it looks either notably ambiguous itself, or else suspiciously like the romanticism from which they are so eager to dissociate themselves.

Client co-option: a revolutionary manifesto?

Social workers themselves were correct in suspecting that uncomfortably mixed up with the liberalism of deviancy theory was a degree of romanticism. They saw the deviant co-opted as hero in a series of revolutionary struggles as deviancy theorists rushed around to find in the actions and—with greater difficulty—the words of football hooligans, vandals, rapists, bank robbers and kidnappers signs of militancy and class consciousness. In some quarters prisoners were seen as being in the vanguard of the revolutionary struggle, homosexuals as precursors of the destruction of the bourgeois capitalist family, and schizophrenics as visionary prophets of man's alienation. In retrospect it is not difficult to see why such attributions were made: from the middle of the nineteen sixties onwards, various of the previously despised and pathetic groups among the deprived and the deviant, did become more organized, vocal and likely to build up collective defences to the stigmatized positions that the powerful had cast them in. Gay liberation, ideological drug users, tenants' associations, squatters, prisoners' unions and more recently mental patients' unions, were calling the tunes. In a real sense these groups were becoming politicized and it was (and still is) impossible for any sociologist to avoid trying to make sense of these developments.

Equally impossible, however, is it to accept the way in which the brand of deviancy theory evolved by contemporary 'hip Marxists' seized upon these groups and elevated them to the status of political without any clear thought about the conceptual problems involved.[3] Having rejected the legacy of positivism, having conveniently (so they thought) disposed of the notion of deviant as victim, they now urged sociologists to join hands with their subjects and social workers with their clients in a joyous storming of the Bastille of social control. The hip Marxists could sit in their universities and conferences while the social workers (and the occasional activist involved in a tenants' association) would spread the message to the people. Deviants of the world unite, you have nothing to lose but your stigmas.

Unfortunately not only was this approach excessively romantic in conception but—like the radical non-intervention model—carried remarkably few prescriptions that could actually be followed by social workers in any practical sense. Indeed this supposed radical alternative to traditional social work was often extremely evasive about what sort of gains the clients could expect from their new workers. I rely again on journals such as *Case Con* and personal contacts over the last five years with many of these social workers and sociologists to try to analyse what alternative models of action were actually being offered.

In examining the programmes of movements, such as Case Con, I am interested less in matters of internal consistency or ideological 'correctness' than in what sort of help the radical social worker might get from absorbing the message. The Case Con type of programme seems to consist of three separate strands which I will call *theory*, *self-help* and *client co-option*. The first strand stresses the need for a total socio-political theory (obviously Marxism, but some are a little coy about the label) which would inform action. It is continually emphasized that part of being a radical social worker is to have such an ongoing analysis to provide a critique of the welfare state and a guard against not being conned by the system. To quote an early statement of aims, '. . . We believe that the first step to the solution of many of the problems facing social workers' clients—such as poverty, inadequate housing, inadequate welfare services, isolation and alienation—lies in the replacement through working-class struggle of capitalism by socialism.' This strand of the programme—in the Case Con version at least—is backed up by the standard polemics about a world in which international capitalism is always on the edge of a crisis and in which every government measure, down to obscure clauses in the Mental Health or Childrens Acts, is an attack on the working class.

[3] For a critique of this brand of theory see Cohen and L. Taylor (forthcoming).

The second strand in the programme stresses the social workers' own internal organization. In order to be radical, one's training course and the profession itself must be democratically organized, which—in this version—is taken to mean the forging of alliances with the relevant unions, rank-and-file involvement in NALGO, militancy about pay and conditions, protecting victimized colleagues.

The third strand—the one most relevant to this discussion—is to find a work role for the social worker as something other than an agent of control, buttressing up the system. A Case Con statement of aims arrives at this alternative: 'We support the attempts of social workers to engage in community action and encourage the activities of grass roots organizations such as claimants' unions and tenants' associations.' This forging of links with various militant groups of deviants and dependants, together with general support for anything identified as the 'working-class struggle' is the main basis of radical social-work activity.

Given acceptance of the Marxist model, each of these elements makes some sense. Working outwards from what most social workers actually do, though, they represent something less than a guideline for action. Not only do they leave out those very groups which because of their lack of organization, grass roots activity, and militancy make up the bulk of social workers clients but, in the case of the first and last strands (the second is largely irrelevant to the discussion), they can be incompatible. Before going on to this let me take a case from personal experience which was instrumental in leading me away from a career in psychiatric social work into the safe world of sociology.

Mrs X was the mother of a five-year-old boy who had been referred for gross 'behaviour problems' to the child guidance clinic in which I was working. The child was clearly unmanageable at home and school. The mother was a middle-aged Cypriot woman. She'd married the father of the child, a British soldier, and he'd left her soon after the child was born. She followed him to England but could not persuade him to return to her. She was now living with the child in one room in Kilburn, and had been joined there by her blind mother, a semi-invalid who could not speak any English. It was a nightmare situation: the poor woman, her blind mother and a hyperactive five-year-old locked in one room. On reporting my first so-called 'diagnostic' interview to my supervisor, I concluded that there was nothing the clinic could do until we badgered the housing department to get somewhere for the family to live. My supervisor thought otherwise and I was queried about whether I'd gone into the psychodynamics of the woman's relationship with her ex-husband (was she perhaps punishing herself for something?) and had I noticed the obsessional way she had been holding her handbag?

Then, as now, one couldn't but see the futility of a purely individualistic casework approach. But then, as now, one could also see some role for the social worker to help the distressed, the powerless, the helpless. Now while it would be wholly unfair to argue that revolutionaries are inhuman monsters wholly obsessed with Marxist dogma, it seems to me an inescapable conclusion from all their writings, that in cases like these (or perhaps ones a little less obvious) the radical social worker will not only be able to derive very little from his theory, but in fact will also encounter a line of argument that mere practical help is in fact undesirable. He will end up—like the Freudian caseworker—doing very little in the way of immediate help or more long-term community action. Such help by improving the client's material condition is seen as dangerous because it blunts the contradictions in the system. In practice, of course, most revolutionary or any other social workers would probably have helped Mrs X in the obvious ways, but it must be remembered that her plight is not made any more helpfully understandable to her by reference to contradictions in the system and the crisis in late capitalism than it is by talking about masochistic personality traits and identity crises.

Let me deal more fully with these practical and theoretical problems. On the practical level it must be said that with the two notable exceptions of housing and welfare rights—through tenants' associations and claimants' unions respectively—there is very little indication in Case Con circles of how the revolutionary social worker would operate very differently from his non-revolutionary colleagues. Having satisfied oneself that one's clients struggles are actually part of the working-class movement—and this is somewhat unlikely in most cases of the disabled, the old, the unhappy, the sick—what would support for this struggle actually look like? As in the non-intervention model, there is very little attempt to spell out what the alternative support or control system would look like, unless of course one is sustained by the thought that, come the revolution, there will be no casualties, miseries or distress. There are only rare attempts in the pages of *Case Con* itself actually to recognize what social workers, radical or otherwise, are really doing—that is, such tasks as mopping up casualties and offering patronage to clients unable to get resources themselves. I found only one brave attempt (Taylor, 1972) to spell out a concrete alternative strategy, one which makes no bones about transforming client help into client co-option.

What Taylor suggests (1972, 5) is that the social worker should refuse to

accept the client as a client—in terms of a symptom, or a case—but rather
'. . . should accept the new "cases" continually being thrown up by the
crisis in the system as political allies "in need of protection and care" only in
the sense that the system has them pinpointed for processing through the
courts, through the SS, through the hands of City Hall and so on.' The
notion that the social workers' clients—Taylor gives such examples as the
unemployed, the mother on probation for stealing children's clothes—are
'thrown up by the crisis in the system' (whatever this may mean) leads onto
the suggestion that social workers must look after their clients' political as
well as other interests. The argument is that the social worker should *defend*
his client by acting as lawyer, organizer and information-provider in
helping him fight the system which has created his problem. In this defender
role he refuses to accept the client as a client but rather sees him as an ally
against the system. Thus—on an analogous ground to my refusal to deal with
Mrs X in casework terms—one refuses to spend hours with a soccer hooligan
discussing his emotional problems and rather ensures that he receives the
right material help. But you must demonstrate that this is all being done on
political grounds. This will expose the division that exists between the
master institutions (the probation officer is not always in league with the
policeman) and this knowledge will eventually politicize the street corner
kids. Taylor sees 'striking alliances' developing out of the politicization of
the social-work relationship and suggests that his various defence strategies
(for example, seeing not just the delinquent but the whole of working-class
culture on trial in the courtroom) '. . . throws up for question the very
ideological basis of social control under capitalism. If such a strategy were to
mushroom, at a time when courts are full to bursting at any case, the
working of the machinery itself could also be thrown into doubt.' (1972, 9.)

This attempt to spell out an alternative strategy is, as I've said, a brave one,
because it is nothing if not explicit. Much of it makes sociological and
political sense and styles of work such as defender, organizer, and
information-provider are the ones which the best social workers—for
example, in experimental youth work—have spontaneously evolved for
themselves anyway. But beyond this, the policy becomes somewhat
unrealistic.

Leaving aside scepticism about whether most or even many clients are
'thrown up by the crisis in the system' and are likely allies in any working-
class struggle, real or potential, what if these clients refuse to see themselves
in this way? What Taylor implies is that if the client refuses to accept the
social worker's refusal to accept him as client, then he should get no help at
all. Indeed Taylor is quite explicit about this in noting—in passing—that the

client-refusal strategy provides the radical social worker for a basis of discriminating within his case load! Not only are we back to the elitism of the psychoanalytically derived casework—whatever you say, we really know best what your problem is—but we end up with another form of non-intervention or benign neglect: only this time, one reserved for the unfortunate few who refuse to see themselves as the social worker's political allies. What if the client actually wants something looking like casework? A case of false consciousness, no doubt. One can only hope that social workers who take this strategy literally will also respect a client's refusal to have anything to do with them.

To return to the more theoretical obstacle—the existence in some Marxist social-work theory of a strand of thought suspicious of *any* attempt (and this presumably includes the client-refusal strategy) to support clients. The first problem is one that most activists are well aware of: that social workers and their clients might be, because of their respective class positions, quite marginal to the working-class struggle. Social workers themselves are part of the welfare state apparatus which protects ruling-class interests while the clients are the powerless, being unemployed, old, disabled, ill, institutionalized. Typically this paradox is avoided in revolutionary social-work circles and, after some rather diffuse talk about repression and the crisis in late capitalism, eventually the client (or consumer) organization is often completely rejected in the belief that such groups cannot after all be slotted into the history of the working-class movement. (Some groups such as Gay Liberation, hippies and druggies have always been an embarrassment to the organized left, who have yet to decide whether to disown them or to co-opt them.)

A problem less clearly recognized by outsiders—because it depends on an extremely orthodox adherence indeed to the doctrine—is that even the likeliest candidates for co-option can be refused support on the grounds that this would be counter revolutionary. The argument is that the working class are not yet equipped to lead a radical movement and although they should be given guidance, simply 'organizing people around poverty, although effective in terms of improving the material existence of the poor, is generally not in the interests of the total working class' (Hague, 1973). Working with tenants and claimants (and one shudders to think what this orthodoxy makes of the freaks, the lonely, the misfits), so the line goes, is alienated from the needs of the genuine working class. Are there *any* genuine community organizations which can be co-opted into the struggle? Yes, those which have 'a solid theoretical framework, an on-going socialist analysis and an in-depth understanding of the working class situation'

(Hague, 1973). Otherwise, and it is worth quoting the catechism at length:

Issues concerning consumer community services are essentially peripheral to the basic contradictions in capitalist society, to the class struggle between the working and ruling classes. Organizing around such issues is therefore very much secondary to organizing around productive relations in the work place and can be misleading and diversionary, siphoning off radical energy and obscuring the real nature of capitalism. . . . On a simple level, community action aims to improve the material condition of the working class and hence tends to blunt the basic contradictions in our society. Its value as a revolutionary tool is therefore doubtful to say the least. (Hague, 1973, 7)

This is not the place to discuss this particular view of society. All I am concerned to show is that it has some very peculiar implications indeed for social-work practice. These implications differ depending on whether one is dealing with this orthodox view, which virtually negates all social work, or with the revisionist view (clearly the one influenced by the new deviancy theory) which is selective about which clients or organizations to co-opt. In either case—and I use this extreme judgement with great reluctance—the social.worker is asked to develop an *exploitative* relationship towards his clients. Their problems are not interesting in themselves, but as signs of something else, such as the crisis in the system: the solutions are not important in themselves unless they help something else, that is, the working-class struggle.

In a highly schematic way, which is not meant to depict any one individual's position that I know of, but to distil the message that might be received by a social-work audience, let me summarize the problems so far before considering briefly a more positive strategy. A social worker is involved in running an imaginative adventure playground in a deprived working-class area. What do our models tell him?

1 *Weak deviancy theory/non-interventionism*
   Be careful of possible stigmatizing and stereotyping.

2 *Strong deviancy theory/non-interventionism*
   Perhaps you shouldn't be doing this at all: there is no hard evidence that adventure playgrounds decrease delinquency rates.

3 *Revisionist Marxism/revolutionary social work*
   Politicize the kids: they are your allies in the struggle.

4 *Orthodox Marxism/revolutionary social work*
   Perhaps you shouldn't be doing this at all: it simply prevents the kids and their parents from realizing how the system exploits them.

'The unfinished'

The least that one can say for the first as opposed to the other three solutions, is that it doesn't ignore the present problem and that it doesn't prematurely close the debate. What it of course does lack, compared with the other three, is a clear positive strategy and not just a set of recommendations about what to avoid. It should be apparent that the strategy I want to suggest is one which does not (like authoritarian Marxism) make people expendable and which does not write off all short-scale intervention. The long versus short-term issue is critical, because to support (as I did at the outset), the radical view of exploitation, power and inequality should not carry the prescription of abandoning all else. A possible way out of this impasse has been suggested by the Norwegian sociologist Thomas Mathiesen (1974), and I want to take his account of his involvement with the prisoners' union there and its fight against the prison system, as a paradigm for change in some other parts of the welfare and control system.

'The unfinished' is a programme based on what does not yet exist. From the beginning Mathiesen is quite clear about the dangers of going for short-term goals only: taking up reformist positions in the system—as a humane prison governor, an advocate of inmate councils—cannot but lead to absorption and an abandonment of the long-range goals of changing the system totally. As every social worker well knows, absorption eventually takes place through all sorts of subtle ways of incorporation, initiation into the agency's secrets, compromising for too long. On the other hand there are some very effective short-term possibilities, not just through humanitarian work but in conscious policies of raiding the establishment for resources, contributing to its crises, unmasking and embarrassing its ideologies and pretensions. Any such effectiveness can be lost by finishing. One must be able to live with ambiguity and refuse to accept what the *others*, the authorities, demand—a choice between revolution and reform.

It was correct, Mathiesen suggests, for the Norwegian prison union, KROM, after a long struggle about going to either extreme, to have kept open the relation between revolution and reform. To make this choice is really 'the choice between being "defined out" as irrelevant and "defined in" as undangerous' (1974, 23). Only an authoritarian political programme cannot tolerate this ambiguity and is constantly looking (like the revolutionary social-work movement here) for clarity about 'the way ahead'. The point is to remain open and capable of growth, to see some ambiguities as irrelevant, never to let oneself be placed. KROM realized that to be revolutionary was to lose the power of competition, but that to be exclusively reformist it would lose its character of contradicting the establishment. In either case, it would be neutralized. The old system is not threatened by a counter-organization that becomes incorporated, but it is threatened by counter-organizing. As long as one is in transition, there are no normative expectations to define your behaviour: 'The adversary does not know where you are heading. The only thing that he knows is that you are heading somewhere, because you are organizing. At this moment, the power of the system is threatened, because you are yourself neither powerless nor fully incorporated in a fully developed positive contributing relationship.' (1974, 199.)

If someone defines himself as revolutionary it becomes illicit to adopt near-at-hand pressing changes (as we saw in the Case Con line) and this must separate him from those he wants to work for. If he defines himself as reformist, the danger is that anything really radical is seen as inadmissible, wild, irresponsible. The choice is not to let yourself be forced to make the choice—let the clients take as their points of departure reforms which are closest to them and will change their lives now. Only then can one move on to wider political questions when the group become dissatisfied. This is not a simple plea for humanitarian work, for although Mathiesen is aware that there are greater pulls in this direction because results are more visible, this can lead to politically unsound short-term choices and to expedient changes which leave the overall structure intact. There are clear and well-documented examples of this in the prison reform area, where short-term humanizing reforms, particularly those which accepted the rhetoric of rehabilitation and the help of psychiatrists, have arguably led to changes which have made the system even more repressive (Cohen, 1974).

Mathiesen sustains the idea of 'the unfinished' throughout a complex analysis of how one may change the system and organize from below. To avoid working for short-term goals is politically impossible and paralyses action, but reform alone will corrupt long-term work; to work within the system is to risk legitimating it, but to stay out would be wrong: 'we did not wish to sacrifice the short-term interests of the prisoners on the altar of general system abolition.' (Mathiesen, 1974, 115.)

There is one other strand in his argument that provides a guide to *which* reforms to work for: this is the notion of the politics of abolition. One must always work at what is close at hand and always in the direction of abolition. Concentrate first on abolishing whatever gives legitimacy to a system one regards as wrong, whatever masks it uses to disguise its true nature. Again 'the unfinished' applies: abolition cannot wait until the alternatives are established. Mathiesen uses the examples of the campaign to get rid of the Norwegian Vagrancy Act. An example I would cite from my own work is the attempt to abolish the forcible use of psychotropic drugs in prisons. When the establishment demands 'alternatives' before contemplating any changes, they know in advance that they can already lay down the framework for the discussion. The conservative aims remain taken for granted—in the one case to get rid of vagrants, in the other to control prisoners' behaviour—and only the means are debated. The demand for alternatives, then, has a conserving effect. Real opposition-values because of their nature must be long-term and uncertain. So when the opponent is presented with the choice of specifying alternatives he finds it difficult to avoid coming close to the prevailing order in what he suggests (reform) or emphasizing completely different values and thereby being defined away as irresponsible or unrealistic. The answer is to always go for abolition and actually to resist the pressure to make positive refoms.

I've suggested this as a paradigm for social-work action. This is not to say it will fit every case, but it seems to me that the notion of 'the unfinished' is the most appropriate one for radical social workers to adopt in welfare-state or social-democratic systems. It has the critical advantage of not exploiting or selling out one's clients. As a footnote to Mathiesen's strategy, I would also commend the notion of 'the unfinished' as relevant to the image we transmit of our 'subjects'. Clients and deviants should not be too easily placed on such continua as 'sick' and 'normal', 'militant' or 'passive'. The new deviancy theory has, quite rightly, been systematically hacking away at the positivist picture of the deviant as pathologically constrained by forces beyond his control. And the treatment ideology which follows from this is correctly seen as the most insidious enemy to radical social change. But alternative images of the deviant—either in the feeble version of the unconstrained delinquent in Schur's 'neo-antideterminism' or the excessively romantic version in the new-criminology-hip-Marxist-radical-social-work version of the rebel against the system—are beyond credibility. I believe that they must discredit in advance any radical policy.

Here, cryptically, would be some of my suggestions for a radical social work programme:

1   Tell those sociologists who urge you to be theoretically more sophisticated to get off your backs. (They are the same sociologists who want to turn their own subject into matters of epistemology and philosophy.)

2   Refuse the ideology of casework, but always think of cases: your constituency is not just claimants' unions, tenants' associations, but also

mothers of autisitic children, suicidal housewives in council tower blocks, derelict old vagrants. . . . You don't have to be sentimental about these people but neither should you write them off.

3   Take the insights of deviancy theory—however low level they may sound to your superior academic sages—seriously. Think very concretely about how to avoid stigmatizing your clients, unwittingly facilitating their drift into further troubles, trapping them in cycles of rejection.

4   Stay in your agency or organization, but don't let it seduce you. Take every opportunity to unmask its pretensions and euphemisms, use its resources in a defensive way for your clients, work for abolition.

5   In practice and in theory, stay 'unfinished'. Don't be ashamed of working for short-term humanitarian or libertarian goals, but always keep in mind the long-term political prospects. This might mean living with the uncomfortable ambiguity that your most radical work will be outside your day-to-day job.

6   Most important: don't sell out your clients' interests for the sake of ideological purity or theoretical neatness.

And keep telling sociologists and political theorists 'it's all right for you to talk.'

6
Homosexuality: Sexual Needs and Social Problems

Don Milligan

There is no doubt that the people who are distressed or in trouble because they are homosexual need help. But what kind of help and who should provide it? The help provided by Gay Liberation and the Campaign for Homosexual Equality is not enough. Both individual and group counsellors must value homosexual erotic experience, and understand what it feels like to be gay. They must proceed from a felt rejection of the ideas of heterosexual superiority that permeate our culture.

People become aware of their homosexuality at different times. Some during childhood or adolescence and others not until they are adult. However, individual awareness of homosexuality and personal acknowledgement that you are homosexual are distinct experiences. Awareness of homosexual desires and fantasies, even of actual homosexual behaviour during childhood or adolescence, is often not sufficient to evince a personal understanding that you are homosexual. Generally it has to be spoken about to a close friend—a confidant—or written about in letters or a diary. This 'confession' is often very difficult and always confusing. But it is crucial because the awareness that one feels with all its physical urgency and emotional longing has to cease being cerebral. It has to break out of your private thoughts and seek some response in the world outside your head.

Once this awareness of insubstantial sensations, of vague fantasies and of theoretic significance of people of your own sex is talked about or written about it is transformed into a selfconscious knowledge that you are homosexual. But this does not necessarily mean acceptance of one's gayness. The contempt, disgust and hostility meted out to lesbians and 'poufs' cannot escape anyone's notice, least of all those who experience intense homosexual feelings. For many the time when homosexuality is acknowledged is the time when psychiatric treatment is applied for, family doctors are consulted and desperate marriages are contracted. A time of nervous breakdowns, overdoses and terror, or simply of numbness.

Heterosexuality is the result of a 'healthy' childhood: it is 'natural'. It is with this belief, finely taught and deeply ingrained, that homosexuals discover the implications of their emotional attachments and sexual longings. They discover their sexuality alone and unsupported by any positive social assumptions. This isolation frequently robs homosexual people of their self-esteem and confidence, rendering them vulnerable to the idea that their sexuality is sick and degraded.

Most people grow up sharing the basic sexual assumptions of their relatives and friends. It is assumed that they find, and will continue to find, members of the opposite sex physically attractive. The behaviour appropriate for the male and female gender is learned very early indeed and it is understood that gender must correspond with the appropriate genitals. Girls in the fourth form know the penalties of being suspected of being a 'les' as much as little boys fear the label 'sissy'. All homosexuals are brought up as heterosexuals in a heterosexual world. The 'rightness' of heterosexuality is confirmed in every classroom, game, street, park, pub, cinema, dance hall, daily paper, and on every juke-box, radio, television and advertising poster.

Homosexuality is quite simply the desire and ability to relate sexually and emotionally to members of your own sex. But heterosexual domination ensures that it is seen as an incapacity to form what are called normal sexual relationships. 'Normal' sexual activity must involve intercourse and 'the essential criterion of normal intercourse is that it is one that tends to fertilize the women' (Allen, 1962). Wilhelm Reich (1931) argued that 'it can be established that sexual satisfaction for a healthy heterosexual is more intense than sexual satisfaction for a homosexual.' One wonders how he found out! The desire to deny the value of forms of sexuality other than heterosexual ones is urgent and insistent. Arthur Janov (1972, 322) echoes Reich's patronizing sympathy: 'The homosexual act is not a sexual one. It is based on the denial of real sexuality and the acting out symbolically through sex of a need for love.' However absurd such formulations appear, they are the intellectual expression of ideas thoroughly taught and commonly held by heterosexual people throughout our society. Matey psychologists at conferences, honest jazz musicians and arts writers for the *Guardian* who shrink from calling a 'spade a nigger' are never so coy about 'queers'. What passes for the intelligentsia in Great Britain simply articulates the prejudices of working people without their honesty.

So, the sexuality of gay people is denied in many ways. And the spurious sympathy of concerned thinking-people is the most disarming and insidious form of denial. Gay sexuality is seen as inferior and masturbatory. It is a substitute for real sex: 'a grown-up must not masturbate because it is, or should be, in his power to do the real thing' (Schwartz, 1949, 32). The term 'wanker' is commonly used as an insult to indicate complete contempt. To be a 'wanker' is to be ineffectual and unproductive. It is obvious that because it is theoretically possible for us all to do the real thing—by engaging in heterosexual coitus—that persistent mutual masturbation between people of the same sex must be pathological: 'Pathological masturbants usually link this act with fantasies that are not realizable in normal intercourse, and are mostly people with a sadistic or masochistic disposition or perverts of another kind.' (Hurschfield, no date, 127.) Gay people are, of course, all 'pathological masturbants'.

As gay people stumble from awareness of the erotic attraction of their own sex towards selfconscious understanding that they are homosexual, the first painful confrontation with anti-gay values is experienced. By the time that most gay people know that they are homosexual they have already internalized heterosexual values. Many believe that they are inadequate or obscene. The spirited defence of a gay boy to reactions of passengers on a Bradford bus makes it clear! 'Don't worry, dear! It could happen to the best of us!' Full of camp irony and courage he defended himself with his own sense of affliction. Fighting back with blunt weapons.

The internalization by gay people of the belief in heterosexual superiority forms the roots of self-oppression. Heterosexuality is 'normal'. It is not simply the most common form of sexual expression, it is dominant; and society admits no legitimate alternatives. Moreover, heterosexuality is essential for marriage. And marriage is the passport to children, legal recognition, social approval and consequently to self-respect. It is also important because it is believed that the penalty for remaining unmarried is loneliness. The best response to these feelings has been given in *With Downcast Gays* (Hodges and Hutter, 1974):

It is a basic mistake to accept heterosexual conventions as God-given criteria by which gay people may be judged. Instead we should use the insights that we have gained as homosexuals to criticize a sexist and hypocritical society. An example of the failure to do this can be seen when the fact that gay couples are childless is pleaded as an excuse for their relationships ending; and our spokesmen fail to point out that, if married couples stay together only for what they imagine to be the benefit of their children, they are not models of permanence but of thwarted impermanence. Instead of comparing our freedom unfavourably with such unions, homosexuals should feel pity for heterosexuals who find themselves trapped in an unhappy marriage and rejoice in the liberty their own homosexuality bestows. (pp. 7–8.)

Apparently marriage is biologically natural, emotionally fulfilling and socially mature. Isolated homosexuals are as vulnerable as most heterosexual people to the apparent advantages and securities offered by marriage.

Heterosexuality is not only considered natural; in its monogamous form it is the hallmark of maturity: 'the sexual association in its mature and perfect form, which is marriage, is meant to be enduring.' This is the key to the sense of loss and deprivation cultivated in most homosexual people. The heterosexual act is not valued simply because of its supposed superiority—it is the social dimensions of heterosexuality that are valued. But homosexual people can have alternative values—alternatives that the counsellor must present to the so-called 'client':

Gay people have no reason to envy the institutionalized sexuality available to heterosexuals, cluttered as it is with ceremonies of courtship and marriage and further poisoned by a division of roles which condemns the man to dominate and the woman to submit. A heterosexual pick-up is fraught with implications of the man conquering and the woman surrendering; it is unlikely to enjoy the sense of mutual agreement enjoyed by gay people. For this reason it is easier for homosexuals to make sexual contacts, and once made there is no tedious process of persuasion—no ritualized escalation of intimacy to be carried out before sexual pleasure is reached.   (Hodges and Hutter. 1974, 8.)

Because the sexuality of gay people is dismissed as, at best, a perversion and, at worst, as a sign of inadequacy, homosexuality is not supported by any positive cultural expression and has no institutional protection. The response of many gay people to this negation of their sexuality and the denial of its social expression is to marry, while many more remain hopelessly unmarried. Family life is difficult enough for heterosexuals, but for gay people it is impossible without major concessions to heterosexual norms, which in turn intensify the contradictions.

Most homosexual people are living with their husbands or wives, or their parents, or quietly alone with little social contact with other gay people. Only a minority of gay people live a more or less openly gay life in the conventional gay social ghetto or on its political periphery. This means that counselling will inevitably be concerned with helping people trapped in a web of heterosexual social relationships which are probably far from supportive. In order to be of any assistance a counsellor must be aware that the feelings of social inadequacy, and the sense of their own obscurity are the most important obstacles to overcome for gay people seeking help.

While desperately wanting homosexual friends and lovers, gay people who come to see a counsellor often have a real desire to dissociate themselves from other homosexuals. The stereotypes of 'queers' held in society as butch lesbians, screaming queens and effeminate pansies revolt many isolated gay people. This revulsion disarms them and leads them to ape heterosexual norms of behaviour in a desperate attempt to appear 'straight'. However, the point about most stereotypes is that they are true. Many gay people who live more or less openly are 'butch' lesbians, screaming 'queens' and effeminate 'pansies'. The scene of revulsion felt by the isolated homosexual must be transformed into a sense of pride. Because prevailing concepts of dignity are heterosexual, anyone who steps outside these patterns of behaviour is inevitably thought of as absurd and contemptible: 'Occasionally one comes across a . . . boy who wants to be a girl and, if this desire is strong enough, adopts a female mentality which may lead to all sorts of absurdities in later life, such as homosexuality, dressing as a woman, or even the wish to be transformed into a woman by means of operations.' (Schwarz, 1949, 48–9.) One's behaviour must correspond with the behaviour appropriate to the gender divisions of the society. If your genitals are female you have no choice; your gender is automatically ascribed—you must be feminine. A gay woman whatever her mannerism or social behaviour breaks the cardinal rule of femininity—she does not desire to be sexually subordinate to a man. Similarly the heterosexual Women's Liberationist who may be severe and bitter will be dismissed by most men as 'in need of a good poke'.

Gay people whose mannerisms are stereotyped are implicitly rejecting the ascription of gender roles and asserting their right to be feminine or masculine irrespective of their genitals. Their 'crime' is simply that they reject heterosexual stereotypes. They are homosexual and they are not afraid to acknowledge their gayness—they flaunt their sexuality. In this, openly gay people are very similar to heterosexuals who flaunt their sexuality all the time. But ostentatious weddings, walking hand in hand, and the myriad other affirmations of heterosexuality are not thought of as 'flaunting' sexuality. These manifestations of heterosexuality are part of the normal life of 'normal' people. While virtually everybody knows the meaning of the word *homosexuality*, many 'normal' people simply do not know what the word *heterosexual* means. Why should they? They have no need to use clinical terms for themselves—they are just people. Heterosexual people can be amused, disturbed or annoyed by openly gay behaviour. But that really is their problem. Stereotyped or not, gay people have a need and a right to live openly and a counsellor who does not understand this can be of no assistance to a closeted or isolated homosexual.

It has been said (Righton, 1973, 21) that 'full integration of the homosexual into society is, of course, the end towards which to work.' But however well meant, this object can only weaken gay people. Integration, whatever is literally meant by it, in practice always means cultural submission of the minority to the majority. For ethnic minorities integration means assimilation. It means the destruction of their culture. That's what all ethnic groups in Great Britain, irrespective of colour, resist so tenaciously. If you want to be integrated you must seek approval from the majority. At present that means being 'English'. It also means being heterosexual. And if you are not heterosexual you must pass for one, because you must not offend the sensibilities of heterosexual society by flaunting your gayness. Lord Arran (quoted in Hyde, 1972, 303) welcoming the passage of the Sexual Offences Act in 1967 made the position clear when he both threatened and asked

those who have, as it were, been in bondage and for whom the prison doors are now open to show their thanks by comporting themselves quietly with dignity. This is no occasion for jubilation; certainly not for celebration. Any form of public flaunting, would be utterly distasteful and would, I believe, make the sponsors of the Bill regret that they have done what they have done.

The internalization by openly gay people of particular forms of behaviour is both an assertion and a defence of their homosexuality. Stereotyped behaviour in the gay community says simply, 'I don't give a damn what you think of me—I am what I am!' By whistling in the dark people narrow their fear and broaden their courage. Isolated homosexual people hate stereotyped and camp behaviour mainly because they fear public acknowledgement of homosexuality. They identify with heterosexual values and heterosexual stereotypes. By chopping their lives up in bits they seek approval from straight society saying—what I want to do in bed has nothing to do with the rest of my life or my general social interaction. This attitude merely points up the contradictions and makes things worse.

Of course, there are apparently good reasons for concealment. One's children might be taken into care or access denied because one is 'morally unfit'. Jobs and flats are also put in jeopardy if it is known that one is homosexual. But the security offered by concealment is vulnerable to discovery at any time, while the inevitable lies and furtiveness strengthen the suspicion that perhaps, after all, there really is something rather nasty about homosexuality. The security achieved by concealment is more than an illusion, it undermines confidence in one's sexuality and erodes pride and self-respect. Concealment cripples many gay people's lives both socially and sexually: it also makes participation in any struggle to defend and improve our situation impossible. Concealment intensifies loneliness and isolation and keeps us in our place—which for gay women is nowhere—and for men is the cottage (public lavatory) and the comedy show.

Coming out and living openly in a limited sense within the gay community or in a slightly wider sense within radical gay organizations is difficult. The gay community is not a true community. Composed simply of bars and clubs, the gay scene is a social ghetto with specific limitations. It is not residentially concentrated and it has no class, racial, occupational or sexual homogeneity. The position of lesbians is tenuous within the clubs and bars. Gay women experience the same problems as their heterosexual sisters because it is very difficult for women to go into pubs, dance halls or clubs alone. A woman as a rule cannot just drop into a bar. She is much more likely to go with her 'affair' or with a group of friends. Consequently lesbians find it harder to develop informal and casual social relationships in gay bars which are used largely by men. The gay community in many areas is cleaved in two and women are very restricted in all their social options, having to maintain a network of supportive relationships and contacts in a more personal and private manner. As a result the social life of gay women is inaccessible to the isolated lesbian, and loneliness and the sense of being cut-off is more difficult for women to overcome.

However, criticisms of the gay ghetto, of social relations within it, and of camp and stereotyped behaviour are not very relevant when they come from heterosexuals and isolated gays. The social ghetto inhabited by many gay people has severe limitations, but it exists because homosexuals who have to deal with a hostile society need it. The implications of camp humour and stereotyped behaviour cannot be the concern of heterosexual social workers nor can social relations within the gay community. Only gay people and their social and political organizations can identify the problems or begin to tackle them. Social workers and counsellors who are concerned to criticize the forms of behaviour adopted by gay people only strengthen the 'value' of heterosexual stereotypes and impair the confidence of the isolated homosexual who comes to them for help.

It is true that social relations in gay bars and clubs—shellacked with sentiment—are often competitive and brittle. However, the gay ghetto is supportive to quite a large minority of gay men and to not a few women. The world of gay bars and clubs must not be romanticized; neither should it be attacked from the outside because to many isolated gay people it offers the only available chance of sex, support and friendship. The object of counselling is to render individuals capable of living, loving and working in a hostile environment. This objective can only be achieved by helping gay people in isolation overcome their fear and hatred of their openly homosexual sisters and brothers.

The context in which people are aware and become conscious of their gayness, the denial of their sexuality and its social expression, and the contradiction between their heterosexual values and homosexual desires, creates many specific problems. These problems have no easy solutions. Isolated gay people cannot simply be directed to the nearest gay bar. People do not learn to swim by being thrown in at the deep end. If you're not careful they drown. Glib solutions are useless because the aim of counselling and other supportive work is of course to increase confidence and self-respect, while the presentation of alternative courses of action which are all extremely difficult as being 'a piece of cake' always makes things worse.

Of course a counsellor must never tell a person outright what to do, but the idea of almost neutral so-called 'client-centred' counselling is equally dangerous. This arises most critically with gay people who desire to be 'cured' of homosexuality. Homosexuality is not a disease, illness or behavioural disorder; all that the available forms of 'treatment' achieve is great confusion—a confusion which often befuddles and sometimes destroys an individual's sexuality rendering them incapable of forming sexual relationships of any kind. A person who wants to be 'cured' must be dissuaded by a presentation of these facts.

The Family Doctor pamphlet *Homosexuality* (Kenyon, 1973) published by the British Medical Association is a good example of the insidious propaganda both counsellors and isolated gay people need to guard against. It starts off well:

Public attitudes are more enlightened these days and homosexuality has come to be accepted as a 'variation from normal' rather than something abnormal, to be sneered at or condemned. And yet there is still a lot of prejudice, misunderstanding and even fear surrounding the subject. This booklet, which is factual and non-moralizing, is intended to disperse the many false impressions and put the subject into proper perspective. (p. 2.)

Apart from word-games like 'variation from the normal' one could reasonably suppose that it would reject anti-gay ideas. In fact the superficial impression created by the pamphlet led a number of Campaign for Homosexual Equality groups to recommend and distribute it.

The pamphlet is fairly representative of the attitudes of 'enlightened' social workers, doctors and psychiatrists. For this reason it is not non-moralizing, factual or intended to disperse false impressions. Its object is to allay the fears of heterosexuals, while its effect is to disarm and demoralize homosexual people. For example: 'The more aggressive type (of lesbian) may seek direct competition with males and go for the managerial executive-type jobs.' But don't worry, 'not all "bossy" managing types of women are lesbians, nor are all Scout Leaders and such-like homosexuals. It is easy to blacken and denigrate any movement which seems a potential threat to the established order by insinuating sexual deviancy.' (Kenyon, 1973, 14.) Well, if nothing else, it comes as a relief to know that the Boy Scouts are not going to threaten the established order!

The author of the pamphlet, F. E. Kenyon, treats us to three personal stories. The first concerns Ann (aged 18) who 'thought she was turning into a lesbian. She had read an article about lesbianism in a woman's magazine when she was sixteen.' She 'fancied herself falling in love with a well-known female singer who often appeared on TV.' But Ann 'was a late developer.' And, 'her mother was in her late forties and herself a very anxious and emotional person, particularly since the death of her first husband.' Kenyon saw Ann on six visits, 'during this period she was treated with a minor tranquillizer and reassurance. She was encouraged to pay attention to her diet, and was given treatment for her facial acne and hair on her face.' This story ended 'happily' because apparently Ann 'realized that her attraction to the female pop star was not really a sexual one but at the time she stood for all the things that she most envied—i.e. good looks, sophistication, popularity. She fully accepted, too, that she was a normal girl and that she had been temporarily overwhelmed by a rather late but rapid adolescent phase.' (pp. 16–17.)

Lesley (aged 27) married with two children. 'Lesley had been following her (female doctor) about, came with obviously trumped-up symptoms, culminating in a terrible scene in the surgery when Lesley put her arms around her (doctor) and said she loved her.' Kenyon gathered that this 'terrible' behaviour resulted from depression that 'had come on shortly after the birth of her last child, and then made worse by her father's death.' Lesley had had a couple of homosexual relationships in the army but she was 'accepted for out-patient treatment and had twenty-five one-hour psychotherapy sessions spread over two years, as well as three months' treatment with anti-depressant drugs. She made very good progress, lost all her lesbian inclinations, and coped with her mother much better. Gradually her relationship with her husband improved, she began to enjoy sexual intercourse, and all round became a much happier wife and mother.' (p. 17.)

The last of the three cases cited concerns Barry (aged 25), a postgraduate student. 'The main aim of treatment here was to help Barry to come to terms with his homosexuality. As a start, and because of his religious background, he was advised to read Norman Pittenger's book *Time for consent: a christian's approach to homosexuality*. At the same time, the medical aspects were discussed with him. He rapidly became less depressed, began to regain his self-esteem and felt less like a freak.' Barry 'faced up to his parents' not, however, by saying he was gay but 'by saying that he preferred to remain a bachelor for the foreseeable future.' After six sessions Barry was relaxed and happy. 'He had met another student for whom he felt "a great natural affinity" . . . they had now decided to share a flat and at last Barry could accept himself as a perfectly ordinary, well-integrated member of society.' (pp. 18–19.)

These three cases are very instructive. This doctor and his 'treatment' worked on a set of entirely negative assumptions about homosexuality. Ann was immature, had acne, facial hair and an anxious mum. She also had a crush on a woman TV star whom she envied. Her sexuality was presented to her as immature and her love was disposed of as envy. Lesley suffered from post-natal depression, the death of her father, an unloving mum and the bad influence of some gay women when she was in the army. Barry had a sheltered up-bringing, was shy with women, had a possessive mum and a 'fussy, strict, unemotional' dad. What is more his younger sister 'could never keep a boyfriend for long as she was a rather moody, unsociable sort of a person and not particularly attractive as she was painfully thin.' Barry's sister was obviously not a social success while he 'reacted poorly to the rough and tumble (of school).' And 'hated all forms of games and sport' (p. 18).

People such as Kenyon have to ask why individuals are gay because they see homosexuality as a behavioural disorder. They never once question what causes heterosexuality and the inability of the majority of people to form homosexual relationships. This is because they don't believe that homosexuality is a rewarding form of sexual expression. At best gayness is seen as a temporary lapse from grace and at worst as something that can be concealed from the world as a 'great natural affinity' with a member of your own sex—plus a desire to stay single.

Frightened and bewildered homosexuals do commonly go to see their family doctor and a minority are referred for psychiatric treatment. Invariably they will be harmed not helped. They will be injured by actual physical ill-treatment masquerading as a 'cure'—aversion therapy—or simply by verbal and authoritative confirmation of ideas of inadequacy learned throughout childhood and adolescence. The defence offered by doctors, psychologists and psychiatrists that homosexuals have to be 'treated' because they ask for it is in reality no defence. When lonely, devout, heterosexual Methodists go to the doctor because they're afflicted with sexual fantasies and generalized randyness it does not enter the doctor's head to prescribe repressive therapy. They are reassured and encouraged to participate in social activities that will objectively increase their sexual opportunities. Lonely gay people need similar advice.

Counsellors must aim to replace doctors. And doctors must learn to refer distressed homosexuals to counselling and befriending agencies. Most doctors are hopelessly ignorant about homosexuality and the problems confronting gay people. There is no reason why somebody with a medical training should be considered qualified to counsel people on any social problem, particularly one which results from oppression which the medical profession is actively involved in perpetuating. Even on the odd occasion that a doctor has a positive approach to gayness, she or he is still the person that you go to see when you are sick. It is this continual association between sickness and homosexuality that does the most harm.

Most general practitioners if they are not openly hostile, will assume an attitude of breezy acceptance or indifference towards the patients' distress—assuring them that they have nothing much to worry about. 'It's just like having one leg really; nothing to be ashamed of!' Dr James Hemming (1974) has perhaps a more typical and more sympathetic approach:

There are about the same number of colour-blind people as there are homosexuals. Well, you shouldn't really feel guilty, or ashamed or put-down because you're colour-blind, you just happen to be colour-blind. Well, if you're homosexual you really needn't feel any more deviant than a colour-blind person.

Such reassurance does not take positive form. Its assumption is that to be gay is to be disabled. Hemming also thinks that heterosexual marriage is perfectly suitable for gay people, as long as they 'talk it through' with their fiancées before marriage and 'don't expect it (homosexuality) to clear up because you get married.' Quite apart from his implicit repressiveness Hemming's rather bland irresponsibility is astonishing. People who are not only aware of homosexual feelings but know that homosexuality is an important if not exclusive aspect of their sexuality should not get married under any circumstances.

Pat Sullivan of *Friend*, a counselling organization, talks about the consequences (1974): 'I know from personal experience—people I've met—where the women got married at 17, have had two or three kids and their life is absolute hell. And there's just no escape from it except, in a lot of cases, suicide. But even then they've got pressures not to commit suicide because of the kids. If she's got a girl-friend already who's prepared to live with her, OK. If she hasn't she's got nothing to go to. So she tells herself she's got to stick with it. Financially she's not secure. And there's really nothing she can do. She's either got to decide to stay with the family or go off and be

[1] Private letter, received February, 1973.

by herself. Even if she has got somebody to go with very often the man will want the child. She doesn't want to leave the child.'

Pat Sullivan goes on to talk about a particular case of a woman who wanted to leave her husband and go to live with her girlfriend in Liverpool. 'But she couldn't take the kids with her, because they couldn't afford to look after the kids. And she didn't want to lose the kids. What could she do? She was stuck. She had to stay with her husband and the kids. There was no other way out for her. Also in a lot of divorce cases if they find out the correspondent's a woman—you know with the wife—the judge is quite likely to give custody of the children to the man.'

This is the real situation for gay people who are married. The situation for men is better than for women. Men are likely to be financially better off—even paying maintenance. But the social, legal and emotional pressures against breaking up a family are still enormous. Alternatively if a gay man stays with his heterosexual wife her oppression will merely be intensified by his. While her husband cruises cottages, parks and bars in search of sexual satisfaction, her chances of being left in front of the telly, baby-sitting night in and night out are greatly increased. In this situation a full sexual relationship is impossible for him. Either way the woman remains sexually unfulfilled and trapped.

The question of bisexuality in this situation does not seriously arise. If somebody is sufficiently concerned about their homosexuality to find their way in front of a doctor or a counsellor then the problems they have are the same as those who see themselves as homosexual. Bisexuality is often a defensive description used by people who are afraid of the label homosexual. However, bisexual people who are married are simply people whose 'infidelity' is complicated by the fact that their lover is of the same sex. If they accept their bisexuality a conventional marriage cannot be a rational arrangement, but merely an insurance against the insecurities of being single and a defence against being thought of as 'queer'. For both the bisexual and the homosexual marriage is a glaringly stupid and oppressive social arrangement. However, as long as homosexuality is despised and penalized, many homosexuals and bisexuals will contract marriages with all the confusion and much misery sewn in. Faced with married gay people, particularly those with children, a counsellor can do little but draw out the inconsistencies and contradictions of the individual's situation and present the person with possible alternatives. One thing is unavoidable—somebody, and often everybody, will get hurt whether the marriage is stuck together or pulled apart.

Once a gay person is married and has children the problems become truly intractable. This is why the positive counselling of adolescent and young gay people is so important. It is often thought that girls of 16 and 17 cannot be sure they are really homosexual. They can't know their own mind. This may be so. By the same token they can't be sure they are heterosexual either. If a young person is worried about their homosexual feelings it is irresponsible and cruel to argue them into 'feeling' heterosexual. On the contrary the rightness of their sexual feelings needs to be confirmed and supported. Too often the response young people receive is like this:

Dear Jim,

I know what you are doing is *not right*. You are a man in every sense of the word and fully developed in that way. The first thing I did was to get some books on the subject and there is plenty of medical treatment available with hormones and hypnosis etc. I know that at the moment you don't want to know, but I hope before it gets too great a hold on you, you will. I read that it mostly stems from a bad experience with a girl in early puberty and when that is overcome in the mind everything comes right. It broke my heart to see you looking so obviously what you say you are which hasn't been apparent before. I hope and pray you will find strength to remove yourself from the influence of this person and come home and we will find the absolute best man in London to help you no matter what it costs. It is obvious that those that practice this are going to persuade you that there is nothing shameful or wrong in this and I hope you are not too weak to realize this. Some people are not developed and have a make-up that can't help it but I am convinced it is not so with you.

William is coming home for the weekend with a girl friend. He phoned me this morning. Please think about this letter and write soon.

Your loving
Mother[2]

Fortunately 'Jim' was just 21. He did not go home—he joined the Gay Liberation Front instead. But many young homosexuals faced with such a response seek help only to be told by doctors and even counsellors[3] that they are probably not really homosexual. It is not the business of the counsellor to question the authenticity of a person's homosexuality—however young they are. The legal problems of men under 21 are considerable and a counsellor needs to warn sympathetically individuals of this, and to help them feel confident enough to meet other homosexual men in social situations. With the advice and companionship of other gay people the boy

[2] Private letter, dated 5 April, 1974, received in May, 1974.

[3] An instance of this occurred at the Bradford CHE Symposium, 9 March, 1974. A discussion workshop report suggested that, in most cases, young people who come for counselling should be encouraged to attempt heterosexual relationships.

will hopefully explore his sexuality. The legal problems are obvious, and inevitably involve the counsellor in taking sides. If the counsellor is to be supportive and encouraging the law must be condemned and evaded.

The attitude of the counsellor to the law is particularly important. The Sexual Offences Act (1967) is essential reading. It legalized homosexual acts between two men who are willing and over 21. The law does not apply to members of the Armed Forces or to relationships between crew members aboard British merchant ships throughout the world. Nor does it apply to anybody in Scotland and occupied Ireland where homosexual relations between men remain entirely illegal. In 1971 Lord Reid ruled that there is 'a material difference between merely exempting certain conduct from criminal penalties and making it lawful in the full sense.'[4] In other words, two homosexual men over 21 may have sexual relations in private without fear of penalty, but it is not fully lawful. There is no legal way in which gay men can get into bed with each other, because this usually involves a suggestion or a request that can only be defined as 'importuning'.

Many gay men do spend their time looking for sexual contacts by 'cottaging' in public lavatories or strolling the parks. These activities are illegal, but social workers and counsellors will not assist anybody by condemning them. Cottaging is practised and enjoyed because of the social situation of gay men. The reasons for cottaging are complex and cannot be explained away as the result of people 'having nowehere else to go'. Sexual contact in a public lavatory enables gay men to have sex that is exciting and erotic without emotional entanglements. The risks are calculated and often thought worth it. Cottaging is strengthened by the difficulties experienced by a gay man having social as well as sexual relations with another man.

A social as well as an erotic relationship between two men inevitably involves being seen in the pub and at the cinema together. It means being seen in cafés or restaurants and perhaps going on holiday together. A social relationship between two men who are lovers involves risks far greater than being caught cottaging. Cottaging presents less of a threat to your marriage, your job, or your painfully constructed emotional independence. The moralizing of people who condemn cottaging does more harm than good. Gay men who cottage are victims not villains and deserve our solidarity against police harassment and intimidation. There is no way that people who believe in obeying the Sexual Offences Act or the relevant parts of Common Law can help gay men.

The relationship between the specific oppression of homosexual people and major social and legal institutions in our society gives homosexual

[4] See *Gay News* 2.

counselling a political significance. It is through political struggle that homosexual people have taken control of who they are. In the same way that 'niggers' are Beautiful and Black, 'queers' are Glad to be Gay. Many oppressed people are heartily sick of being told who they are and what they are by those with power. Oppressed people need to define themselves.

A necessary part of this process is the open organization of homosexual doctors, psychiatrists, teachers, probation officers and social workers. Heterosexual people who work in these fields can best help us by making it clear both in the work situation and through their trades' unions and associations that they will actively defend the job security of gay people. In this way it will be possible to ensure that distressed and isolated gay people who seek help will be counselled by fellow homosexuals. Of course, there is a need for both individual and group counselling. The form that these should take is detailed in *Counselling homosexuals*, compiled by Peter Righton and published by The National Council of Social Service. Apart from the assumption and acceptance that individual counsellors will be heterosexual (Righton, 1973, 25–8) the specific suggestions made in this pamphlet could hardly be bettered.

Although counselling homosexuals and gay political action are distinct activities they are interdependent. The purpose of political action is to defend and extend the freedom of homosexual people to enjoy their sexuality. On the other hand, the object of counselling must be to render individuals capable of living, loving and working in a hostile environment. Political struggle and counselling depend on each other. An isolated gay person is unlikely to develop the pride and self-confidence necessary to live openly without the sort of individual help offered by counselling and befriending agencies.

However, these agencies owe their existence directly to the political action of gay people themselves. The counselling of gay people was not seriously considered until homosexual people began to struggle for social as well as legal change. Recognition of the need for counselling has grown as a result of political struggle. More importantly the activity of gay people has created new ideas and attitudes to counter our oppression. Without these alternative ideas counselling would exist only in the form of support for repressive psychotherapy and clinical 'treatment'.

Some United Kingdom contacts

Gay Switchboard
01–837–7324
Every evening 18.00 to 22.30
Complete national gay information service

Friend
Friend is a national counselling and befriending agency with fifteen groups
in seven regions.
P.O. Box 427, Spring Gardens, Manchester M60 2EL
Telephone—evenings only: 061–225–0058 or 061–445–9629

Cara
Irish counselling organization
Gay Liberation Society, Students' Union, Queen's University, Belfast

Parents Enquiry
Ms Rose Robertson, 16 Honley Road, London SE6 2HZ

Icebreakers
01–274–9590
19.30 to 22.30 every evening of the year

Further Reading

The Well of Loneliness. A novel by Radclyffe Hall. Jonathan Cape, London,
   1928.
A Single Man. A novel by Christopher Isherwood. Simon and Schuster, New
   York, 1964.
Psychiatry and the Homosexual. A pamphlet (32 pp.). Pomegranate Press, 165
   Gloucester Avenue, London NW1, 1973. (Price 15p.)
With Downcast Gays. A pamphlet (40 pp.) by Andrew Hodges and David
   Hutter. Pomegranate Press, 165 Gloucester Avenue, London, NW1, 1974.
   (Price 20p.)
Politics of Homosexuality. A pamphlet (19 pp.) by Don Milligan. Pluto Press,
   London, 1973. (Price 20p.)
The Joke's Over. A pamphlet (24 pp.). Gayprints/Ratstudies, Box GP, 197
   Kings Cross Road, London WC1, 1973. (Price 15p.)
Counselling Homosexuals. A pamphlet (36 pp.) compiled by Peter Righton.
   Bedford Square Press of The National Council of Social Service, 26
   Bedford Square, London WC1, 1973. (Price 30p.)

7
Welfare Rights and Wrongs
Crescy Cannan

Radicalization

The increasing militancy of social workers (including community workers
and probation officers) is part of a general rank and file militancy in
industrial, service and white collar sectors. In the United Kingdom, papers
pressing for greater democracy in the trade unions have mushroomed:
Hospital Worker, *The Car Worker*, NALGO (*National and Local Government
Officers Association*), *Action News* and *Rank and File Teacher* are just a few, and
community and tenants' newspapers are part of the same concern with
grassroots democracy and control. Other papers like *Red Rat* and *Humpty
Dumpty* for psychologists, or *Case Con* for social workers, cut across trade
union boundaries and have been concerned with critiques of traditional
ways of working and thinking, and especially the notion of the expert and
professionalism. *Case Con* first appeared in 1970 and has been important in
reflecting and developing the growing dissatisfaction of social workers with
the repressive elements in the work they do, and with the disparity between
the sorts of problems they are asked to solve and the resources they are given.
For social workers, just like teachers and nurses, are directly involved with
the consumption of their services, and their militancy has taken the form not
just of demanding better pay and conditions, but of looking to changed
services in the consumers' interests, not those of a local bureaucratic system,
or of capitalism as a whole.

Apart from the criticisms of the ideology of casework and the cries of the
welfare state, what have radical social workers achieved in practice? In many
London boroughs social workers have been prepared to show publicly their
solidarity with homeless families or squatters in their struggle for better
housing; some have refused to ask for contributions to the cost of temporary
accommodation, or to help clients fill in rent rebate forms under the Housing
Finance Act. There has been work with gypsies harassed by local councils,
with battered wives, members of the Mental Patients' Union and with
claimants' unions. In many parts of the country there has been militancy over
office conditions, better conditions for residential workers, the struggle over

standby pay for emergency duties, and strike action over the London weighting allowance. Many social-work students have agitated for the removal of exams and the introduction of coursework that is more relevant to social problems than casework. And as well as Case Con there are social-workers' action groups, the NAPO (National Association of Probation Officers) action group, Treaclestick in the Midlands, and many Case Con groups have merged with NALGO action groups to forge links in the public sector.

Community workers, too, are questioning the initial assumptions of community work which is seen traditionally as a way of mobilizing community resources and coordinating social services to help the 'inadequate' and deprived. For instance:

> . . . problems of multi-deprivation have to be redefined and reinterpreted in terms of structural constraints rather than psychological motivations, external rather than internal factors. The (Community Development) project teams are increasingly clear that the symptoms of disadvantage in their 12 areas cannot be explained adequately by any abnormal preponderance of individuals or families whose behaviour could be defined as 'pathological'. Even where social 'malaise' is apparent, it does not seem best explained principally in terms of personal deficiencies, so much as the product of external pressures in the wider environment.[1]

The radical social worker is no longer willing to paper over the cracks, but seeks ways of diverting power to client groups so that they can challenge, if not change, the status quo. The fact that the social services as a whole have an ideological and repressive function does not mean that grass-roots social workers necessarily have as well, and much of the work of groups like Case Con has been to define carefully the repressive elements in the job. But apart from the left wing, there are many liberals, represented for instance by the professionals' British Association of Social Workers (BASW), or the CPAG, who also frankly accept poverty as an explanation for clients' problems, and much of whose day-to-day strategies may sound little different from those of the left-wingers.

Welfare rights is a strategy that has been enthusiastically accepted across the liberal-left spectrum, and it is a seductive one for radicals for it can embody a refusal to interpret the client's view of the problem in an 'expert' way, and it gives short-term rewards of material benefit to those in poverty. It is assumed to be a 'good' strategy, but we find in it very little discussion of the nature of poverty, how it can be changed, or the role of the state.

[1] Community Development Projects, *Inter-Project Report to the Home Office*, paragraph 2.6.

Welfare rights is often described as a strategy for social change, but there is little analysis of the way that day-to-day struggles for individual benefits relate to the longer term, nor of the function of supplements and rebates in propping up a low-wage, high-rent system. The way rights are fought for is crucially important for social change: and because there is little discussion of this issue, the welfare-rights strategy has a radical coat covering merely liberal practice. Tony Lynes (1969) rightly said that 'One might perhaps describe it as the new Fabianism, in that it seems to offer a means of achieving gradual progress without upsetting the basic value assumptions of our society.' Of course any radical social worker automatically and correctly helps clients to get as much in the way of benefits as possible, but to claim that this is a process of social change is quite another matter. Anyone who is serious about social change needs an analysis of the role of welfare in capitalism, and of concepts of poverty.

The cycle of deprivation theory

Social policies embody the dominant conception of the nature and causes of the social problems they seek to affect. Social workers using the casework approach see poverty as the result of personal pathology—the client is considered unable to make full use of the opportunities and benefits that are available, and through various forms of self-defeating behaviour, confirms his or her position as inadequate and poor. The wide impact of the 'rediscovery of poverty' in the nineteen sixties led to a new conception of the poor as victims of a rigged social structure. Pressure groups like the Child Poverty Action Group and many social workers worked for greater access to welfare benefits, the rights to which exists in legislation if not always in practice. In both the psychological/casework approach, and this materialistic approach, the poor are victims, and professional intervention is considered necessary and useful.

At the moment the vogue concept of poverty is the cycle of deprivation. It owes much to the idea of a culture of poverty, a subculture of the poor, handed down from generation to generation through the family, producing particular attitudes and personality structures, in particular a fatalistic apathy, a resistance to change. The cycle of deprivation concept neatly combines the psychological, materialistic, and cultural explanations of poverty. It fits very nicely with the new family casework Seebohm social services departments; it encourages welfare rights as a strategy for social workers and as a self-help activity for clients and claimants. It is the underlying idea of community development programmes too. The miracle ingredient is the claim that all the elements in the poverty environment interact with and exacerbate each other. Poor housing, low pay, insecure employment, poor schooling, inadequate community institutions like nursery schools or health facilities, all combine to reinforce the cycle. Overlaying these are a transmitted culture of poverty, providing the apathy to prevent self-improvement, and on the psychological level, detrimental patterns of child rearing, poor genetic endowment and low ego-strength to compound the problem. The place of casework in the generic social worker's training is therefore secure, and the emphasis on the psychological dynamics of the individual or family allows social workers to adopt materialistic stances while retaining individual relationships with clients.

Because this theory defines poverty as something very complex, posing many interacting causes and effects, 'experimental' anti-poverty projects are justified to discover the particular dynamics of special, exceptional, areas, and what the most effective use of existing and extra resources might be. For instance, introducing the United Kingdom urban programme in 1968, the then Home Secretary, Mr Callaghan (see Meacher, 1974), said, 'There remain areas of severe social deprivation in a number of our cities and towns—often scattered in relatively small pockets. They require special help to meet their social needs and to bring their physical services to an adequate level.' Clearly environmental stress and cultural deprivation do coincide with poverty, but all this discussion of the effects of poverty, seen also in the definition of educational priority areas, merely diverts the discussion from the question of why some people earn a great deal less than others. The blots are defined as the problem, not what produces them; the poor are the problem, not inequality; 'immigrants', not white racialism; homelessness, not the housing market. That positive discrimination programmes do little more than give the government the appearance of determination to eradicate the evils of our society is seen in their very low cost: for 1972–3, the urban programme represented 0·05 per cent of totalled programmed public expenditure, and 0·1 per cent of social services expenditure. The community development project was even smaller by proportion. Educational priority area expenditure was just over one per cent of the total educational budget for 1972–3 (Meacher, 1974, 5).

Michael Meacher (1974, 7) has written about the political functions of positive discrimination programmes:

The provision of selectively focused expenditure, even in minute amounts, can be used to justify political claims about urgent concern for the poor and deprived without in any way impugning the structure of rewards in society or demanding any significant sacrifices from the privileged. It is the equivalent, on a territorial basis, of income support in extreme cases through means testing, and similar political claims have recently been mounted regarding family income supplement and the new rent rebates. In the case of the PDPs [Positive Discrimination Programmes], this trend has most strikingly been demonstrated by the increasing emphasis in later phases of the Urban Programme on projects to aid the casualties of the housing market, such as hostels and advisory centres, at exactly the same time as wider political ideologies were being brought to bear against the public sector of the housing market which brought overall house building to the lowest point for a decade which, together with all time high prices, actively pushed up the number of casualties.

The idea of the cycle of deprivation and positive discrimination goes with a trend towards selectivity in welfare, for the assumption is that the mass of people get along all right, and that only a few need special help. Social services and community development programmes 'resocialize' people into making better use of existing welfare (and educational) resources. 'Better communication' is a phrase that crops up in the community-work literature over and over again, and the Gulbenkian Report (1968) claims that people 'grow as persons' once communication is achieved, presumably a rather odd way of saying that people develop more tolerant attitudes to the status quo.

But while community work can be criticized for concentrating on the local, for seeking adaptation to unpleasant environmental conditions, and for trying to cope with bureaucratic malfunctioning (instead of changing these things), many community projects have meant the better articulation of local grievance. The way this grievance is channelled is affected by the kind of leadership that community workers can give, many of whom are committed radicals, if not revolutionaries. Grassroots activity can be used to stimulate morale among people who feel frustrated and who cannot see a way out; but this may simply pre-empt militant activity—the fate of welfare rights programmes which allow claimants to let off steam but not to change their situations. As I describe below, this function was very much in the policy makers' minds in the United States anti-poverty programmes. And Marjorie Mayo in the following chapter describes how imperialist powers use community development programmes. It is only through an analysis of the political motivations behind programmes that fieldworkers can put their radical ideas into practice.

A comparison of the United Kingdom Labour and Conservative parties reveals little difference in their views of poverty. The Conservatives are rather more concerned with genetic inheritance and socialization: Sir Keith Joseph, for example, referred (see Meacher, 1974, 7) in 1972 to 'personal factors arising from illness or accident or genetic endowment. And there are many factors which affect patterns of child rearing.' Accordingly Joseph sought measures that would reach families with young children—playgroups, compensatory education, family-planning facilities—and in doing so help to limit the size of poor families (and increase social-work intervention in the family). Labour have been more concerned with the fact that health, education, and employment impinge on individuals, but their policies have not differed significantly from the Conservatives'. Roy Jenkins, for instance, relies (see Holman, 1973a) on the 'generosity of all men and women of goodwill, irrespective of their economic interests or class position' in the fight to eradicate poverty. It was, after all, the 1964 Labour Government that began to dismantle the system of welfare set up in the 1940s, and their programme of cuts in public expenditure and use of wage freezes in attempting to curb inflation have been virtually identical to the Conservatives'. The 1966 Ministry of Social Security Act did nothing to bring the Supplementary Benefits Commission under democratic control and maintained its protection of secrecy. It was this act that contained the repressive measures now so well known and widely criticized, for instance the unreasonable rent rule, the cohabitation rule and the wage stop. I shall now look briefly at anti-poverty programmes in the United States, for it is upon them, their experience and concepts, that so much British policy is based.

Anti-poverty programmes and welfare rights in the United States

Like the British programmes that followed them, United States anti-poverty programmes set out to be effective in breaking the poverty cycle by tackling the main elements—employment opportunities, health facilities, education, housing, welfare rights:

The Economic Opportunity Act defines community action as a programme which combines the resources of an urban or rural area in actions which promise to reduce poverty or its causes—'through developing employment opportunities, improving human performance, motivation and productivity, or bettering the conditions under which people live, learn and work.' It is to be organized by a public or private non-profit agency, and to be 'developed, conducted, and administered with the maximum feasible participation of the residents of the areas and members of the groups served'.   (Marris and Rein, 1974, 265.)

Consumer views were taken seriously, above professional judgements, in order to promote controlled institutional change, while social science expertise was used to evaluate the programmes. These were conceived within an experimental framework so that premature large-scale commitment could be avoided and limited resources apparently used to fulfil urgent, but ill-defined, goals. In fact earlier more ambitious projects that aimed to tackle poverty as a totality of deprivations had been found too expensive and smaller grants for specific programmes were offered in compensation. The poverty cycle theory is not clear about the exact interrelationship of all the elements like bad housing and poor schooling, so that the withdrawal from intervention in all the elements is not necessarily seen as an abandonment of the fight. In the British positive discrimination programmes we also see the elements being fought piecemeal: the programmes are supposed to be complementary, but exactly how is left vague.

As in Great Britain, a major source of grievance to emerge in the community centres was the hardship and humiliation of life dependent on welfare. The Civil Rights' Movement earlier in the 1960s influenced the setting up of the National Coordinating Committee of Welfare Rights' Groups in 1966, and social workers and lawyers began to use litigation as an instrument of social change. The most celebrated use of law for social reform was in the winning of the Supreme Court rulings that 'children could not be denied welfare on the grounds that their mother was living with a man to whom she was not married; that welfare could not be cut off before the recipient had exercised her right to a fair hearing; that states could not apply length-of-residence conditions in the granting of welfare.' (Marris and Rein, 1974, 355.) Cases were fought to establish precedents that would define and extend the right to welfare. Although a variety of different tactics was employed, the creation of an economic and political crisis through the overloading of the welfare bureaucracy was seen as a precondition for the kind of reverberations that would secure reforms at the national level. Welfare rights groups called attention to the misuse of public expenditure in many anti-poverty programmes that did more to ensure bureaucratic reshaping of the various welfare services than to alleviate the day-to-day experience of being on welfare, and they objected to the forcing of people into low-wage work.

United States welfare rights groups have been very militant, their mainstay usually being black unsupported mothers. They soon found that mass claims achieved more than individual advocacy and used sit-ins and demonstrations to advantage. In 1967 New York special grants totalled $3m., in 1968, $13m. (Piven and Cloward, 1972, chapter 10.) Welfare departments had the choice of calling the police and risking mass (possibly racial) violence, or paying out money.

Welfare rolls increased sharply in the 1960s partly because of militant action by claimants and would-be claimants. But the welfare rights movement was itself given aid from federal sources: the Office of Economic Opportunity which oversaw all anti-poverty programmes gave grants to local anti-poverty programmes, and were quite aware that a substantial part of the money would go to strengthening local welfare rights groups. The federal government openly financed an organization of the poor which was militantly harassing local welfare departments. What were their motives? The anti-poverty programmes were partly an attempt by federal government to intervene in local affairs over and above local political interests, and the Democrat administration in Washington had been eager to win black votes. Holman (1974) has shown how the poverty programme fared under the Nixon administration; although such state interference conflicts with aggressive Republican individualism, nevertheless the poverty programmes had useful political functions:

Thus by the end of his first administration, President Nixon had a poverty programme which, if the political climate made it appropriate, could continue in its new directions, initiating research, cooperating with local government, and running a limited number of service programmes. It could serve as evidence that the government was taking action against certain social problems without being the kind of action to promote hostility amongst the government's supporters.

While expenditure on action and initiation of projects was cut, that on research became the largest proportion.

During the 1960s the fear of black militancy provided another reason for the financing of welfare programmes. When federal agencies 'attempted to make gains for blacks in housing and health care and education and employment, resistance was stiff and sometimes virulent, for other groups in the cities had major stakes in these services and resources. But there were few other major groups in the cities with direct and immediate interests in welfare. (Giving welfare was also cheaper, at least in the short run, than building housing, for example.) Consequently, relief-giving turned out to be the most expeditious way to deal with the political pressures created by a dislocated poor, just as it had been many times in the past.' (Piven and Cloward, 1972, 285–6.)

Racial violence was not the only threat to the establishment—so-called urban renewal with the uprooting of poor families was another major, often related, problem. A more considered slum clearance programme was not envisaged, instead it was to the welfare agencies that the administration turned. The increasing numbers eligible for welfare meant that programmes seeking to enable greater access of the poor to benefits were fostered: the Office of Economic Development set up 'community action agencies'—neighbourhood service centres. Federal intervention established welfare rights services, promoted litigation and nourished grass-roots pressure by the poor themselves. This meant that the degradation and demoralization of the poor and thus their hostility to the state, were largely pre-empted. A Department of Health, Education and Welfare report suggests that

Although there is no direct evidence, CAP [Community Action Project] programs may have helped the poor understand their rights under existing public assistance policies and may have lowered the amount of *personal* stigma recipients felt. There is evidence showing that CAP programs are associated with reduced feelings of helplessness. CAP expenditures per 1,000 poor persons were inversely related to powerlessness (the more a city received CAP funds, the fewer the number of recipients feeling helpless). (Piven and Cloward, 1972, 289.)

Between 1964 and 1969 the rolls in the 78 northern urban counties rose by 80 per cent. As the applications rose, so did the proportion of acceptances. Modernization, migration, urban unemployment, family breakup, and rising grant levels, created a large pool of eligible families in the 1950s and '60s, but the rolls did not rise until the '60s and then largely as a result of government programmes designed to moderate political unrest among the black poor. Such concessions were largely symbolic but came at a time when ghetto unrest was at a peak, and, when this unrest began to wane, they could be viewed in retrospect as major liberal reforms.[2]

Claimants and claimants' unions

As in the United States so in Great Britain the system of social security has come under increasing strain in the face of structural impingements on people's lives: for instance, redevelopment has meant the loss of much cheap accommodation and multiplied homeless families; structural unemployment has produced more long-term unemployed; and the greater life expectancy of the old has increased the number of pensioners who need supplementary benefits, their pensions being so small. Rein and Heclo (1974) have shown that the proportion of people on welfare in the United States rose to seven per cent of the population in 1972, in Sweden, after remaining at or near 4

[2] For full descriptions of American anti-poverty programmes and welfare rights see Piven and Cloward, 1972, chapter 10, and Marris and Rein, 1974, chapter 9.

per cent for most of the post-war period, the proportion rose to 6·3 per cent in 1971—higher than at any time in the preceding 23 years. In Great Britain, the percentage rose gradually from 3·9 in 1950 to almost 5·5 in the mid 1960s, 7·2 in 1967 (following the 1966 Ministry of Social Security Act) and reaching 8·4 per cent in 1972. There are striking differences when we look at one-parent families—the section that is fastest growing in the British claiming population. In Great Britain these families were 16 per cent of all welfare recipients (1971–2), in Sweden 24 per cent (1968–9), and in the United States 60 per cent (1971–2). In Great Britain in 1964 2,774,000 were dependent on supplementary benefit, in 1972 4,563,000—an increase of over 65 per cent (Field, 1974). Much of this increase is accounted for by the diminishing real value of national insurance benefits, so that more and more people have had to turn to supplementary benefits. And some of the increase is accounted for by the proliferation of means-tested benefits like Family Income Supplement that draw ever more people into the claiming category, including the fully employed who are on low wages. There are also the local authority benefits that affect more and more people— rent and rates rebates, rent allowances, school meals and uniform allowances, and so on. What about claimants' unions?

In an anonymous pamphlet called 'The Ostrich—have claimants' unions got a future?', some CU members argue that one factor which weakens CUS is the wish to think of claimants as an homogeneous body. This results in a false notion of revolutionary potential, and at worst, a belief that only claimants have 'true' revolutionary consciousness, having rejected the work ethic. 'Claimants' is a general term for a variety of categories—unsupported mothers, the old, the short-term unemployed, the sick, the chronic sick, the disabled, and those who choose to claim rather than work. All they have in common is living at subsistence level, and facing the harassment and inefficiency of social security officials. But even here there are differences, for some people are seen by the officials as more deserving than others: the 'deserving' covers those like widows, the old, the disabled, in other words those who cannot be expected to work; the 'undeserving' covers the unemployed, the short-term sick—those who are seen as being able to work. Frank Field (1974) has shown that in the United Kingdom the 1974 Labour budget improved benefits for the former group while those for the unemployed and short-term sick have not been increased equivalently (this is not to imply of course that the 'deserving' claimants receive anything like adequate benefits). An important group of claimants are the low-paid employed, who by becoming eligible for supplementation are split off from the organized and productive sector of the working class, and whose functions are to depress wage levels, to provide a reserve army of labour for industry, and to perform low-status service jobs. Clearly this is quite a different problem from the old or unsupported mothers, people who cannot work.

Claimants are also atomized by the wide use of discretion in assessments they are given:

> Massive discretion provides the conditions for day-to-day struggle around which CUs formed. At one stroke, it both created the possibility of successful battles of solidarity, and atomized the coherence of claimants as a category: since every case is a special case, every fight is an individual fight. Collective victory *over single cases*, so long as it doesn't affect the treatment of *groups* of claimants, is acceptable to the system (if not to its individual members); which is why the principle of precedent has never been accepted by the SBC [Supplementary Benefits Commission].

This individualism in claimants, produced by a discretionary system, has been reflected in our reactions to that system as a kind of anti-cult of the personality: the collection of minutiae about such-and-such a supervisor's foibles, the cultivation of hate campaigns against particularly vicious managers, etc. Unless one sees one's own oppression as part of a collective situation, it's hard to understand that the SBC structure is an expression of class interests.

CU action is thus often the collective form of individual mystifications: not, or not only through a failure of critical awareness on the part of revolutionaries active in CUs—but because the '66 act *defines* the situation in this way (naturally enough). ('The Ostrich', p. 13.)

CU ideology is a vague and uncritical populism. The immediate fighting of social-security decisions can take precedence over long-term strategy; long-term ineffectuality tends to be obscured by an optimistic faith in 'people', not organization. Ultra-radicalism and reformism can join hands only too easily as 'The Ostrich' shows in the cohabitation campaign. The CUs did not prevent the media taking up the campaign as a sob story, indeed they encouraged them to do so: there is no harm to the system in focusing attention on special cases, one victim, one remaining pocket of injustice. Without a clear analysis of what they are up against, how change is achieved, and of what the role of welfare under capitalism is, CUs, like other community groups, will be vulnerable to pre-emption by well-meaning liberals, for example in community development projects or the media. I bring together these criticisms in order the more effectively to support CUs, and not in any way to deny them that support.

Newton Abbot CU, composed mainly of unemployed workers wishing to overcome the stigma of laziness and scrounging that goes with claiming, started cooperative food production and distribution (Jordan, 1973a, Chapter 2). This meant that the traditional dichotomy of worker-management was questioned by those involved, but it hardly posed any threat to the system that produces unemployment or stigmatizes those who are unemployed. The CU entertained romantic notions of cooperative work, with overtones of the revival of the craft community; when they organized a system of voluntary work to do odd jobs, it was not surprising that the local trades council should angrily describe it as blackleg labour. They worsened relations with the very people who had the power to organize militant industrial action about unemployment in the area. The *National Federation of Claimants' Unions Guidebook* (p. 17) state, that all CUs must try to establish links with organized workers, especially during strikes. Many CUs attempt to affiliate to the local trades council. This is important as trades councils are represented on SBC appeals tribunals.

The tribunals are the main arena of activity for both CUs and for professional representatives such as those from the Child Poverty Action Group, and Hilary Rose (1973) has compared the forms of representation. She noted that a form of middle-class co-option may emerge 'whereby the educated and the expert enter into a compassionate complicity, where the chairman and the well-briefed middle-class representative retreat into an expert's world, leaving the appellant no longer an actor in his own destiny, but merely the object of the case at issue.' Both CU and Child Poverty Action Group representatives can be guilty of this distancing, but the CUs try to avoid situations in which particular people become experts, and aim for everyone to learn and practise relevant skills. The CUs see fighting an appeal as part of a long-term strategy to raise claimants' consciousness and confidence so that they can defend themselves; the immediate and long-term struggles are truly part of the same process. But for the Child Poverty Action Group, or the liberal social worker, the claimant's involvement is not crucial (indeed it may be considered detrimental if the claimant is rather uncouth), but just a matter of courtesy, for the immediate aim is material relief of need. Reform and change for liberals takes place elsewhere—by pressure group politics, using the media and aimed at the government, and not by the power of the mass of people. A CU appellant asks for representation by a CU member as a right, and expects one day to be able to represent others in return; the Child Poverty Action Group advocate makes a decision about whether or not to support an appeal, and as the expert he decides what the most appropriate line of argument might be. 'The advocate model is basically that of the expert who will use his skills to defend the defenceless, the training programme [of the CPAG] is mainly one of training professionals as Galahads rather than one of training people to defend themselves.' (Rose, 1973.) The claimant is discussed as if he were not in the room, and his position as an object confirmed. But the CU representative, who shares a common condition of life with the appellant and therefore a common attitude to the tribunal, cannot thus patronize or exclude the appellant, whose position becomes not an object but a participant.

In the *Handbook for strikers* the following Golden Rules are given, which are useful advice for social workers:

1 Don't negotiate over a claimant's head
2 Support everyone *unconditionally*
3 —don't judge
   —don't try to 'weed out those who are trying it on'
   —don't look for 'special hardship cases'
4 Don't worry about lightening the Ministry's burden—it's *always* chaos anyway, and your demands will help to change the system for the benefit of *all* claimants. (p. 7.)

And direct advice is given to social workers in the *Claimants' Union Guidebook*:

a Refuse to discuss confidential information about a Claimant with the SS unless the Claimant has agreed. They should not collude with local SS staff, or bargain over the Claimant's head.

b They should support all Claimants unconditionally and refuse to make value judgements about deservingness or undeservingness.

c They should refuse to administer any local authority Means Test and instead pay Section I (Children's Act) money to Claimants pending their appeals.

d Explain to all Claimants and fellow workers exactly what a CU is and does. They should fight in their own organizations, BASW, NALGO and Case Con for a Guaranteed Income for All without a Means Test. (p. 21.)

Social workers and social security

The Seebohm report (1968)[3] was an attempt at an administrative solution to the failure of social services' departments at the time to get to grips with the problems of need and deprivation, and a confirmation that poverty would be tackled not through fiscal measures, but by increased social services. In the report, poverty was seen as a family problem, pathological socialization

[3] For a discussion see the preface to Marris and Rein, 1974.

perpetuating the cycle of deprivation: social workers were to become family caseworkers, seeking within the family the reasons for and the solutions to school truancy, rent arrears, long-term dependence on social security, and mental illness. The report recognized that resources allocated to social services would be far short of what was necessary to tackle deprivation effectively, and community self-help projects were thus to become an important part of the generic social worker's job. Contemporary criticisms of casework, and the move towards more materialistic attitudes among social workers, fitted in admirably with the new departments initiated after the report. Freudianism had apparently been overthrown in favour of another approach, but it would be quite misleading to assume that the new materialistic ideology has in practice resulted in radical departures from the underlying social work ideology. Issues still become cases; poverty or housing stress are redefined as social, not economic problems; hence social workers proliferate. And the idea of 'self-help' should be seen for what it is—a withdrawal from the principle of state responsibility for the poor, disabled and disadvantaged.

As social security offices become more inaccessible and centralized, social workers are increasingly involved in mediating between them and the claimant. In contacting them on behalf of a claimant to query an assessment, or in helping claimants to appeal, the social worker has made an assessment of the case that the social security office has neither staff nor time to do. But the sorts of questions that social workers ask about family circumstances are no doubt more surprising to claimants than those of social security visitors. 'Radical' social workers have always assumed that their increased involvement in material help is to their clients' advantage, a view that can only be maintained while social services are seen in isolation from the system of social security and income maintenance as a whole. The increasing complexity and inefficiency of social security offices and the absence especially of a satisfactory emergency payment system have brought social workers into this area of work. One reason for this is the very vagueness of the generic social worker's job, so that new duties can continuously be slipped in. Income maintenance slipped in very easily, aided by 'radical' social workers who optimistically believed that people prefer to be dealt with by sympathetic social workers than by mean and nasty social security officers. But at least social security is statutorily defined and, however difficult to get, the rights do exist and can be checked in the legislation. Social services never make it clear what is offered, what to do to get it, what to do to appeal if dissatisfied. Bill Jordan (1973b) has argued persuasively against the involvement of social workers in income maintenance, and against the suggestion now in vogue that welfare rights officers should be employed in social services departments:

Radical social workers who accuse traditionalists of 'creating' clients by translating material problems into emotional terms should become equally aware of the danger of artificially created financial problems being accepted as suitable material for social-work intervention. Presumably a case opened under these circumstances (loss of a pension book in the post, or failure of DHSS to despatch a Giro) could develop, by the inexorable process of casework deviance amplification, into a full-fledged welfare or child-care case.

Jordan suggests that, rather than creating welfare rights officers which would encourage the United Kingdom Department of Health and Social Security to shed yet more of its responsibilities, social workers should demand that the DHSS recognize its responsibilities for emergency and exceptional needs under the 1966 Act, that it set up proper local emergency facilities, and halt immediately its programme for centralization. I would add that just as social workers took industrial action over their stand-by duties, social security officers should do the same, demanding a decently paid emergency system so that emergencies do not get referred to duty social workers.

Those who are concerned with rights and social security often ignore the fact that social services departments operate one of the most discretionary benefits of all—payments under the 1963 Children and Young Persons Act, often made as substitutes for social security emergency payments or exceptional needs grants. And money from charities is used in the same way. The sudden gift-like payment out of the blue confirms the dependency of the client on the social worker, something that the client is often blamed for. Worse still, it encourages feelings of personal gratitude to the social worker who has secured this 'present', for such it seems, as there is absolutely no way of claiming entitlement to it or asking for more. Even more confusing, the social worker sometimes reappears asking for it back, and then has to help the client to budget. While social workers should obviously do their best to get as much as possible for clients, it is crucial that they explain exactly what the source of the money is, the terms on which it is given or loaned, whether it is discretionary or a right, and at the same time put clients in touch with consumer groups—tenants' associations, claimants' unions, women's groups, trades unions, squatting groups and so on—so that the judgement of individual inadequacy cannot be conferred. Many social workers, of course, already do this.

As far as community work is concerned, the erosion of people's civil liberties, especially over housing, and the exemption of tribunals from the usual safeguards that operate in courts of law (ineligibility of appellants to legal aid, no rule of precedent, proceedings in camera, no right of appeal, admissibility of hearsay evidence, for instance) has meant that the few legal and advice centres that have been set up have flourished. At the Hillfields Information and Opinion Centre, set up under the Coventry Community Development Programme, it was found during June, July and August 1972 that enquiries about social security were 29·68 per cent of callers, the highest single category (followed by gas, 14·46 per cent and housing 10·47 per cent). Enquiries about social security had also been top throughout the preceding 16 months. In 13·44 per cent of the social security enquiries evidence of mismanagement was found—late Giro payments, books late, benefit calculated wrongly and so on (Bond, 1973). While it is clearly essential that we have more of these centres so that people can find out their rights and get help in their defence, it is disturbing that government departments are setting up yet more bodies to cope with the inefficiencies of and abuses by other departments, and of course by private operators like property speculators and developers. We see willingness to tackle results, but not causes.

That enthusiasts can maintain their optimism about welfare rights as a strategy for social change is a result of the divorce in their discussion between immediate strategy and pressure-group politics. Pressure after all has not prevented the very considerable dismantling of measures like free school milk, free prescriptions, and the introduction of the Housing Finance Act or the Industrial Relations Act. The state is not a neutral entity that can be made better by the introduction of more welfare benefits, but acts on behalf of well-defined and powerful interests. Subsistence benefits, low pay, and the system of income distribution must be seen as parts of a whole, the function of benefits and supplements being to depress wage levels, while enabling people to carry on consuming as prices and rents, and therefore profits, rise. Industrial discipline is a key characteristic of national insurance and social security legislation (industrial misconduct rule, four week rule, ineligibility of strikers to benefit, unreasonable rent rule, voluntary unemployment rule, persistent refusal to maintain one's family, and so on). As far as the national insurance commissioners are concerned, hearsay evidence that would not be admissible in a court of law is admissible in cases of industrial misconduct, which covers dismissal for dishonesty, or negligence in work, a breach of rules at work, absenteeism and lateness. There have been cases where refusal to do work blacked by the union, or biding by demarcation agreements, or refusing to work in bad conditions, have been judged as voluntary unemployment (Kincaid, 1973, chapter 12). It is utopian to assume that

changes can be made to eradicate poverty without a fundamental
transformation of the structure of society. Because social workers are in the
front lines in the attempt to control the effects of poverty and environmental
stress, they are subjected to particularly pernicious ideologies: only by
constant awareness of these will they be able to use that position in the fight
for real changes.

Additional references

Whatever happened to the welfare state? George Clark, City Poverty
   Committee, London, 1974.

Poverty: the forgotten Englishmen, Ken Coates and Richard Silburn,
   Harmondsworth, Penguin, 1970.

Social security and society, Victor George, London, Routledge and Kegan
   Paul, 1973.

Stories from the dole queue, Tony Gould and Joe Kenyon, editors, London,
   Temple Smith, 1972.

'Poverty, welfare rights and social work', Robert Holman, *Social Work
   Today* 4 (12), 6 September, 1973.

'Deprived cycle', Bill Jordan, *New Society*, 10 May, 1973.

Community action, Anne Lapping, editor, London, Fabian Society, 1970.

The Penguin guide to supplementary benefits, Tony Lynes, Harmondsworth,
   Penguin, 1972.

'Who is being radical?', Gerald Popplestone, *Case Con* 7, April, 1972.

'The ideology of professional community workers', Gerald Popplestone,
   British Journal of Social Work 1 (1), April, 1971.

'Client refusal: a political strategy for radical social work.' Ian Taylor,
   Case Con 7, April, 1972.

8
Community Development
A Radical Alternative?

Marjorie Mayo

Community development has become a boom industry. Jobs have been multiplying increasingly rapidly in new projects and job-settings, in government projects and particularly in local authority social service departments like the councils of social service (see Bryers, 1972). And of course old job descriptions are being revitalized with new names—run-down schools in deprived inner city areas are 'community schools' or, even more euphemistically, 'children's homes'; and borstals become 'community homes'.

So why has this notion of 'community' acquired such euphoric connotations, both with governments and local authorities of differing political persuasions and with the student and young professional proponents of community action? This chapter will attempt to analyse the implications of community development in terms of its own development and in relation to the problems to which it is supposed to provide more effective solutions than traditional social work. It should then be clearer why the term has appealed so much to apparently disparate sections of society and, more significantly, what its limitations and possibilities are as a radical alternative to social work.

Where has the notion of community development sprung from?

Although this chapter will refer to projects which include substantial ingredients of other aspects of community work—for example, community organization or coordination between different welfare agencies, as in the poverty and community development programmes—it will concentrate primarily on the community development aspects. This is mainly because it has been the self-help and resident/client participation forms of community development which have been most attractive to those professionals in search of an alternative to the more directly hierarchical and paternalistic traditional approach of the 'helping professions'. As the most seductive form of community work, community development is thus most directly in need of critical analysis from an alternative perspective.

Definitions are typically abstract and general. The standard United Nations definition (1955),[1] for instance, states that 'community development is a process designed to create conditions of economic and social progress for the whole community with its active participation.' This simply begs the question, since development, progress, community and participation are all problematic terms—development and progress of what kind, for whose benefit in what type of community, composed graphically or in class terms, participating in what and with what degree of real power or influence? A clearer understanding can be achieved by adding practical and specific analysis of the concrete experience of community development as developed by Western 'social democracies'—particularly by Great Britain in her colonies and by the United States both in depressed inner city areas at home and in external 'spheres of influence' particularly in Southeast Asia, Latin America and the Middle East.

The British concocted the term community development out of their attempts to develop 'basic education' later called 'mass education' and social welfare in the colonies.[2] But why, after 30 or 40 years or so of colonial influence or rule in Africa (and very much longer in India), this dramatic increase in concern for the 'development', 'education' and 'welfare' of the subject colonial peoples? Colonial rule had, after all, been based on principles of metropolitan self-interest as well as benevolent paternalism—the dual mandate to 'civilize' while exploiting, which was recognized quite explicitly by that well-known colonial administrator and theorist, Lord Lugard (1922).[3]

At the political level, there were clearly self-interested reasons for Great Britain's increasing concern for colonial social or community development. During the interwar period, the fear of the possible implications of self-government for the colonies began to be felt in earnest in the metropolis. In India this process had begun even in the 1930s; in Africa it began later although, before the end of the second world war, there is evidence of the first recognition of the distant but eventual possibility of successful independence demands in that continent, too. The Colonial Office began to consider ways of coping with these demands by promoting the

[1] (Misc. no. 523—February, 1955.) Report of the Ashbridge conference on social development.

[2] The titles of Colonial Office documentation bear out this parentage: *Educational policy in British political Africa* (1925), *Mass education in African society* (1944) and *Social development in the British colonial territories* (1948).

[3] See also Margery Perham's biography of Lugard for an account of his role in the development of that peculiarly British form of colonial administration, indirect rule.

'development of political institutions' or more generally of that most ambiguous term 'political development'.

The British wanted 'to encourage democracy and local initiative', and 'to establish solid foundations for the approaching self-government' (see Brockensha and Hodge, 1969, 164) which, as the United Nations (1958–9) explained, meant bringing the colonies in line with 'political, economic and social standards as established in the majority of democratic countries.' In other words, the colonies were to be protected from communism or from other potentially unstable political regimes (which might eventually be too weak to contain the emergence of that same spectre of communism). One of the best known consequences of British policy was the Indian community development programme. This was developed by both British and United States protagonists before independence in 1947 and taken up (merged by then with the non-violent and anti-communist ideology of Ghandi) as a major plank of the Congress Party in 1952. The whole programme was quite explicitly an attempt to create plausibly democratic institutions without serious dislocation of the vested interests of the status quo.

During the second world war the British had become increasingly concerned about the political crisis with which they might have to deal at its end. What, the colonial administrator F. L. Brayne (1944) asked, would become of the returned soldier?—would he 'explode and become either a fervent reformer or red-hot enemy of all government or a violent and dangerous criminal?' The answer he thought, lay in a balanced community development and national reconstruction programme. 'A comprehensive programme of economic and social betterment that kept everyone busy, body and mind, would do more than anything else to ease the solution of the constitutional problem.'

An idealized and supposedly democratic version of village life, the 'Panchayat', was to be recreated, as part of this scheme to promote rural development without offering any explicit challenge to existing property or power and caste relationships (Brayne, 1945; Mayer, et al. 1958). Nehru himself (1957) made this quite clear in his own statements on the community development programme: 'We want an integrated India, not only politically but emotionally' (i.e., ideologically). Existing property (and particularly land-ownership patterns) were thus to be left undisturbed; Nehru would not give official support even to 'voluntary' programmes for land re-distribution. 'It is obvious,' he affirmed, 'that no government can go about asking people to give up their land.'

Yet, as Barrington Moore (1966) has commented, to attempt in India 'to democratize the villages without altering property relationships is simply absurd.' As the United Nations evaluation team on their visit in the late 1950s were forced to recognize, despite all the efforts of the community development teams, the poorer peasants still lacked incentives, while the richer peasants and landlords were still able to appropriate their surplus, not to mention the additional material benefits that had been available from the community development programme. Thus social and economic divisions have actually widened and the underdevelopment of the poorer peasants' plots increased as a result of five years of community development. Nor was the Indian programme alone in having such political and social ideological intentions. Similar conclusions can be drawn, for instance, about British efforts in part of Africa and Malaya where, by 1953, there were 450 'new community development villages' as a result of the emergency resettlement of half a million people as part of the military operations against the communists.

The political implications of community development as an attempt to build up local bulwarks (and vested interests) opposed to communism, can be traced in the possibly even cruder policies of Britain's successor as an imperial power, the United States. As Brokensha and Hodge (1969) have explained, ' by far the greatest American expenditures on community development occur in those countries (Vietnam, Thailand, Laos) considered to be most threatened by communism.' Often community development is used to disguise counter-insurgency activities, including perhaps those projects as part of aid programmes to Latin America. 'The Alliance for Progress' and all the non-government sponsored United States projects are concentrated in politically tense, yet economically vital areas, for instance, in the Middle East—Jordan, Lebanon and Iran—and Greece, another critical sphere for political and military influence. Greece received community development programmes from the United States both before and after the second world war and the civil war, between communists and their allies and the right-wing groups supported by the United States and Great Britain. On the political level, then, as an American critic (Erasmus, 1968) has commented, community development clearly has been used by both countries 'as a pacifier in the hopes of avoiding disagreeable agitation'.

Underlying the political dimension and critically and causally linked to it, economic motivation has also been of key significance in the development of the colonial ideology of community development. The colonies had, after all, a crucial economic function for the metropolitan power (see Lenin, 1966). Imperialism was economically vital for a variety of reasons, as a means of combating falling rates of profit at home by the more profitable export of capital abroad, but also, for instance, to provide and guarantee the supply of raw materials cheaply and to facilitate the export of metropolitan manufactured goods on favourable terms of trade. The British preferred to ensure that native labour was available to produce these raw materials and to facilitate this trade by economic pressure, for example, taxes to force peasants into wage labour and the use of ideological pressure rather than by the Portuguese method of naked brute force—forced labour. Even so there were exceptions made to the 1933 International Labour Organization ordinance forbidding this practice, exceptions which were inserted partly as a result of British pressure—and these were exploited by the British up to 1956, for example, in what was then Bechuanaland, Kenya, Uganda and Tanganyika. Lugard (1965) even justified forced labour as an African tradition—the native ruling class having also been able to extract unpaid labour from their peasants in various areas, for example, northern Nigeria.

Community development was a more subtle, potentially less troublesome way of achieving the same ends—the extraction of 'voluntary' and, of course, still unpaid native labour, to build up the infrastructure for further economic development exploitation. So the typical colonial project involved drilling wells to irrigate the cash crops, and road and bridge building to facilitate their transportation to the port of embarkation.

During the second world war, the production of raw materials in the colonies took on a new importance for Great Britain, because of the 'reverse lend lease' arrangement made with the United States (Rodney, 1972). By this agreement, Great Britain was able to repay war loans, not in dollars, but in raw materials from the British colonies. Most important of these were tin and rubber from Malaya, followed by cocoa from West Africa. In other words, Great Britain was bailed out of her economic difficulties at least partly through the efforts of her colonies. As a result British investment in colonial development was heavily slanted towards facilitating this process: the Colonial Development and Welfare Fund (set up in 1940 and administering loans and grants from 1944) concentrated on the infrastructure for this increasing export of raw materials—developing ports, railways and electric power plants. In addition, African currency had to be based on 'sterling reserves' banked in the United Kingdom and invested in British government stock. By 1955, Africa had contributed £1,446 million, which was over half the total gold and dollar reserves of Great Britain and the Commonwealth combined—another way in which the former relied upon her colonies and the earnings from the export of their raw materials to support her own economy when it was in difficulties. In this process, then, community development had a certain degree of direct economic influence, for example, through projects which built up the economic infrastructure

and stimulated the production of key raw materials, such as the campaigns to improve cocoa farming in Ghana in the 1950s (du Sautoy, 1958).
Community development was also significant, ideologically, in encouraging favourable institutions and attitudes, and in discouraging those unfavourable ones that might lead to the development of a radical challenge. To the economic and political establishment community development thus represented an attempt to create a capitalist 'free market', economic development on the cheap (development for the metropolitan interests anyway, even if that entailed underdevelopment for the colonized country), and colonized peoples sufficiently indoctrinated to participate voluntarily in accelerating this process (see Frank, 1969, for an explanation of this term, 'underdevelopment'.)

Community development as applied in contemporary United States and British urban situations from the Deep South during 'reconstruction' to the United States 'poverty programme' and the British community development programme

Could such a concept as community development have been applied for radically different goals in the very dissimilar situation of the cities of the West? In practice, the evidence from official programmes and the establishment community development literature in Great Britain and the United States demonstrates striking parallels with—despite the obvious differences from—the colonial and neocolonial experience.

These links can be traced particularly clearly in the programme to 'develop' the depressed black minority population in the United States. After the Civil War, in order to oust the southern Democrats the Republican party was anxious to secure the newly available votes (at least until the blacks lost the vote again, in the subsequent period of reaction from the late 1870s onwards when the Jim Crow laws were passed and the Ku Klux Klan developed). So various Republicans were willing to support and encourage black self-help projects, as long as these were designed to develop agricultural productivity and a better skilled and disciplined black industrial labour force—not of course to generate black political or social demands. Some wealthy southern conservatives were also willing to support schemes of this nature. Probably the best known black leader of this 'self-help only' genre was Booker T. Washington (1967; Weisberger, 1972). From 1881, he ran a black teacher training college in Alabama, Tuskegee, which became from the point of view of the wealthy whites the model for black self-advancement. As Washington explained, black education for agriculture and factory work could produce a more docile labour force 'without the strikes and labour wars' which were becoming endemic amongst the white proletariat in the north; and he was quite explicit in making no social or political demands. 'The wisest among my race understand,' he said, during the Alabama address which made his fame, 'that the agitation for social equality is the extremest folly.' After this speech, Washington became more popular with the whites and his projects enjoyed better funding than ever before. He was invited on a trip to Europe which included tea with Queen Victoria. As the militant black leader W. DuBois (1971) assessed him 'Mr Washington represents in Negro thought, the old attitude of adjustment and submission. His doctrine has tended to make the whites, north and south, shift the burden of the negro problem to the negroes' shoulders and stand aside as critical and rather pessimistic spectators.'

Formally, the politically situation was reversed in the 1960s when community action emerged as a major strand in the war on poverty. This time it was the Democratic party which was interested in keeping the votes of the black migrants, who had shifted to the ghettoes of the northern and western cities. Alinsky (1965) has described this war on poverty as 'political pornography', a 'huge political pork barrel' patronage in the form of jobs and funds to be handed out to supporters—i.e., to liberal academics and social and community workers—whereas, in terms of the real issues of the redistribution of economic opportunities and of the redistribution of physical resources (such as adequate housing) and of political power, the programme represented, he considered, no more than mere tokenism. And, as tokenism, Alinsky thought it should be resisted to the death.

Even less vehement critics have had to admit that the war on poverty was an attempt to initiate reform in the inner cities without actually committing any major resources (see Marris and Rein, 1971). Instead, self-help and resident participation were to stimulate cheaper solutions—a theme which, despite some of the negative conclusions of the American experience, has been taken up in contemporary British attempts at community development. As the Home Office explained in the early papers,

The underlying general aims of all these forms of social action would be to create a more integrated community, supported by services more integrated in their concepts and practices (even though some of them will remain separately organized); and to take some of the load off the statutory services by generating a fund of voluntary social welfare activity and mutual help amongst the individuals, families and social groups in the neighbourhood, supported by the voluntary agencies providing services within it. . . . It is not therefore to be expected that social action in an experimental area will involve the provision of facilities which are individually, large, expensive or wholly new in conception. The project cannot for example, hope to secure the provision of a new comprehensive school or the rehousing of the whole neighbourhood; . . . Nor is it its purpose to do so. Large-scale remedies belong to the steady evolution, as resources permit, of familiar general policies.[4]

In practice, however, at least in the United States, the theme of resident participation has been one of the most contentious, and it has certainly had a radical dimension. On the other hand it is equally certain that it was not universally seen in these terms among the initiators of the war on poverty (or of the community development programme for that matter). L. Cottrell, for instance, an influential thinker behind OEO, was apparently interested in community development for the development of 'responsible leadership' and the affirmation of 'American values' (see Knapp and Polk, 1971). This is another striking parallel with the form of community control used in the colonies and in the Deep South, in the reconstruction period).

The movement for the development of community self-help can also be related to particular notions about the causation of poverty in the inner cities, and to theories of a poverty cycle or a cycle of transmitted deprivation or a culture of poverty (see Moyniham, 1969). Essentially, for the proponents of these views, the absence of real opportunities is not so much the problem as the failure of certain types of individuals and families to take advantage of them. The remedy for families concentrated in inner city slums was community development to overcome their current alienation. Mike Miller and Martin Rein (in press) have criticized this interest in community development and citizen participation as 'community psycho-therapy' as opposed to an attack on the real structural problems underlying this alienation.

The notions behind community development are, however, still deeply embedded, having had a long history in western social thought. Some of their clearest manifestations can be found in a book which was until very recently considered a classic in the field: Biddle and Biddle (1968) define community development as 'a group method for expediting personality growth', i.e., another method of social work.[5] Thus, on a project in a depressed area in the southern states they comment, 'Today there is little evidence that the problems of the area have been solved but, there is abundant evidence that the people have changed their attitudes . . . [for the poor and] alienated must overcome their inner handicaps, partially through

[4] Home Office, mimeographed report, 'Objectives and strategy'.
[5] See Valentine (1968) for a contrary view.

the cultivation of their own initiative.' Lest there be any remaining doubt
about the political implications of such a conception, Biddle and Biddle
(1965) are even more explicit. For them the objectives 'are found in Judaeo-
Christian teaching as it emerges in the democratic tradition . . . the concept
of political democracy being itself an outgrowth of the Judaeo-Christian
belief in men and women as the children of God . . .' or again, 'Community
action that involves conflict against someone limits the spreading
inclusiveness of the community. . . . The all-inclusive community calls for a
multiple approach [i.e. consensus-cooperation]. The two-way division [i.e.
conflict] is more reminiscent of the Marxian class struggle than of the reality
of American pluralism. . . . Whereas the community development worker
should NOT be or should nevei become a destroyer of the social order. By
using or endorsing the idea of revolution, he can find himself disqualified to
act as a mediator between factions in controversy.'

By this time the non-radical (i.e. the reactionary and repressive) aspects of
community development should be sufficiently obvious. As a relatively
cheap and typically ideological attempt to resolve various economic, social
and political problems it has clearly been attractive to governments and
voluntary agencies both national and international for use not just in the
Third World but also among racial minorities and indigenous poor
at home.

So why has community development appealed so much to apparently
radical groups, particularly among students and young professionals? Part of
the explanation seems to lie in the problems to which it is currently posed as a
solution. Both the United States and the British official programmes
recognize that all is not well with the present administrative and political
structures of Western social democracies. Miller and Rein (in press) make
this quite explicit: all the attempts at improved coordination between
welfare departments and better communication between departments at
central and local levels are merely symptomatic of these basic failures of the
administrative and political systems. Part of this increasingly evident failure
of the state mechanisms seems to be due to the increasing scale of state
intervention. In economic terms in Great Britain this increase can be
measured in terms of public expenditure as a percentage of gross national
product—13·5 per cent before the first world war in 1913 and over 52 per
cent in 1968 (Brown, 1972). This dramatic increase, of course, has been
substantially due to nationalization. But it has also been due to the British
political situation and the scale of the demands of the 'welfare state'
(currently 26 per cent of GNP) (see Wedderburn, 1965). In its attempts to
regulate contemporary capitalism the state has thus been forced to intervene

into more and more areas of the economy and also more deeply into an increasing number and range of social, political and ideological institutions. The more complex and technical its interventions and planning processes, the more difficult these become to oversee through the formal political processes which are increasingly seen as peripheral to the real sources of power and decision-making.

Meanwhile, in face of this evidently far from popular growth in official bureaucracy, western social democracies have been concerned to offer official antidotes in the form of citizen or public participation, community action and community development—to name only the most popular at present. These notions have enjoyed considerable popularity just because they do contain in part, if in idealized form, the outlines of potential counter-institutions. Their appeal, however, has probably been strongest among the growing numbers of young professionals and subprofessionals, themselves employed to operate the expanding central and local government services in question. Free schools and community schools have appealed to certain teachers; community action has appealed most particularly to planners (*Skeffington Report*, 1969). Similarly processes are evident in participation in medical policy for doctors and nurses and in the personal social services for social and community workers. Beneath the apparent contradictions, such notions do not necessarily actually cut across the professional self-interest of the young activists concerned. For that professional self-interest is itself contradictory, particularly at the lower end where the supposedly professional part of the job content is clearly becoming depreciated: the young professional is thus less clearly a professional and more obviously just another local (or central) government employee (Mandel, 1972). These pressures are typically compounded with the frustrations caused by the gap between their actual job content and their professional aspirations. As a result more and more young professionals are joining trade unions (for example, NALGO) and professional ginger groups (for example, Case Con). And these same pressures have also been pushing them to look for other ways of making their jobs more satisfying; which is why the notion of a return to the client population, implied in community development, has been so appealing.

But can community development be more radical than this: can it be more than a booster for the flagging egos of liberal students and young professionals who are unwilling to accept this devaluation of their professional status?

In practice, of course, any projects which dabble in social change can and frequently have backfired on the sponsoring agencies. The very ambiguity of the goals beneath the ideological rhetoric can be and has been exploited for other, more radical objectives. Even where in the short term official goals have apparently been attained, such changes can trigger off other, more far-reaching processes. So in the colonies, where community development led to successful promotion of popular education, this newly acquired literacy frequently became a source of strength to the emerging nationalist movements: in Ghana, for example, the mass literacy plank in the community development programme to improve cocoa growing in the 1950s was used to considerable advantage by Nkrumah's party in the struggle for independence (Fitch and Oppenheimer, 1966).

Some of the most reactionary writers have also clearly been aware of the potential danger that their ideological weapons might be used for other ends. Biddle and Biddle, for instance, admitted that the community development 'process' could be hard to control, because once social change was on the agenda Pandora's box would have been opened. As I have already been suggesting, it is clear from the experience of the war on poverty that some of the poverty warriors also saw this very early on, and planned to use the projects for more radical ends. Richard Cloward, in particular, related his own ideas to the considerably less radical, presidential interest in delinquency control, in the early period of the Kennedy administration; and he proceeded to use the ensuing experiments as a spring board for putting into practice his own, more radical ideas about changing not individuals so much as the opportunity structure.

Once citizen participation was let loose that too became part of a wider, more radical debate; and, despite official reaction in favour of putting control firmly back in the hands of city hall (as in the Model Cities programme), citizen participation could not altogether be conjured away. And of course all sorts of radical individuals and groups used Office of Economic Opportunity resources for other, more political ends. The Black Panther party grew around the North Oakland poverty programme office which hired Bobby Searle as foreman in the summer youth work programme in 1966!

Yet in spite of all manner of pockets of radicalism, the verdict on the achievement of community action in the United States so far seems to be that it did not offer any widespread or overall challenge to the established interests of power and influence. As a whole it has been incorporated by the status quo. 'So far from challenging established power,' Marris and Rein (1971) concluded, 'community action turned out to be merely another instrument of social services, essentially patronizing and conservative.'

The limitations of community action

Pockets of challenge are just not enough. Local community issues are probably the easiest to incorporate anyway: the groups can be isolated and ignored by the very fact of their local base and their consequent lack of wider, less fragmented support. Or their demands can met by shifting the problem somewhere else. This process can be seen particularly clearly in traffic issues, for example in contemporary community action experience in Great Britain—closing one road or set of roads which typically diverts the traffic into those neighbouring roads which haven't protested loudly enough—or in housing maintenance issues, the best organized estate getting priority from the same inadequate supply of building resources, while the least organized suffer even longer delays as a result. Community action can so easily become divisive in these circumstances when the authorities can play off one group against another. It is typically a more effective weapon for middle-class consumer and amenity groups who have greater access to and facility in using the media and other pressure-group tactics, compared with most working-class community organizations.

Of course, the very fact that community campaigns revolve around consumption issues—as opposed to work-place campaigns around issues in the process of production—means that they involve less potential bargaining power for the working class. However effectively organized it may be, a rent strike normally lacks the bargaining power which comes from industrial action, which is where the working class can make an impact on their employers where it hurts. Without real links with organized labour to back them up, working-class community campaigns usually remain at the level of pressure-group type politics—getting publicity through militant tactics, and influencing or alarming the powerful, rather than bargaining in situations where the working class can really use its collective strength to full advantage (see Binns, 1973).

The potential role of the radical community worker

As individuals even the most radical community workers are not in a very strong position either to resist the tendency for community action to become a predominantly middle-class weapon for shifting various local problems elsewhere, or to overcome the fragmentation and isolation of each working-class attempt at community action both from every other attempt and from the mainstream of working-class organizations around the point of production.

On a practical level, though, there are several essential steps which they can take to strengthen their ability to resist these difficulties. For instance, they can become unionized themselves and take part in local union activity, for example in local NALGO branches. Apart from strengthening their own vulnerable position with their employers this can help to bring them into a meaningful practical dialogue with other trade unionists, particularly the militants in the area. From inside the trades council they can also be in a better position to press for closer links between tenants and other community groups (for example, pensioners' unions, claimants' unions and unemployed workers' unions) and the trades' council itself.

Not that the community worker *per se* could or should take on the leadership of local working-class politics. Nor is it likely that the local leadership would allow this to happen. Professional knowledge and skills clearly have their value as back-up for community action campaigns—for instance legal and planning expertise around a planning issue. But this is still no argument for putting the professional provider of this information into a position of political leadership which must remain dependent on political rather than professional skills and on the leaders' standing in their community. Yet, on the other hand, even to be professionally most useful the social worker does still need, without aspiring to political leadership, to develop and think through his own political position, if only to avoid some of the most obvious pitfalls of incorporation.

Explicit recognition of the national (and international) political implications of community development is also essential if any real challenge is to be offered to the ways in which governments and international bodies have used it for their own ends, predominantly among the poor both at home and in the Third World. But for many community workers this involves massive shifts in their own ideological positions, so that idealized visions of a return to the small community as a retreat from an answer to the encroachment of large-scale bureaucracies have to be recognized for the cosy romanticisms they are, and more realistic analyses substituted in their place. Similarly, sentimental faith in 'the people' has to be replaced by an analysis of the actual potential of different sections (i.e. classes) of 'the people' given their economic, political social and cultural starting-points, from within their own concrete situations.

Historically, 'back to the people', populist movements, have frequently represented conservative reactions—attempts to retreat to an idealized past, the nineteenth-century version of populism in the United States, for example. On the other hand populist movements have also fostered radical elements. The 'Narodniks', in late nineteenth-century Russia, a predominantly student and intellectual middle-class movement for a return to the people in idealized village communities (Venturi, 1960), has many points in common with contemporary community development and action movements (Gellner and Ionesco, 1969). Yet they also contained genuinely radical potential. It thus seems rash and doctrinaire to conclude that despite its official exploitation its local disadvantages in the fragmented nature of its base and the prevalent ideologies of many of its practitioners, community development has absolutely no possibilities as a radical alternative to social work.

Conclusion

It would take a further chapter to do any justice to the crucial task of spelling out what such a radical role for the community worker might entail. This chapter has attempted to fulfil a different function, to look at the development of the concept of community development and to set its contemporary manifestations in a realistic context. As I argued at the outset, it has been essential to attempt this reappraisal to counteract the current fashionable euphoria. Only when the co-optive and repressive aspects of community development have been analysed, can any radical potential be properly realized. Indeed one implication of this chapter may be that, if radical social change is the prime objective, community development is not a specially favourable starting point at all: nor does it have any automatic advantage over social work of the casework variety—indeed in some instances it may be, and has been, *more* repressive.

On the other hand, having stressed the limitations of community work as a radical alternative to social work I think it would be a mistake to deny it any radical potential whatsoever. Community organizing can be, and has been, used as part of a movement for radical social change. Even small local campaigns can build up local, working-class organizations and develop their political capacity and understanding; and every link-up with other parts of the labour movement has potential for the development of that movement too.

In any case, working-class community organizations (like the trade union movement itself) are necessary at the defensive level, quite apart from the question of further political development. The most pressing current example, the housing crisis, leaves no doubt about that. Even if radical community workers do not see their work-situation as the spearhead of the movement for fundamental change in the economic, social and political structure of society, they need have fewer doubts about the potential contribution they can make to the struggles around the immediate needs of their working-class clientele. The problem for them to explore must be the relationship between these short-term, albeit critical, problems and the development of that longer-term political movement.

As Ken Coates (1973, 157) has said, a specifically socialist view of community action should 'support anything which increased the solidarity and self-confidence of working people and their dependants.' But 'what consciousness can be aroused in such struggles will remain *sectional* unless it is keyed into an embracing political strategy involving *all* the poor, *all* the ill-housed, *all* the deprived.'

Appendix: Case Con Manifesto

No easy answers

Every day of the week, every week of the year, social workers (including probation officers, educational social workers, hospital social workers, community workers and local authority social workers) see the utter failure of social work to meet the real needs of the people it purports to help. Faced with this failure, some social workers despair and leave to do other jobs, some hide behind the façade of professionalism and scramble up the social work ladder regardless; and some grit their teeth and just get on with the job, remaining helplessly aware of the dismal reality. Of course, some do not see anything wrong in the first place.

CASE CON is an organization of social workers (in the broadest sense), attempting to give an answer to the contradictions that we face. Case Con offers no magic solutions, no way in which you can go to work tomorrow and practise some miraculous new form of social work which *does* meet the needs of your 'clients'. It would be nice if there were such an answer, but we believe that the problems and frustrations we face daily are inextricably linked to the society we live in, and that we can only understand what needs to be done if we understand how the welfare state, of which social services are a part, has developed, and what pressures it is subject to. It is the purpose of this manifesto to trace briefly this development, to see how it affects us and our relationships to the rest of society, and above all to start working out what we can do about it.

The 'welfare state'

The welfare state was set up partly in response to working-class agitation and mainly to stabilize the upheavals generated by wartime conditions. It was recognized that improvements in the living conditions of workers helped provide capitalism with a more efficient work force and could nip militancy in the bud. Furthermore, the threat of withdrawal of benefits under certain conditions (being on strike or cohabiting, for example) could be a useful technique of social control. During the post-war boom, wage rises came fairly easily; in the euphoria about the supposed end of inequality, means tests were gradually reintroduced and the principle of universal entitlement to social, educational and health services was eroded. As the boom subsided, cuts in welfare expenditure were justified in the attempt to control inflation and are now used ideologically to create an impression of scarcity as an explanation for the crisis of capitalism. Cuts have taken three main forms:

1   Actual and direct cuts in expenditure—prescription charges, withdrawal of free school milk, cut-backs in building programmes, etc.

2   The drawing of resources from the working class itself via operations like the Housing Finance Act, and the widespread introduction of means-testing.

3   The rationalization of all services on a long-term basis—for example, The National Health Service, and even the 'hiving off' of certain sections to private enterprise, for example, pensions.

In the social services, the Seebohm Report was the main agent of this rationalization process. Specialized social work (mental health, child care, etc.) was abolished and replaced by generic social work, placing the emphasis of responsibility for welfare on the *family* not on the state. The new generic workers were supposed to be 'helping individuals and families cope with their problems and so achieve at any given time a better personal service and social equilibrium, a better chance to face challenges and accept responsibility.' In other words, to persuade the 'client' that his problems are of his own making, and to learn to face up to them.

It was also decided to utilize the resources of the community itself to tackle social problems at both an individual and a community level. Thus, a new category of worker was proposed to discover and promote these resources within the community and to emphasize the importance of people doing things for themselves rather than depending on the corporation or on the government. This can be seen also in recent changes in legislation dealing with criminal offenders, for example, community service orders and intermediate treatment schemes. The encouragement of voluntary organizations was another important facet of the new strategy, and official dependence on such organizations as Child Poverty Action Group and Shelter is increasing. Even claimants' unions and squatters have been successfully co-opted by the state.

Professionalism

It is important to examine the 'professional approach' that has been accentuated by Seebohm and happily accepted by social service hierarchies and workers alike. 'Professionalism' firstly implies the acquisition of a specialism—knowledge and skills not possessed by untrained workers. This isolates the social worker from the population at large. Secondly, social workers come to see themselves as part of an accepted specialist group on a par with doctors and lawyers. Thirdly, it encourages the introduction of businesslike career structures, where 'correct' and 'professional' behaviour (such as 'detachment' and 'controlled emotional involvement') is rewarded with advancement. Clearly, such an approach is welcomed by the ruling class.

One important tool of professional social work has been casework—a pseudo-science—that blames individual inadequacies for poverty and so mystifies and diverts attention from the real causes—slums, homelessness and economic exploitation. The casework ideology forces clients to be seen as needing to be changed to fit society. Social work has now expanded to include new (and not so new) tricks, such as community work, group work, welfare rights work, etc., which, when professionalized, end up by becoming the same sort of mechanism of control as traditional casework, often with the additional merit of being less expensive for the ruling class. Professionalism is a particularly dangerous development specifically because social workers look to it for an answer to many of the problems and contradictions of the job itself—i.e. being unable to solve the basic inadequacy of society through social work. It must be fought at every opportunity.

How we must organize

Organizing independently of the state

The idea of the state as a neutral arbiter between different sections of society who may have some minor temporary differences is wholly inadequate if we are to understand the development of the welfare state and the role of the social worker. An understanding of the state is a vital prerequisite to effective action because, far from being neutral, the state in any class society represents the interests of the *ruling* class and has at its disposal the instruments necessary to keep it in power. Thus, in Britain, the state safeguards the interests and development of British capitalism. Only on this basis can we make sense of the developments in the welfare state since the war and understand *how we must organize*. If the state cannot be neutral, it is important to analyse the expectations placed on social workers by the state, as our employer, and to assess, in the light of this, where and how action supporting the class struggle is most effective.

We are supposed to 'help' our 'clients' by making them 'accept responsibility'—in other words, *come to terms* as individuals with basically unacceptable situations. We must counterpose this to the possibility of *changing* their situation by *collective* action. We can only do this by acting collectively ourselves.

Therefore, we do not merely concentrate on democratizing a few of the state's outposts (such as social service departments) for all this does is to make them more efficient. We should fight for powers of veto over any decisions which are against our best interests and the interests of the people we are supposed to serve. We should also constantly demand the provision of improved services, geared to the real needs of the community. To be in a position to do this requires a lot more than office meetings and working parties. The crux of all our actions must be to organize independently of the state and in the interests of the working class. These interests are in opposition to those of capitalism and its administrative tool—the state.

The trade unions

We should seek to pressurize the union leadership and fight for official positions ourselves, but our priority is to promote the development of rank-and-file organization through fighting for democratic control by ordinary members at all levels of union organization. We support the trade-union leaders to the extent that they support the struggles of the rank and file, but we must beware of letting the union leaders take the struggle out of our hands and out of our control. To achieve real long-term gains we believe that the creation of a national rank-and-file organization, uniting trade unionists at shop-floor level, is absolutely essential.

All social workers should join NALGO where possible, since this is the union that actually negotiates on behalf of most social workers. But obviously other organizations, such as NAPO for probation officers, will be more appropriate to some Case Con supporters. Social workers can make the union more democratic at a local level by setting up departmental committees and forging them into shop stewards' committees. But the fight for democratic control on any other level requires linking up with other militants. This should be done by joining or setting up a local NALGO action group or NAPO members' action group, and drawing on the experience of other militants through a national organization. Links should be forged with other rank-and-file groups (e.g. Rank-and-File Teachers, the Hospital Worker, Nurses' Action Group), militant tenants groups and squatters.

We must beware of allowing our struggle to become one of passing motions in our union branches. We have to take concrete action to fight for what we believe in. For instance, on housing we should fight for local government workers to refuse to implement rent rises caused by the Housing Finance Act, support squatters who are taking direct action on the 'housing problem', refuse to put people into bed and breakfast temporary accommodation, and demand adequate housing for all. In relation to racialism we should join the other public sector unions in refusing to have anything to do with anti-black legislation (for example, the Tory 'pass laws'). In the fight against repression we should insist that our union branches take up specific instances and join in the fight against them actively through pickets, conferences, industrial action, etc.

We must also beware of leaving behind our views when we come face to face with our 'clients'. Our social-work practice must be in line with our stand as trade unionists on issues such as racism, homelessness and repression. Our principles must come before individualism, professionalism and careerism.

A socialist conclusion

Case Con believes that the problems of our 'clients' are rooted in the society in which we live, not in supposed individual inadequacies. Until this society, based on private ownership, profit and the needs of a minority ruling class, is replaced by a workers' state, based on the interests of the vast majority of the population, the fundamental causes of social problems will remain. It is therefore our aim to join the struggle for this workers' state.

References

Alfero, L. A. 1972: Conscientization. *New Themes in Social Work Education,* proceedings of the XVIth International Congress of Schools of Social Work, The Hague. International Association of Schools of Social Work, New York.

Alinsky, S. 1965: The war on poverty—political pornography. *Journal of Social Issues* (January), 41–7.

Allen, C. 1962: *A textbook of psychosexual disorders.* London: Oxford University Press.

Armistead, N., editor, 1974: *Reconstructing social psychology.* Harmondsworth: Penguin.

Auden, W. H. 1964: *Selected essays.* London: Faber & Faber.

Baker, R. 1974: Letters. *Social Work Today* 5(6), 192.

Basaglia, F., editor, 1974: *The crimes of peace.* Turin: Einaudi.

Bartlett, H. M. 1970: *The common base of social work practice.* London: National Association of Social Workers.

Becker, H. S. *et al.,* 1961: *Boys in white: student culture in medical school.* Chicago: University of Chicago Press.

Becker, H. S., *et al.,* 1968: *Institutions and the person.* Chicago: Aldine.

Berger, P. L. 1966: *Invitation to sociology.* Harmondsworth: Penguin.

von Bertalanffy, L. 1971: *General systems theory.* Harmondsworth: Penguin.

Biddle, W. W. and **Biddle, L. J.** 1965: *The community development process: the rediscovery of local initiative.* New York: Holt, Reinhart and Winston.

1968: *Encouraging community development.* New York: Holt, Reinhart and Winston.

Biestek, F. P. 1961: *The casework relationship.* London: Allen and Unwin.

Binns, I. 1973: What are we trying to achieve through community action? *Community Action* (Spring).

Blackburn, R., editor, 1974: *Ideology in social science*. Glasgow: Fontana.

Bolton, C. and **Kammeyer, K.** 1968: The decision to use a family agency. *The Family Co-ordinator* 17.

Bond, N. 1973: *The Hillfields Information and Opinion Centre—the evolution of a social agency controlled by local residents*. London: Community Development Project Occasional Paper.

Borensweig, H. 1971: Social work and psychoanalytic theory. *Social Work* 16, 1.

Brayne, F. L. 1944: *Winning the peace*. London: Oxford University Press. 1945: *Better villages*. Bombay: Oxford University Press.

Briar, S. 1966: Welfare from below: recipients' views of the public welfare system. *California Law Review* 54, 370–85.

Brokensha, D. and **Hodge, P.** 1969: *Community development: an interpretation*. New York: Chandler (Intext Group).

Brown, J. 1968: Charles Booth and the labour colonies. *Economic History Review* 21(2).

Brown, M. Barrat 1972: *From labourism to socialism*. London: Spokesman Books.

Bryers, P. 1972: Analysis of community development job advertisements. In Jones, K., editor, *Yearbook of Social Policy*. London: Routledge and Kegan Paul.

Cannan, C. 1970: Deviants—victims or rebels? *Case Con* 1 (January).

Cannan, C. 1972: Social Workers; training and professionalism. In Pateman, T., editor, *Countercourse—a handbook for course criticism*. Harmondsworth: Penguin Education Special.

Castaneda, C. 1972: *The teachings of Don Juan*. Harmondsworth: Penguin. 1973a: *A separate reality*. Harmondsworth: Penguin. 1973b: *Journey to Ixtlan*. London: Bodley Head.

Claimants' Union 1971: *Claimants' handbook for strikers*. London: Action Books.

Clark, G. 1974· *Whatever happened to the welfare state?* London: City Poverty Committee.

Coates, K. 1973: Socialists and the Labour party. In Miliband, R. and Saville, J, editors, *Socialist Register*. London: Merlin Press.

Coates, K. and **Silburn, R.** 1970: *Poverty: the forgotten Englishman*. Harmondsworth: Penguin.

Cockburn, C. 1973: *The devil's decade*. London: Sidgwick & Jackson.

Cohen, S., editor, 1971: *Images of deviance*. Harmondsworth: Penguin.

Cohen, S. 1974: A futuristic scenario for the penal system. In Basaglia, F., editor, *The crimes of peace*, Turin: Einaudi.

Coser, L. 1962: The sociology of poverty. *Social Problems* 10, 140–48.

Davies, B. 1968: Social needs and resources in local services. London: Michael Joseph.

Davis, F. 1968: Professional socialization as subjective experience: the process of doctrinal conversion among student nurses. In Becker, H. S. *et al.*, *Institutions and the person*, Chicago: Aldine, 235–51.

DuBois, W. 1971: *The seventh son.* (Collected works.) New York: Vintage Books.

Edginton, J. 1974: The Batley battle. *New Society*, 5 September.

Emerson, R. 1970: *Judging delinquents.* Chicago: Aldine.

Erasmus, C. 1968: (Article in) *Human organization* 27(1), 65–74.

Field, F. 1974: No party for the poor. *The Guardian*, 2 April.

Fitch, B. and **Oppenheimer, M.** 1968: *Ghana: end of an illusion.* London: Monthly Review Press.

Frank, A. G. 1969: *Capitalism and underdevelopment.* London: Monthly Review Press.

Friere, P. 1972a: *Cultural action for freedom.* Harmondsworth: Penguin.
1972b: *Pedagogy of the oppressed.* Harmondsworth: Penguin.

Gellner, E. and **Ionescu, G.**, editors 1969: *Populism.* London: Weidenfeld and Nicolson.

George, V. 1973: *Social security and society.* London: Routledge and Kegan Paul.

Glastonbury, B. Burdett, M. and **Austin, R.** 1973: Community perceptions and the personal social services. *Policy and Politics* 1(3), 194.

Goddard, D. 1972: Anthropology: the limits of functionalism. In Blackburn, R., editor, *Ideology in social science*. Glasgow: Fontana, 61–75.

Goetschius, G. W. and **Tash, J. M.** 1967: *Working with unattached youth*, London: Routledge and Kegan Paul.

Goldstein, H. 1973: *Social work practice: a unitary approach.* University of South Carolina Press.

Goffman, E. 1969: *The presentation of self in everyday life.* Harmondsworth: Penguin.

Gottesfeld, H. 1965: Professionals and delinquents evaluate professional methods with delinquents. *Social Problems* 13.

Gouldner, A. 1971: *The coming crisis of western sociology.* London: Heinemann.
1974: Marxism and social theory. *Theory and Society* 1 (Amsterdam).

Gould, T. and **Kenyon, J.**, editors 1972: *Stories from the dole queue.* London: Temple Smith.

Gulbenkian Report 1968: *Community work and social change: a report on training*. Harlow: Longman.

Hague, G. 1973: Community work: a carrot for radicals. *Case Con* 10 (January) 8.

Hall, Radclyffe 1928: *The well of loneliness: a novel*. London: Cape.

Halmos, P. 1965: *The faith of the counsellors*. London: Constable.

1970: *The personal services society*. London: Constable.

Handler, J. 1968: The coercive children's officer. *New Society*, October.

Hemming, J. 1974: *Coming out*. BBC Radio 4, 25 April.

Hobsbawm, E. J. 1964: *Labouring men*. London: Weidenfeld and Nicolson.

1969: *Bandits*. London: Weidenfeld (Penguin edition, 1972).

1971: *Primitive rebels* (3rd edition). Manchester University Press. (First published 1959.)

Hobsbawm, E. J. and **Rudé, G.** 1973: *Captain Swing*. Harmondsworth: Penguin. (First published 1969 by Lawrence & Wishart, London.)

Hodges, A. and **Hutter, D.** 1974: *With downcast gays*. London: Pomegranate Press.

Holman, R. 1970: *Socially deprived families in Britain*. London: Beford Square Press.

1973a: Poverty, consensus and alternatives. *British Journal of Social Work* 3(4).

1973b: Poverty, welfare rights and social work. *Social Work Today* 4(12).

1974: The American poverty programme 1969–71. *Journal of Social Policy* 3, 21–38.

Horton, J. 1968: Order and conflict theories of social problems. *A.S.R.* (May).

Hurschfeld, M. no date: *Sexual anomalies and perversions*. London: Aldor.

Hyde, M. 1972: *The other love*. London: Mayflower Books. (First edition, 1970, London: Heinemann.)

Isherwood, C. 1964: *A single man: a novel*. New York: Simon & Schuster. (Paperback edition, Harmondsworth: Penguin.)

Janov, A. 1972: *The primal scream*. New York: Dell.

Jones, H., editor 1974: *Towards a new social work*. London: Routledge and Kegan Paul.

Jones, K., editor 1972: *Yearbook of social policy*. London: Routledge and Kegan Paul.

Jordan, W. 1973a: *Paupers: the making of the new claiming class*. London: Routledge and Kegan Paul.

1973b: Emergency payments. *Social Work Today*.

Jordan, W.,—*cont.* 1973c: Deprived cycle. *New Society*, 10 May.

Kenyon, F. E. 1973: *Homosexuality*. London: British Medical Association.

Kincaid, J. 1973: *Poverty and equality in Britain: a study of social security and taxation*. Harmondsworth: Penguin.

Kitson, F. 1971: *Low intensity operations*. London: Faber & Faber.

Knapp, D. and **Polk, K.** 1971: *Scouting the war on poverty*. Lexington: D. C. Heath.

Kuhn, M. 1962: The Interview and the professional relationship. In Rose, A. M., editor, *Human behaviour and social processes*. London: Routledge and Kegal Paul; New York: Houghton Mifflin.

Lapping, A., editor 1970: *Community action*. London: Fabian Society.

Land, H. 1969: Large families in London. *Occasional Papers in Social Administration* 32. London: Bell.

Leonard, P. 1965: Social control, class values and social work practice. *Social work* (October).

Lévi-Strauss, C. 1973: *Tristes tropiques*. Translated by Weightman, J. and Weightman, D. London: Cape.

Lenin, V. I. 1963: *What is to be done?* Oxford: Clarendon Press.
  1966: *Imperialism: the highest stage of capitalism*. Collected works 22. Moscow: Progress Publishers. (First published Moscow 1916.)

Lipset, S. M. 1963: Working-class authoritarianism. In Lipset, S. M., editor, 1963: *Political man: the social bases of politics*. New York: Anchor Books, 87–126.

Lugard, F. 1922: The dual mandate in British tropical Africa. London: Cass. (Reissued, 1965.)

Lynes, T. 1969: *Welfare rights*. London: Fabian Society.
  1972: *The Penguin guide to supplementary benefits*. Harmondsworth: Penguin.

Macarov, D. 1974: Client-worker agreement. *Social Work Today* 5(24), 775.

Maclean, U. 1973: Sources of help. *New Society*, 5 April, 16–18.

McKay, A., Goldberg, E. M. and **Fruib, D. J.** 1973: Consumers and a social services department. *Social Work Today* 4(16), 486–91.

Mandel, E. 1972: The changing role of the bourgeois-university. In Patement, T., editor, *Countercourse: a handbook for course criticism*. Harmondsworth: Penguin Education.

Marris, P. and **Rein, M.** 1971; 1974: *Dilemmas of social reform*. London: Routledge and Kegan Paul; Harmondsworth: Penguin (second edition).

Marsden, D. 1969: *Mothers alone: poverty and the fatherless family*. London: Allen Lane.

Marx, K. and **Engels, F.** 1965: *The German ideology*. London: Lawrence & Wishart; New York: International Publishers.

   1952: *Manifesto of the Communist party*. Moscow: Progress Publishers. (First published 1848.)

Mathiesen, T. 1974: *The politics of abolition*. London: Martin Robertson.

Matza, D. 1969: *Becoming deviant*. Englewood Cliffs, New Jersey: Prentice-Hall.

Mayer, A. C. *et al.* 1958: *Pilot project India*. View of California.

Mayer, J. E. and **Timms, N.** 1970: *The client speaks*. London: Routledge and Kegal Paul.

Meacher, M. 1974: The politics of positive discrimination. In Glennerster, H. and Hatch, S., editors, *Positive discrimination and inequality*. London: Fabian Society.

Meyer, C. H. 1970: *Social work practice: a response to the urban crisis*. New York: Free Press

Miller, W. B. 1959: Implications of urban lower-class culture for social work. *Social Service Review* 32(3).

Miller, M. and **Rein, M.** (in press): *Community work* volume 2. London: Routledge and Kegan Paul.

Milligan, D. 1975: *Politics of homosexuality*. London: Pluto Press.

Moore, B. Jr 1966: *Social origins of dictatorship and democracy*. Harmondsworth: Penguin.

Morgan, I. 1974: Paupers and bureaucrats. *Social Work Today* 5(2), 54–6.

Morris, P., Cooper, J. and **Byles, A.** 1973: Public attitudes to problem definition and problem solving: a pilot study. *British Journal of Social Work* 3(3).

Morris, N. and **Hawkins, G.** 1970: *The honest politician's guide to crime control*. Chicago: University of Chicago Press.

Moynihan, D. 1969: *Maximum feasible misunderstanding*. New York: Free Press; London: Macmillan.

Munday, B. 1972: What is happening to social work students? *Social Work Today* 3(6).

Nehru, P. J. 1957: *Speeches on community*. New Delhi: Ministry of Community Development.

Neill, J. E., Fruin, D., Goldberg, E. M. and **Warburton, R.** 1973: Reactions to integration. *Social Work Today* 4(15) 458–65.

Oleson, V. L. and **Whittaker, E. W.** 1968: *The silent dialogue*. San Francisco: Jossey-Bass.

Parker, G., editor, 1973: *Casework within social work*. University of Newcastle-upon-Tyne Press.

Parsons, T. 1951: *The Social System*. New York: Free Press.

Pateman, T., editor 1972: *Countercourse—a handbook for course criticism*. Harmondsworth: Penguin.

Paul, B. and **Miller, W. B.**, editors, 1955: *Health, culture and community*. New York: Russell Sage.

Pearce, F. 1973a: The British road to incorporation. *The Writing on the Wall* 2.

   1973b: The rule of law: a bourgeois myth. *The Writing on the Wall* 1.

Pearson, G. 1973: Social work as the privatized solution to public ills, *British Journal of Social Work* 3(2), 209–23.

   1974a: The politics of uncertainty: a study in the socialization of the social worker. In Jones, H., editor, *Towards a new social work*. London: Routledge and Kegan Paul.

   1974b: Prisons of love: the reification of the family in family therapy. In Armistead, N., editor, *Reconstructing social psychology*, Harmondsworth: Penguin, 137–56.

   1975: *The deviant imagination*. London: Macmillan.

Perham, M. and **Bull, M.**, editors, 1959–1963: *Lord Lugard's Diaries*. Four volumes. London: Faber & Faber.

Perlman, H, H. 1970: Casework and the 'diminished man'. *Social Casework* 51(4), 216–24.

   1973: Social casework in social work. In Parker, G., editor, *Casework within social work*, University of Newcastle-upon-Tyne Press.

Phillipson, M. and **Roche, M.** 1974: Phenomenology, sociology, and the study of deviance. In Rock, P. and McIntosh, M., editors, *Deviance and social control*, London: Tavistock.

Pincus, A. and **Minahan, A.** 1973: *Social work practice: model and method*. Itasca, Illinois: Peacock.

Pinker, R. 1971: *Social theory and social policy*. London: Heinemann.

Piven, F. F. and **Cloward, R. A.** 1972: *Regulating the poor: the functions of public welfare*. London: Tavistock.

Platt, A. 1969: *The child savers*. Chicago: University of Chicago Press.

Popplestone, G. 1971: The ideology of professional community workers. *British Journal of Social Work* 1(1).

   1972: Who is being radical? *Case Con* 7.

Prins, H. 1974: 'Motivation in social work', *Social Work Today* 5(2), 42.

Priestley, P. 1974: New careers: power sharing in social work. In

Jones, H., editor, *Towards a new social work*, London: Routledge and Kegan Paul.

Rainwater, L. 1974: *Social problems and public policy: deviance and liberty*. Chicago: Aldine.

Rees, S. J. 1973: Clients' perspectives of social work services. Unpublished paper, University of Aberdeen.

1974a: Interpreting outcome. Unpublished paper, University of Aberdeen.

1974b: No more than contact: an outcome of social work. *British Journal of Social Work* 4(3).

Rees, S. J. and **Edwards, F. E.** 1973: Power and influence in social work. *Social Work Today* 3(21), 17–20.

Reich, Wilhelm 1972: *The sexual struggle of youth*. London: Socialist Reproductions. (First published 1931.)

Reid, W. and **Shapiro, B.** 1969: Client reactions to advice. *Social Service Review* 43(2).

Rein, M. and **Heclo, H.** 1974: Welfare: a comparison. *New Society*, 24 January.

Reynolds, B. C. 1934: Between client and community. *Smith College Studies in Social Work* 5(1).

Righton, P. 1973: *Counselling homosexuals*. London: Bedford Square Press of The National Council of Social Service.

Rock, P. and **McIntosh, M.**, editors, 1974: *Deviance and social control*. London: Tavistock.

Rodney, W. 1972: *How Europe Underdeveloped Africa*.

Rose, A. M., editor, 1962: *Human Behavior and social processes*. London: Routledge and Kegan Paul; New York: Houghton Mifflin.

Rose, H. 1973: Who can de-label the claimant? Welfare rights from the claimant's perspective. *Social Work Today* 4(13).

Rosenburg, D.: *Social work and social control*. Unpublished M.Ph. thesis, Bristol University.

du Sautoy, P. 1958: *Community development in Ghana*.

Schwarz, O. 1949: *The psychology of sex*. Harmondsworth: Penguin.

Scheff, T. J. 1969: Negotiating reality: notes on power in the Assessment of Responsibility. *Social Problems* 16(1).

Schur, E. M. 1965: *Crimes without victims: deviant behaviour and public policy*. Englewood Cliffs, New Jersey: Prentice-Hall.

1973: *Radical non-intervention: rethinking the delinquency problem*. Englewood Cliffs, New Jersey: Prentice-Hall.

Scott, R. A. 1969a: Professional employees in a bureaucratic structure. In

A. Etzioni, editor, *The Semi-professions and their Organization*. New York: Free Press.

1969b: *The making of blind men*. New York: Russell Sage.

Seebohm Committee 1968: *Local authority and allied personal social services*. London: HMSO.

Shepherd, M., Oppenheim, A. N. and **Mitchell, S.** 1966: Childhood behaviour disorders and the child guidance clinic: an epidemiological study. *Journal of Child Psychology and Psychiatry* 7, 39–52.

Sinfield, A. 1969: *Which way for social work?* London: Fabian Society.

Skeffington Report 1969: *People and planning*. Report of the Committee on Public Participation in Planning, London: HMSO.

Smith, G. 1973: *Ideologies, beliefs and patterns of administration in the organization of social work practice: a study with special reference to the concept of social need*. Unpublished Ph.D. dissertation, University of Aberdeen.

Smith, G. and **Harris, R.** 1972: Ideologies of need and the organization of social work departments. *British Journal of Social Work* 2(1).

Spencer, H. 1906: *Principles of sociology*, volume 1. London: Williams and Norgate.

Stedman Jones, G. 1971: *Outcast London*. Oxford: Clarendon Press.

Stevenson, O. 1974: 'Editorial'. *British Journal of Social Work* 4(1).

Strauss, A. L., Schatsman, L., Bucher, R., Ehrlich, D. and **Sabshin, M.** 1964: Psychiatric institutions, ideologies and professions. In Strauss, A. L. *et al.*, *Psychiatric Ideologies and Institutions*. New York: Free Press

Sullivan, P. 1974: *Coming out*. BBC Radio 4, 25 April.

Taber, M. 1970: Social work as interference in problem definitions. *Applied Social Studies* 2, 59–68.

Taylor. I. 1972: Client refusal: a political strategy for radical social work. *Case Con* 7, 5–10.

Taylor, I. *et al.*, 1973: *The new criminology*. London: Routledge and Kegan Paul.

Taylor, I., Walton, P. and **Young, J.** 1975: Critical criminology in Britain: review and prospects. In Taylor, I., Walton, P. and Young, J., editors, *Critical criminology*, London: Routledge and Kegan Paul.

Taylor. I. and **Walton, P.** 1971: Industrial sabotage: motives and meanings. In Cohen, S., editor, *Images of deviance*, Harmondsworth: Penguin, 219–45.

Townsend, P. and **Abel Smith, B.** 1965: *The poor and the poorest*. London· Bell.

Timms, N. 1962: The public and the social worker. *Social Work* 19(1).

Titmuss, R. M. 1960: *Income distribution and social change*. London: Allen & Unwin.

United Nations 1958: *Evaluation of Indian Community Development*. New York: United Nations.

Valentine, C. 1968: *Culture and poverty*. Chicago: University of Chicago Press.

Venturi, F. 1960: ⎸*Roots of revolution*.

Waldron, F. 1961: The choice of goals in casework treatment: a case study. *British Journal of Psychiatric Social Work* (2).

Washington, Booker T. 1967: *Up from slavery*. New York: Airmont. (UK editions published by Longman and Oxford University Press.)

Wedderburn, D. 1965: Facts and theories of the Welfare State. In R. Miliband and J. Saville, editors, *Socialist Register*. London: Merlin Press.

Weisberger, B. 1972: *Booker T. Washington*. New York: Mentor Books.

Wilensky, H. L. and **Lebeaux, C. N.** 1965: *Industrial society and social welfare*. New York: Free Press.

Williams, D. 1971: *The Rebecca riots*. Cardiff: University of Wales Press.

Wootton, B. 1959: Contemporary attitudes in social work. In Wootton, B., *Social science and social pathology*, London: Allen & Unwin, chapter 9.

Young, J. 1975: Working-class criminology. In Taylor, I. *et al.*, *Critical criminology*. London, Routledge and Kegan Paul.

Zimmerman, D. H. 1971: The Practicalities of Rule Use. In Douglas, J., editor, *Understanding everyday life*, London: Routledge and Kegan Paul, 221–30.

Notes on Contributors

ROY BAILEY graduated from the University of Leicester in 1963. He began teaching at Enfield College of Technology (now a constituent college of Middlesex Polytechnic, London) in 1964. In 1967 he moved to the University of Bradford as a lecturer in Sociology. He is now head of the department of applied social studies at Sheffield Polytechnic. He is currently concerned with problems of course development as convenor of the course structure project at that polytechnic. From 1970–4 he was a founding member of the editorial board of *Economy and Society*, a social science journal. Since 1968 he has been a member of the executive committee of the National Deviancy Conference. He contributed an article. 'The family and the social management of intolerable dilemmas', to a book he edited with Jock Young, *Contemporary social problems in Britain* (Saxon House, 1973).

MIKE BRAKE spent his early working life in the ballet. In 1967 he graduated from Leeds University in sociology and psychology, he then completed an M.Sc. at the London School of Economics. He has taught at North East London Polytechnic, Middlesex Polytechnic, North London Polytechnic, London University Institute of Education, and has lectured at the California State Universities as Visiting Associate Professor. He has lectured at the University of Bradford in the school of applied social studies and also in the postgraduate department of peace studies at that university. He is at present lecturer at the University of Kent at Canterbury. He has written on youth subcultures, sexual diversity, and is at present writing a book on sexuality. His main interests apart from those mentioned are deviance, sexual politics, community work and radical approaches to psychological damage. He is a member of the National Deviancy Conference.

CRESCY CANNAN: after taking a sociology degree at York University in 1969, Crescy Cannan worked as a research assistant at the North London Polytechnic on an area study and local social services reorganization, and on a study of juvenile delinquency and schools. She now works for East Sussex social services department, and at the time of writing was seconded to Surrey University to take an M.Sc. in applied social studies. She has published articles in *Social and Economic Administration*, *Social Work Today*, *Times Education Supplement*, *Spare Rib*, and *Counter Course* edited by Trevor Patemen (Penguin, 1972). She has written for and been a member of the editorial collective of *Case Con*, the revolutionary magazine for social workers.

STANLEY COHEN is professor of sociology at the University of Essex. He received his undergraduate education in South Africa, worked for a year as a social worker in London, then did his Ph.D. research at the London School of Economics. He lectured in sociology at the University of Durham from 1967–72, and since then has been at Essex. His main publications are *Images of deviance* (editor) (Penguin, 1971); *Folk Devils and moral panics* (Paladin, 1972); with Laurie Taylor, *Psychological survival: the experience of long-term imprisonment* (Penguin, 1973); and with Jock Young, *The manufacture of news: deviance, social problems and the mass media* (Constable, 1973).

PETER LEONARD is professor and chairman of the department of applied social studies in the University of Warwick to which he was appointed in October 1973. Previously he was for some years director of social-work education at the National Institute for Social Work and before that a lecturer in social work at Liverpool University. Before entering the educational field he was a social worker for ten years in child-care, family casework and child-guidance settings. He published a book on the contribution of sociology to social work in 1966, since when he has profoundly changed his political, theoretical and practice orientation. Recently he has been working on philosophical and political issues relating to social work education and practice.

MARJORIE MAYO is working with the Resource Centre of the Joint Docklands Action Group in London on the redevelopment of the dock areas. Before this she taught in the department of sociology at the University of Surrey. She has been a research officer on the Home Office community development project. She has worked as a community worker in Nigeria and is now actively involved in campaigns in the neighbourhood where she lives. With David Jones she is co-editor of two recently published collections of essays on community work.

DON MILLIGAN did not acknowledge his homosexuality until 1971, when at the age of 27 he became active in the Gay Liberation Front. He started work in 1960, took 'A' levels in 1969 and graduated from the University of Lancaster in 1972 where he studied history. He is now studying for an M.A. in Peace Studies at Bradford. His publications include *Politics of homosexuality* (Pluto Press) and *Gay Liberation in a class conscious society* published in *Circles and Arrows, Critical Perspectives in Human Sexuality* (National Press Books, USA).

GEOFFREY PEARSON holds a lectureship at University College, Cardiff, where he teaches courses in human socialization and the social aspects of psychiatry. He was educated at the universities of Cambridge and Sheffield and at the London School of Economics where he qualified as a psychiatric social worker. His experience of social work has covered the mentally ill, old people, physically disabled, vagrants, homosexuals, youth problems and group dynamics work. His publications include several articles and essays and a book, *The deviant imagination*, to be published by Macmillan. A book prepared with G. Mungham, *Working class youth culture*, is to be published by Routledge and Kegan Paul.

STUART REES is a lecturer in social work at the University of Aberdeen. He completed his undergraduate, postgraduate and professional social-work education and training at Southampton University. His career has been split between social work and teaching. He has international experience of probation and parole, having worked as a probation officer in Watford, Hertfordshire, in Vancouver and Revelstoke, British Columbia, and carried out research into the penal system in the United States with particular regard to convicted persons' appraisal of the administration of justice. He has taught social policy and administration in the extra-mural department, University of London, spent two years as a sociology lecturer at Southern Colorado State College, Pueblo, and held his present post since 1969. His recent research has been in community work and into client/social worker perceptions of social-work services. He has contributed articles on social work and social policy and on the sociology of social work to several professional journals in Britain and North America, including two recent papers 'Patronage and participation, problem and paradox, a case study in community work' and 'No more than contact: an outcome of social work' in the *British Journal of Social Work*.

Index